Combating Poverty

Since 1985 the International Center for Economic Growth, a nonprofit organization, has contributed to economic growth and human development in developing and post-socialist countries by strengthening the capacity of indigenous research institutes to provide leadership in policy debates. To accomplish this the Center sponsors a wide range of programs—including research, publications, conferences, seminars, and special projects advising governments—through a network of more than 230 correspondent institutes worldwide. The Center's research and publications program is organized around five series: Sector Studies; Country Studies; Studies in Human Development and Social Welfare; Occasional Papers; and Working Papers.

The Center is affiliated with the Institute for Contemporary Studies, and is headquartered in Panama with the administrative office in San Francisco, California.

For further information, please contact the International Center for Economic Growth, 243 Kearny Street, San Francisco, California, 94108, USA. Phone (415) 981-5353; Fax (415) 986-4878.

ICEG Board of Overseers

Combating Poverty
Innovative Social Reforms in Chile during the 1980s

by Tarsicio Castañeda

An International Center for Economic Growth Publication

ICS PRESS

San Francisco, California

Inquiries, book orders, and catalog requests should be addressed to ICS Press, 243 Kearny Street, San Francisco, California 94108, USA. Telephone: (415) 981-5353; fax: (415) 986-4878. To order call toll-free **(800) 326-0263** in the contiguous United States.

Cover designer: Ben Santora

Copyeditor: Barbara Kendrick

Production editor: Heidi Fritschel

Indexer: Shirley Kessel

Distributed to the trade by National Book Network, Lanham, Maryland.

Library of Congress Cataloging-in-Publication Data

Castañeda, Tarsicio, 1950–
    [Para combatir la pobreza. English]
    Combating poverty : innovative social reforms in Chile during the 1980s / by Tarsicio Castañeda.
      p.   cm.
    Translation of: Para combatir la pobreza.
    Includes bibliographical references and index.
    ISBN 1-55815-192-3—ISBN 1-55815-154-0 (pbk.)
    1. Chile—Social policy. 2. Human services—Chile.
    3. Poor—Chile. 4. Decentralization in government—Chile. I. Title.
HN293.5.C3713 1992
361.6'1'0983--dc20   91-44694

Contents

Foreword

Economists do not have a stamp to mark quality in analytical work on poverty. I would find such a hallmark useful in evaluating this book, for it deserves a high mark in quality.

The study of the economics of poverty continues to be exceedingly nebulous. It lacks an analytical foundation. Meanwhile, poets and historians often reveal basic insights about what it means to be poor; in expressing what being poor implies, our language is more comprehensive than our theory. It is difficult to bridge the gap between moral obligations calling for private and public charity and the economic requirements that could improve the lot of the poor.

Poverty is not endemic to economic modernization. It is not specific to a particular type of economy, market or communist, nor is poverty an economic disease.

The success of Chile's economic reform and the resulting marked increases in real income are becoming well known. Chile has achieved its economic success despite the difficulties inherent in unstable and military governments. Economists and other skilled experts were ever active, and they effectively argued for policies that would create incentives for specialization and trade and thus lead to the increases in income that are possible in a modernizing economy.

This study features neither the economic logic that supports welfare economics nor the logic that seeks to reduce the inequality in the personal distribution of income, as such. Castañeda's approach leads him to observable, income-enhancing components that can be targeted and subsidized by government. Targeting is a process designed to keep these subsidized, income-enhancing components from creeping up the income ladder and thus no longer servicing the poorest of the poor. It is necessary to keep the political process from inducing and supporting such shifts away from the poorest people.

The mechanisms used in the formulation of policies to reduce poverty include reforms in education and schooling, health and nutrition, low-income housing, and social security. The municipal system has been restructured to make the municipalities capable of administering and managing the various reforms. This decentralization allows for increased efficiency in the use of resources. Further decentralization and additional efficiency is attained by using the private sector to take over various economic activities that help reduce poverty.

Castañeda's analysis and findings rest on several important principles: targeting of government subsidies to the poorest segments of the population; provision of additional social services by entities in close proximity to the beneficiaries, namely, municipalities, the private sector, and nonprofit organizations; and the public financing of these social services based on the actual costs that their production and distribution entail.

Castañeda's sharp, inquiring mind is clearly evident. His apprenticeship could not have better prepared him for this study on reducing poverty, and his work is enhanced by his knowledge of recent advances in the economics of the family, of the household, and of human capital. His understanding, gained from experience, of the nature and significance of the interactions between politics and economics has also served him well.

Theodore W. Schultz
Nobel Laureate in Economic Science

Preface

Targeting programs to alleviate poverty so that they actually reach the poor is one of the hardest tasks developing countries face. Existing programs and institutions often must be reshaped or collapsed, complex legal issues addressed, and long-standing benefits taken away from politically powerful interest groups. Constant effort is needed to ensure that subsidies and services meant for the poor are actually available to them and do not escape up the income ladder into less needy hands.

Examples of effective, well-targeted reforms in the social sector are notably few. *Combating Poverty* is about one of them. Over the past fifteen years, Chile has undertaken major structural reforms in nearly every area of its government and economy. Best known are the economic reforms, which, despite rocky periods, are credited with stimulating economic growth and sharply reducing unemployment. Less well known, but just as important, are the innovative reforms Chile has enacted in the social sector—education, health and nutrition, low-income housing, and social security—and in municipal systems, which now administer many social services. These reforms have produced record gains in social indicators such as life expectancy, nutrition, and infant and child mortality rates. Even more impressive, these gains were achieved in years that saw political upheaval, economic instability, and frequent fiscal constraints.

In *Combating Poverty* Tarsicio Castañeda presents a comprehensive review of Chile's social policy changes and structural reforms. His detailed study of each social sector explains the rationale behind the reforms, covers the stages of their implementation, and analyzes the results so far. He gives special attention to the shifting of program administration from the central government to the municipalities, where services can be more closely monitored and equitably delivered, and to the successful transfer of costs from the public sector to the private sector.

These important reforms were not achieved easily; Castañeda gives many examples of the obduracy of bureaucracies and interest groups in the face of change. He points to areas where the new services are functioning less than ideally, recommends improvements, and identifies issues that must be resolved in future planning. His account of the problems encountered and the lessons learned from specific failures and successes will be invaluable to policy makers contemplating similar reforms.

The International Center for Economic Growth is pleased to publish the English edition of this important work, which, in its original Spanish version, received the third place 1991 Sir Antony Fisher International Memorial Award, given annually by the Atlas Foundation for outstanding empirical economic research. We believe that *Combating Poverty* is essential reading for scholars and policy makers around the world.

Nicolás Ardito-Barletta
General Director
International Center for Economic Growth

Panama City, Panama
February 1992

Acknowledgments

This book would not have been possible without the collaboration of many people in Chile. Patricia Matte, Marcelo Astoreca, and Antonio Sancho of the Secretaría de Desarrollo y Asistencia Social were essential in helping me write most of the chapters and in putting together the statistical information. A large part of the work began in 1982, when I started teaching and research at the Department of Economics of the University of Chile in Santiago. I owe much appreciation to the department directors in the period from 1982 to 1985, Professors Alvaro Saieh, Jorge Selume, and Sergio Melnick, who were most supportive of my work and provided me with ideas, comments, and suggestions. With Sergio Melnick and many others, such as Emita Budinic, Cristián Larroulet, Gerardo Jofré, Francisco Covarrubias, and Patricia Matte, I worked at the National Planning Office (ODEPLAN) as an expert on evaluation of social projects, hired by the Organization of American States (OAS). This experience was very valuable for me, because it gave me the opportunity to witness firsthand the functioning of the public sector, including the Ministries of Health, Education, and Housing and several municipal systems.

Numerous people participated in updating some of my previous studies, in preparing excellent drafts and background information, and in thoroughly reviewing the final chapters. These were Beatriz Fried and her research assistant, Sergio Montenegro, of the Department of

Business Administration of the University of Chile (education); Rosa Camhi of the Secretaría de Desarrollo y Asistencia Social (nutrition programs); Jorge Quiroz, graduate student at Duke University; Rodrigo Cood of the Secretaría de Desarrollo y Asistencia Social (housing); Antonio Sancho and Luz María Izquierdo of the Secretaría de Desarrollo y Asistencia Social (social security); and José Miguel Bilbao of the Secretaría de Desarrollo y Asistencia Social (decentralization and municipal development).

Other people who reviewed the chapters included Hernán Büchi, Hernán Larraín, María Teresa Infante, Juan Antonio Guzmán, Rafael Caviedes, Mercedes Cifuentes, Charles Holmes, Alvaro Donoso, Santiago Plant, Juan Ariztía, Cecilia Vivancos, Víctor Hassi, Rámon Yávar, Isabel Vial de Valdés, Fernando Vío, Ernesto Schiefelbein, and Felipe Larraín. Many of my friends and colleagues at the World Bank provided very useful comments and suggestions. These were Guy Pfeffermann, William Paul McGreevey, George Psacharopolous, Luis A. Riveros, John Briscoe, Steve Hoenack, Karen Lashman, Philip Musgrove, Carlos Tobal, and Paul Meo, who took the time for a detailed review of several chapters. I also appreciate the many comments and suggestions of the four anonymous referees who read the manuscript and those of Professor T. W. Schultz of the University of Chicago, who was also so kind to write the foreword to the book.

I would like to thank the International Center for Economic Growth for its interest in my work and for the great effort it devoted to the publication of this book. My thanks go especially to editors Heidi Fritschel and Barbara Kendrick.

I am also grateful to my wife, Rosalba, for her patience and encouragement and for not pressing for vacations during the past two years. Many other friends, such as Alberto and Isabel Valdés, provided continued and much-needed encouragement.

Finally, the findings, interpretations, and conclusions expressed in this book are entirely my own and should not be attributed to the World Bank or to its affiliated organizations.

In Memoriam

This book is dedicated to the memories of Miguel Kast and Marcelo Astoreca, both of whom had enormous influence in the structural changes described herein. Miguel Kast was a leading figure at the National Planning Office (ODEPLAN) when the reforms were planned and began to be implemented. A brilliant and charismatic person, he was able to attract a great number of young professionals to work in the reform program. Marcelo Astoreca was one of his brightest disciples. Miguel died in 1982, when he was only thirty-four years old. Marcelo died in a car accident on April 8, 1989. Both deaths were a tremendous loss for the country they loved, their families, and their friends.

Marcelo had been helping me with this book after I began it in January 1988. His tragic death was a deep loss for me personally and for the book project, mitigated only by Antonio Sancho's great dedication to helping me after Marcelo died. Like Miguel, Marcelo was an honest and most decent person, an excellent son and friend, hard-working, extremely concerned about problems of the poor. Numerous times Marcelo and Miguel rejected easier, more economically rewarding jobs in the private sector to pursue their dreams in public service.

Marcelo started his public service at ODEPLAN in 1978, two years after graduating as a civil engineer from the Catholic University of Chile. He joined the strong team of young, motivated professionals Miguel had built that was crucial in initiating the reforms described in this book. After a short stay at ODEPLAN, Marcelo went to help the government of the Metropolitan Region of Santiago in the Planning Secretariat (SERPLAC), where he was particularly involved in the upgrading and rehabilitation of slums.

At the time of his death, Marcelo was involved in a project in one of the poorest communities in Santiago. It was aimed at helping the municipality improve the quality of education in the schools attended by children in extreme poverty. The idea was to develop a model that could be applied at all schools serving children from extremely poor families, using special financing. Lasting testimonies of Miguel and Marcelo's work are private, nonprofit social assistance foundations created in their names and, in Marcelo's case, a school and square that carry his name, located in La Pintana, one of the poorest municipalities of Santiago.

List of Tables

List of Figures

CHAPTER 1

Introduction

In the past fifteen years, Chile has made major structural reforms in almost every area of its economy and government. The economic reforms are well known and have been credited for the increased exports that have resulted in rapid economic growth and reduced unemployment in the past few years. The reforms in the social sectors (education, health and nutrition, low-income housing, and social security) and in the municipal systems are less well known but are both more profound and unique to Chile; as a result, they will probably have broader, more lasting effects.

Chile has experienced remarkable improvements in its social indicators in the past three decades. From 1960 to 1988, the infant mortality rate went from 119.5 per thousand live births to 18.5, the child mortality rate dropped from 9.1 per thousand to only 0.82, and life expectancy at birth increased by 14.4 years, a world-record gain (Table 1.1).

These trends have been observed in most of Latin America and the developing world, but at a much slower rate than in Chile. The speed at which those indicators and others, such as malnutrition, have been reduced in Chile, especially in the past two decades, is remarkable. In 1973, for instance, Chile still had the second highest child mortality rates in Latin America, but by 1987 it had achieved the second best social indicators (after Costa Rica) (Table 1.2). From 1970 to 1988, the life expectancy at birth increased by ten years. Malnutrition, as measured

1

TABLE 1.1 Key Social Indicators, 1960–1988

Year	Population (millions)	Infant mortality rate (per 1,000 live births)	Child death rate (per 1,000 children 1–4 years old)	Life expectancy at birth[a]	Malnutrition[b] (% of children 0–6 years old)	Daily calories per capita
1960	7.7	119.5	9.06	57.1	n.a.	n.a.
1965	8.5	97.3	5.25		n.a.	2,592
1970	9.3	82.2	3.80	61.5	n.a.	n.a.
1975	10.3	57.6	2.16	64.2	15.5	2,601
1980	11.1	33.0	1.25	65.6	11.5	n.a.
1985	12.1	19.5	0.87	67.1	8.7	2,579
1986	12.3	19.4	0.88		9.1	n.a.
1987	12.5	18.7	0.83		8.8	n.a.
1988	12.7	18.5	0.82	71.5	8.6	n.a.

a. Averages for 1960–1961, 1969–1970, 1970–1975, 1975–1980, 1980–1985, and 1985–1990.
b. Includes those with mild, moderate, and severe malnutrition, as calculated according to the SEMPE scale. See note 1 for this chapter.
n.a. = not available.
SOURCES: National Institute of Statistics (INE); Ministry of Health; World Bank 1988; World Bank 1990.

TABLE 1.2 Social Indicators in Selected Latin American Countries, 1973 and 1987

Country	Infant mortality rate (per 1,000 live births)		Child death rate (per 1,000 children)		Access to safe water (% of population)	
	1973	1987	1973	1985	1973	1987
Chile	74	20	11	1	56	84
Argentina	47	32	3	1	66	57
Brazil	89	64	11	5	77	71
Costa Rica	52	18	6	0	74	84
Colombia	74	46	5	3	63	92
Guatemala	92	60	8	5	39	51
Mexico	67	48	5	3	62	74
Venezuela	48	36	3	2	75	83

SOURCES: UNICEF 1989; World Bank 1988.

by weight for age, was reduced from 15.5 percent of children under six years of age in 1975 (when systematic information was first collected) to 8.6 percent in 1988.[1] Severe malnutrition has virtually disappeared in Chile.

There is some debate on the main reasons for these remarkable improvements. Monckeberg et al. (1987) stress Chile's long tradition in social programs (starting in the mid-1920s), the social awareness of its people and policy makers, and the dedication of its health workers. The improvements in the past decade are attributed to strides in data collection, supplementary food programs, nutrition education programs, family planning programs, special care for pregnant women in rural areas, promotion of breast-feeding, treatment of children suffering from severe malnutrition, and programs for homeless and abandoned children. Taucher (1982) stresses the rapid decline in fertility rates that has occurred since the mid-1960s. Raczynski and Oyarzo (1983) point out the drop in birth rates in the 1970s and modifications in the distribution of birth rates toward groups of lower infant mortality. Castañeda (1985a) cites improvements in the targeting (*focalización*) of primary health interventions (maternal-child programs), food supplementation programs, water and sanitation, and better safety net coordination for the poorest population.

These improvements have come in a period of sharp economic instability, witnessing profound declines in gross domestic product (GDP) 1975 and 1982–1983, a rapid increase in unemployment, a decline in wages, and fiscal constraints.[2] The distribution of labor income probably worsened during the 1970s and most of the 1980s, although improvements have likely occurred recently because of lower unemployment and increased wages. The improvements have also been accompanied by profound policy changes and reforms in the financing and delivery of most social services (such as education, health and nutrition, housing, and social security) and in municipal administration.

Purpose of This Book

The purpose of this book is to review the policy changes and structural reforms in the social sectors and in municipal administration. The book analyzes the rationale for the reforms, examines their implementation, and provides indications, albeit preliminary and crude, of the results to date. It also identifies some key issues for the future of the reforms and makes recommendations for improvements. Considerable space is devoted to describing how things were done. As the reader will find, how programs are implemented often determines the failure or success of the reforms. This narrative account will be useful for policy makers who want to implement similar reforms in other countries. It also shows what a slow and difficult process it is to transform entrenched bureaucracies and interest groups and introduce new ways of operating social services. Targeting subsidies to the poor has been particularly difficult; it has often required reshaping programs and institutions, addressing complex legal aspects, and taking subsidies away from powerful and vocal interest groups.

Although the main focus of the book is on the policies and reforms, each chapter offers a brief review of the behavior of social expenditures during the sharp economic recession Chile suffered during 1982–1983, in order to identify ways in which the government mitigated the costs of adjustment. These included reducing expenditures that did not target the poorest people well—such as university education—so as to protect the programs that were well targeted. The contribution of the private sector is also highlighted, partly because of its great impact in complementing government efforts by providing social services that previously had been handled almost exclusively by the public sector.

Contents of This Book

Each chapter in this book is designed to be a self-contained unit, appropriate for those readers who may be interested only in a particular subject. As a result there is some repetition in the discussion of programs or reforms that overlap two or more sectors. This chapter briefly reviews the economic and social context of the reforms. Chapters 2 through 5 describe the reforms in education, health and nutrition, housing, and social security public systems. The format of each of these chapters is similar: first, there is a short overview of the situation before the reforms, the problems faced, and the government's strategies in addressing those problems; second, a more extensive review of the reforms and how the government implemented them; and third, an assessment of the likely impact of the reforms and the objectives achieved. Finally, each chapter contains a summary, including some discussion of issues for the future of the reforms and specific lessons that can be derived for other countries. Chapter 6 describes the major modifications to decentralization and municipal laws, emphasizing the new role of the municipalities in the provision of social services. Chapter 7 summarizes the main social reforms and provides some lessons and thoughts for other countries trying to implement similar programs.

The Socioeconomic Context of the Reforms

Soon after the military took power at the end of 1973, the main concern of the Chilean government was economic stabilization, to combat the runaway inflation of over 500 percent and the huge fiscal deficit of about 24 percent of GDP. At the same time, the government put a strong emphasis on structural reforms, beginning with price liberalization of most consumer goods, deregulation of the economy, and trade liberalization.[3] The economic program also included tax reform (to introduce the value-added tax and eliminate or reduce others, such as corporate and trade taxes). The government established nominal tariffs ranging between 10 and 35 percent and eliminated all nontariff barriers. In mid-1979, nominal tariffs for all goods (inputs and final goods) were set at 10 percent. In 1983 tariffs were increased to 35 percent, and in 1984 they were lowered to 15 percent. It was estimated that the average equivalent nominal tariff (taking into account nontariff barriers) was 182 percent in 1973, at the end of the government of President Salvador Allende (Hurtado et al. 1987).

The state of the economy in the 1970s and first half of the 1980s was generally unfavorable to social reforms. In 1974–1975, GDP per capita declined by over 15 percent, after a 7 percent decline in 1973. This resulted from the severe fiscal adjustment necessary to stabilize the economy (real public spending dropped by over 60 percent in 1974–1975) and a significant drop in the terms of trade (from an index of 224.4 in 1973 to 100.7 in 1975). In 1982–1983, GDP per capita dropped by 18.2 percent as a result of the deep financial crisis produced during those years by inconsistencies in macroeconomic and exchange rate policies and aggravated by external factors. Consumption per capita declined by almost 30 percent in 1974–1975 and by 17 percent in 1982–1983 (Table 1.3).

Employment and real wages

The effects of the adjustment process on real wages and employment were dramatic. Real minimum wages dropped by about 47 percent (average real wages by 21 percent) in 1973, resulting from lags in adjustment of nominal wages and elimination of indexation classes. After 1974, minimum wages recovered the 1970 level and rose rapidly, but average wages recovered slowly, attaining the 1970 level only in 1982. The real minimum wage declined again from the very high level attained in 1982 (mainly because of automatic wage indexation tied to declining past inflation) to the 1970 level in 1988. The decline in average

TABLE 1.3 Growth Rates of GDP and Government Spending, 1970–1988

Year	GDP per capita (%)	Consumption per capita (%)	Inflation rate (%)	Terms of trade (1977 = 100)	Real public spending (%)	Social spending as % of total spending[a]
1970	0.5	−1.3	34.9	212.9	n.a.	40.0
1973	−7.1	−7.1	508.1	224.4	36.4	27.4
1974	−0.7	−15.9	375.9	181.9	−36.2	39.7
1975	−14.4	−12.9	340.7	100.7	−29.3	45.5
1976	1.8	−1.4	174.3	107.0	−8.6	49.9
1977	8.0	12.2	63.5	100.0	14.7	50.5
1978	6.4	5.8	30.3	98.9	4.7	50.2
1979	6.5	5.3	38.9	110.1	3.4	47.9
1980	6.0	2.6	31.2	106.6	14.1	50.4
1981	3.9	7.1	9.5	100.1	20.7	54.7
1982	−15.8	−12.3	20.7	96.1	−2.5	59.4
1983	−2.4	−4.6	23.1	95.0	−3.8	59.7
1984	4.7	−0.3	23.0	87.2	6.1	61.0
1985	0.8	−2.6	26.4	85.5	3.4	58.6
1986	4.1	2.2	17.4	88.0	4.4	57.0
1987	4.1	2.2	21.5	90.4	−1.2	54.4
1988	5.8	7.4	12.7	108.6	5.4	52.5

a. Social spending includes expenditures on education, health and food supplements, housing, social security, and special employment programs. Figures for 1970 are in relation to 1969.
n.a. = not available.
SOURCE: Central Bank of Chile 1988.

real wage was less dramatic (15 percent), but in 1988 its level was about 10 percent lower than in 1970 (Table 1.4).

Unemployment increased rapidly after 1974 because of a combination of factors, including reduced public employment (due to the fiscal adjustment and structural reforms), the acceleration of the labor-force growth in the 1970s resulting from the baby boom of the late 1950s and early 1960s, and the wage indexation policy mentioned previously. Because inflation started to decline in 1976, albeit more slowly than anticipated, this indexation led to a rise in real wages. Other reasons cited are overvaluation of the exchange rate, very high real interest rates, reductions in import tariffs leading to increased imports, and lower industrial production and employment. There is, of course, debate among economists on the relative contribution of each of these factors.

TABLE 1.4 Unemployment and Real Wages, 1960–1988

	Unemployment rate (%)		Index of real wages (1970 = 100)	
Year	University of Chile[a]	INE[b]	Minimum wage	Average wage
1960	7.1	n.a.	90	56
1970	5.7	n.a.	100	100
1973	4.8	n.a.	53	79
1974	9.2	n.a.	103	59
1975	13.5	14.7	125	60
1976	15.9	12.7	125	61
1977	14.2	11.8	113	71
1978	14.2	13.8	136	76
1979	11.8	10.4	132	84
1980	12.0	10.5	136	90
1981	11.0	11.4	154	94
1982	18.4	19.6[c]	168	104
1983	22.0	14.7	127	87
1984	19.1	13.9	112	89
1985	16.0	12.0	101	84
1986	13.9	8.8	99	84
1987	12.6	7.9	91	84
1988	12.4	6.3	101	89

a. National rate, March each year.
b. National rate, October through December each year.
c. October through November.
n.a. = not available.
SOURCES: Department of Economics, University of Chile; National Institute of Statistics (INE) for unemployment, nominal wages, and CPI of June of each year.

The government responded to the rise in open unemployment by creating emergency employment programs (EEPs). In 1975, the Minimum Employment Program (PEM) was created and covered an average of 4.6 percent of the labor force every year from 1975 to 1981. This program had several implementation problems and induced higher participation in the labor market by people not normally in the labor force. In 1982, the government created new programs that covered about 11 percent of the labor force in 1982 and 13 percent in 1983, when open unemployment skyrocketed to about 20 percent. All EEPs were eliminated in 1989 owing to the sharp decline in open unemployment resulting from the rapid increase in exports and domestic industrial production after 1985.

Government social spending

Table 1.5 shows that the central government's social expenditures have followed the trend of overall government spending, though the declines during the crisis years were less severe. In 1974–1975 and 1982–1983 the share of social in total spending increased considerably. Overall social spending doubled in real terms between 1970 and 1988. As a percentage of GDP, government social spending averaged about 20 percent from 1982 to 1988, an average similar to that of 1971–1973. This ratio is among the highest in Latin America and the developing world, comparable only to that of Costa Rica. In 1970, the ratio was 13 percent; between 1974 and 1981, it was about 16 percent. The main factors responsible for the increase in social spending have been social security and social welfare, which includes the EEPs. Social security expenditures increased, particularly during the 1980s, as a result of the reform that permitted the creation of private pension fund companies. Because of the massive transfer of workers to the new pension fund administration companies, the government had to provide funds to the state pension fund companies (Cajas) to help pay their ongoing pension obligations. Additionally, the government increased the number of assistance pensions granted to individuals from about 35,000 in 1975 to 310,400 in 1987, and the number of people receiving a monthly money income subsidy grew from about 17,400 in 1981 to over 1 million in 1987.

Government spending on key social services such as health, housing, and education has declined, and markedly so in the case of health. There are several reasons for this. First is the drop in wages and salaries of workers. Over 80 percent of expenditures on education and over 55 percent of expenditures on health are devoted to the wage bill. Any decline in real wages results in a decline in expenditures. Second, the

TABLE 1.5 Evolution of Government Expenditures, 1970–1988 (millions of 1988 U.S.$)

Year	Health[a]	Social welfare[b]	Housing[c]	Social security[d]	Education[e]	Regional development[f]	Total social expenditures	Total government expenditures	Social expenditures as % of total	Social expenditures as % of GDP
1970	342.5	61.3	183.9	512.6	792.3	14.2	1,906.8	4,768.5	40.0	13.0
1971	467.4	114.5	383.3	926.2	1,097.7	47.9	3,056.9	6,350.3	48.1	19.2
1972	577.5	59.2	340.8	883.3	1,204.6	42.6	3,107.9	6,742.3	46.1	19.8
1973	553.6	104.3	439.1	514.1	874.0	37.4	2,522.5	9,199.7	27.4	17.0
1974	429.5	101.1	402.1	481.8	866.4	62.8	2,363.7	5,960.9	39.7	15.8
1975	311.7	206.2	164.3	497.2	667.4	69.4	1,916.1	4,215.1	45.5	14.7
1976	262.1	297.7	144.7	436.9	674.0	111.1	1,921.6	3,853.5	49.9	14.2
1977	301.7	266.5	158.6	584.4	824.2	95.2	2,230.5	4,419.3	50.5	15.0
1978	314.8	338.8	122.2	621.6	831.8	93.6	2,322.8	4,625.4	50.2	14.5
1979	298.4	220.9	133.8	678.3	868.5	88.7	2,288.7	4,781.8	47.9	13.1
1980	384.1	392.5	149.7	810.3	921.1	88.8	2,746.5	5,453.9	50.4	14.6
1981	406.5	759.2	144.2	1,090.1	1,107.6	96.1	3,603.7	6,584.3	54.7	18.2
1982	384.3	933.0	51.3	1,265.2	1,131.7	45.4	3,810.9	6,420.7	59.4	22.4
1983	317.3	1,055.2	99.8	1,227.4	970.4	35.2	3,705.4	6,175.9	60.0	21.9
1984	313.7	950.8	155.0	1,563.9	905.9	27.5	4,006.7	6,552.9	61.1	22.3
1985	281.1	880.9	176.3	1,643.9	980.1	15.2	3,977.4	6,775.3	56.7	21.6
1986	261.6	715.8	178.8	1,876.0	976.0	43.7	4,051.8	7,075.5	57.3	20.8
1987	259.0	576.4	208.9	1,792.6	899.6	67.0	3,905.4	6,993.5	54.4	18.5
1988	270.3	471.8	299.4	1,902.3	851.4	78.9	3,874.1	7,572.4	52.5	17.6

a. Health expenditures include contributions to the Ministry of Health institutions: National Health Service, Hospital Facilities Construction Society, National Food and Nutritional Council, and National Health Fund.

b. Social welfare expenditures include contributions to the Ministry of Labor institutions (excluding Social Security Funds), Minimum Employment Program, allowance for additional workshop contracting, National Board of Kindergartens, National Board of School Assistance and Scholarships, National Childhood Service, National Emergency, and the contribution to fireman units.

c. Housing expenditures include contributions to the Ministry of Housing and Urban Development and Metropolitan Region Urbanization.

d. Social security expenditures include the contribution to social funds for the payment of retirements, workers pensions, widows and orphans' pensions, unemployment subsidy, compensations, and social security fund of public employees.

e. Education expenditures include contributions to the Ministry of Education institutions for public and private basic, middle school, and superior education, the National Scientific and Technological Research Commission, Educational Facilities Construction Society, and the National Television Commission.

f. Regional development expenditures include resources assigned to the regions and intended basically for health, extreme poverty, housing, and education.
SOURCE: Ministry of Finance.

policy of the government, particularly in the health sector, was to tap other sources of funding. The number of employers evading their social security contribution was lowered and the cost of services to users was increased, especially in the preferred provider program (see Chapter 6). Thus, total public health expenditures per capita declined less sharply (about 15 percent) than public spending between 1980 and 1987 (Miranda 1990). Third, the reforms themselves had an effect on the way social expenditures are reckoned over time. For example, when people were offered the opportunity to put their payroll contributions in private health insurance companies, they moved, taking revenues (and expenditures) out of the public health system. In 1988, private health insurance companies attended over 1.5 million beneficiaries who, in the absence of this option, had been enrolled in the public system. Taking into account these revenues and expenditures, total expenditures on health increased by almost 30 percent between 1980 and 1986. Another example is housing. In the early 1970s, the Ministry of Housing had a number of activities, ranging from land development, construction, and financing to selection of beneficiaries and the handing out of subsidies. Since the late 1970s, this ministry has left many of these activities (notably land development and construction) to the private sector, in order to concentrate on normative and policy-making roles, financing a system of direct subsidies, and selection of beneficiaries. As a result, many expenditures left the public-sector accounting sphere. The number of people employed in the ministry was also reduced to match the new responsibilities.

The extent of poverty

In view of the sharp deterioration of wages and the high unemployment rates of the 1970s and 1980s, there has been legitimate concern among many researchers about an increase in poverty in Chile. The connection between labor market variables and income distribution has been well established. Further concerns have been raised because, although government spending has been countercyclical, there have been reductions in government social spending in key social services. Measuring poverty is, however, fraught with subjective judgments and political controversy. This has been the case in Chile, where estimates of poverty ranged in 1985 from 14 percent of the population to over 45 percent. Differences in poverty measures arise in Chile, as in most countries, because of different assumptions about poverty lines, sources of income considered, and the value given to social programs.[4]

In Chile, the past government estimate of 14 percent is based on the map of extreme poverty developed on the basis of the 1982 population census. This map follows the same methodology used for estimating a poverty figure of 21 percent of the population in 1970. Extreme poverty is defined according to housing conditions, water and sanitation, overcrowding, and possession of selected durable goods. There have been two other recent estimates of poverty in Chile. One is by J. Rodríguez-Grossi (1985a) of the Latin American Institute on Social Teaching of the Church and Social Studies (ILADES), who estimated the indigent population at about 35 percent of the population in 1983. The other is by A. Torche (1987) of the Department of Economics of the Catholic University of Chile, who estimated poverty at 45 percent of the population (25 percent indigent, 20 percent poor) in 1985, based on the cost of a food basket and estimates of money income. "Indigent" defines those people whose money income is not enough to cover the cost of a food basket that meets minimum caloric requirements, and "poor" refers to those whose current consumption of food does not cover their caloric requirements.

The past government estimates are likely to understate poverty because they do not consider the labor market variables of employment and real wages, although they are good measures of progress in housing conditions, sanitation, and other strong correlates of structural poverty. By contrast, the estimates by Rodríguez-Grossi and Torche are likely to overstate poverty, because they rely almost exclusively on labor market conditions (earned income and money income subsidies) to assess the consumption gap and poverty line. They do not consider other subsidies such as food, which provide substantial supplements to vulnerable groups and poor families. Also, it is well established that poor people are heavily concentrated in activities in the informal sector of the economy—many are self-employed or family workers—where it is difficult to calculate money income.[5] In 1987, over 30 percent of people in the first two deciles of the income distribution were self-employed. One indication of the overestimation of the indigent population is the fact that undernutrition of children up to six years old, a very vulnerable population, has been reduced to very low levels (8.6 percent), and the incidence of low birth weight, a measure of mothers' malnutrition, is now almost nil in Chile. It is doubtful that these levels could have been achieved if 25 percent of the population did not have enough income to buy a food basket with minimum caloric requirements.[6] This underscores the need to consider government programs and the targeting impact of government subsidies in poverty measures. The food assistance programs totaled over U.S. $100 million in 1985, and targeting has improved considerably in recent years, in many instances as a result of the social reforms that this book will describe.[7]

The Social Reforms

All of Chile's social reforms were based on five common principles that defined the roles of the state and the private sector, the main beneficiaries of social programs, and the financing and operation of social programs. First, the government should target subsidies to the poorest segments of the population rather than attempt to meet the basic needs of the entire population, many of whom can provide for their basic needs on their own. Second, social services should be provided by municipalities and the private sector, which are closer to the beneficiaries than is the central government. Third, financing for social services should be based on services provided rather than on historically based budget allocations. Fourth, subsidies should be given directly to beneficiaries rather than to providers and should be in the form of direct, up-front subsidies (such as vouchers) rather than indirect subsidies (such as lower-than-market interest rates). Fifth, the public sector should undertake only those activities that are socially profitable and that no private-sector party is willing to provide.

Based on these principles, Chile undertook its reforms in the various social sectors. In education, the government aimed to increase efficiency and expand opportunities for students by encouraging the private sector to offer more education alternatives and programs. It instituted a new system of financing education based on a per-student payment (or voucher) and channeled money from the university level to the primary and secondary levels. At the university level, for instance, tuition was raised, but loans were also introduced for needy students.

The reforms of the health care system were designed to target health services and food supplements more tightly to the needy population and to increase the efficiency of the public health-care delivery system. The government therefore established a new system for collecting and disbursing money for health services, decentralized the health-care delivery system, and gave workers more choice over their health insurers. The reforms also emphasized primary health care, health- and nutrition-related interventions, and sanitation.

The government designed housing reforms to meet the needs of the poorer population. It introduced vouchers for down payments to replace subsidies given in the form of lower-than-market interest rates or reduced prices for housing units. The role of the public sector was limited to financing and screening the beneficiaries of subsidies and establishing norms and regulations. The private sector was responsible for land development, arrangements for water and sewerage connections, housing construction, and financial intermediation.

To reform the social security system, Chile initiated unified, simple, nondiscriminatory rules regarding the benefits provided, retirement requirements, and eligibility criteria. It created a system of compulsory savings that workers deposit in private companies that administer pension funds. In addition, government subsidies are now targeted to the poorest workers.

Hand in hand with these reforms in the social sectors have come changes in the operation of municipalities, which have gradually gained a larger role in providing social services and combating poverty. Among the activities that have been transferred from the central government to the municipalities are primary education and health care, sanitation, low-income housing, child care, and recreation.

Several important elements of the reform process appear to have contributed to the level of success achieved. First, Chile had a leading institution pressing for policy change: the National Planning Office (ODEPLAN). Since its approval was required for all government investments, this agency had strong influence over the entire public sector. Second, the reform efforts were remarkably constant over time, in part because of the single-mindedness of key personnel in the ministries and the training provided to people at all levels of the public sector. Third, the government initiated an extensive program of incentives for those affected by the reforms. Fourth, the government has developed information systems that allow for better targeting of social assistance. All of these factors will be discussed in more detail in this book.

CHAPTER 2

Reforms in Education

Chile introduced major reforms in primary and secondary education in 1980; these were followed with important changes in university education in 1981. This chapter reviews the reforms and examines the redistributive impact of the changes made during the 1982–1983 crisis in the financing of education, which benefited nonuniversity schooling.

Reforms in Primary and Secondary Education

Before the reforms

By 1980, Chile's well-developed educational system was one of the oldest and most sophisticated in Latin America. During the 1960s, the government had initiated major reforms to extend the compulsory primary education cycle to eight years and to strengthen secondary education. The socialist government of President Allende undertook no major reforms except for a policy of open universities, which led to a substantial increase in enrollment and government spending. Similarly, except for major changes at the management level, the military government made no major changes between 1973 and 1980, although it did create a system of Regional Ministerial Secretariats of Education (SEREMIs) in 1974 as part of the decentralization mandated for all ministries.

Until 1980, the Ministry of Education was the main provider of preprimary, primary, and secondary education. In that year, 80 percent of students were enrolled in public schools, 14 percent in private subsidized schools (*escuelas subvencionadas*), and the remaining 6 percent in private nonsubsidized schools. Of total school enrollment, 6 percent was in preprimary, 74 percent in primary, and 20 percent in secondary. Secondary enrollment in turn consisted of 70 percent in general education and 30 percent in technical/vocational. The Ministry of Education provided 75 percent of the vocational education in its schools throughout the country; the remainder took place at private subsidized schools. Education was provided free of charge to all students in the public and private subsidized schools.

The Ministry of Education's thirteen SEREMIs were responsible for administration and operation of the public schools. Each SEREMI had, in turn, one or more local directorates (*direcciones locales*) charged with supervising and evaluating school performance, using supervision and evaluation norms originating at the central Ministry of Education. The ministry appointed all teachers, paid for all inputs (such as textbooks and teacher aids), and handled school building and repairs through its company for school construction (Sociedad Constructora de Establecimientos Educacionales).

According to the education authorities, this highly centralized and bureaucratic system presented several problems, including low-quality education and low efficiency—as revealed by the high dropout and repetition rates—because school administrators had no incentive to attract and retain students; low teachers' salaries, because the bureaucracy consumed a large part of the budget; inadequate supervision of school administrators and teachers; rigid and inflexible curricula that were not amenable to local adaptation; and minimal community participation in school affairs (ODEPLAN 1981).

The 1980–1981 reforms

To correct these problems, the government implemented major curriculum, administrative, and financing reforms in 1980 and 1981. The curriculum reforms, not dealt with in detail in this chapter, started with Decree 4,002 of May 1980, which modified the primary education study plan, and continued with Decree 300 of December 1981, which introduced changes to the plans for secondary studies. Both these reforms sought to provide more flexibility in the study plans, in order to facilitate adaptation to local needs and to allow students and parents to express their preferences about what subjects the schools would teach.

The administrative and financing reforms consisted of transferring control of the public preprimary, primary, and secondary schools to the municipalities; transferring the public vocational secondary schools to private nonprofit organizations created by associations of employers (for example, agricultural schools to the National Agriculture Association); and encouraging, through a per-student subsidy payment, private individuals and nongovernment organizations to create tuition-free schools.

The transfer of schools to the municipalities was aimed at improving administration, increasing enrollment, and upgrading the quality of education. The transfer of vocational schools to the associations of employers sought to encourage direct private-sector involvement in administration and the design of curricula to make the schools more responsive to actual work demands. The purpose of the per-student subsidy system was to promote competition among the municipalities and private subsidized schools in attracting and retaining students, since enrollment was the basis for obtaining financing from the central government. Another objective was to heighten community participation in education.

In actually transferring the schools, several administrative questions had to be addressed: (1) How should public property be shifted to private institutions and municipalities? (2) How should teachers who were public employees under the Ministry of Education be decentralized or transferred? (3) How should the decentralized schools be supervised? (4) How should those schools be financed?

Transfer of public property.   Decree 1-3063 of June 1980 authorized the Ministry of Education to transfer school infrastructure under a special legal arrangement (called a *comodato*) to the municipalities without charge for up to ninety-nine years. The municipalities would be completely autonomous in administering the material resources and in maintaining schools. In turn, the Ministry of Education would pay the municipalities according to student attendance and would monitor quality of education through achievement tests.

Decree 3,166 of February 1980 authorized the Ministry of Education to enter into contracts (*convenios*) with private organizations for the transfer of the vocational secondary schools, free of charge, including all infrastructure, machinery, and material inputs. These organizations were given complete autonomy to administer these schools and design their curricula but had to accept financial and pedagogic supervision from the Ministry of Education and report on annual enrollment and expenses.

Dealing with the teachers.   Responsibility for the teachers' payrolls in both the vocational and the "municipalized" schools was decentralized from the Ministry of Education to each private corporation and municipality. Before the reform, teachers who were public employees were paid based on the pay scale of the public sector (*escala única*) and were promoted according to the teacher pay scale (*carrera docente*). After the reform, teachers had two options: they could continue being paid according to the public-sector pay scale, with promotions based on this scale and seniority rules, or they could accept the pay system of the private sector, whereby employees and employers negotiate salaries and promotions. Both alternatives were to be regulated by Decree 2,200 (the new labor code introduced in 1979), which stated that the new status of teachers would be private rather than public. Under both alternatives, teachers would get full severance pay (*desahucio*) because they were losing their public employee status. Teachers could also choose early retirement if they had contributed to the social security system for at least twenty years.

One argument for decentralizing the teachers' payroll was the need to provide local authorities with more freedom to allocate resources. Had the Ministry of Education continued to pay all teachers, only a limited amount of money would have been available to allocate locally. The decentralization of payrolls, however, was a more costly process than had been envisioned initially.

Supervision of schools.   As noted, the Ministry of Education continued to supervise all transferred schools. This ensured that the curriculum standards and guidelines were properly applied and that the infrastructure and financial resources were properly utilized.

Financing transferred schools.   The Ministry of Education was to finance the transferred schools with general taxpayers' funds. Municipalized as well as private subsidized schools were to receive the per-student payment.[1] The payment, the same for both types of schools, was to be equal to the average per-student expenditure by the Ministry of Education in 1980, increased by 10 percent in real terms. This provision amounted to a great incentive for the private schools, whose expenditures per student were, according to the Ministry of Education, 70 percent of the average amount spent by the ministry. The vocational schools transferred to private organizations were to receive an amount of money equal in real terms to that which the ministry was spending on those schools at the time of the transfer.

The payments varied according to level of education, grade within a given level, type of education (basic, secondary, special education for disabled students, and vocational education) and type of school (day or evening). For instance, payment for the first and second grades of primary education would be 0.46 Unidad Tributaria Mensual (UTM)[2] (about U.S. $47.70), whereas for grades six and eight it would be 0.56 UTM (U.S. $58) and for secondary general day education, 0.63 UTM (U.S. $65).[3] In addition, the amount of the payments differed by region to provide a hardship allowance for teachers working in remote areas. In 1987, the law was restructured to approximate the relative cost of teaching by grade to simplify the system and to introduce a new unit of account that would increase with the wages and salaries of the public sector.

Implementation of the reforms

The government started transferring the preprimary, primary, and secondary schools to the municipalities at the end of 1980. It had begun to transfer the vocational secondary schools to private organizations in 1978, with one school transferred experimentally as early as 1977.[4] In March 1982 all transfers were suspended because of the budgetary constraints arising from the 1982–1983 crisis; by the end of that year, however, 87 percent of all the public schools had been transferred to the municipalities. These schools accounted for 83 percent of the public school students and employed 78 percent of the teachers in nonprivate schools. As for technical schools, thirty-eight transfers to private organizations were authorized by 1982, of which twenty were implemented. These latter included one-third of the thirty-three industrial public schools, which went to the Society of Manufacturers (Sociedad de Fomento Fabril), and all nine public agricultural schools, which went to the Corporation for Rural Social Development (CODESER), a private nonprofit corporation created in 1976 that is linked to the National Agriculture Association (Sociedad Nacional de Agricultura).

To implement these reforms, the Ministry of Education had to increase its expenditures substantially. Real government expenditures for education rose by 6 percent between 1979 and 1980, 20 percent between 1980 and 1981, and 2 percent between 1981 and 1982, when the transfers were suspended (Central Bank of Chile 1983). Expenditures increased not only because the Ministry of Education had to pay the 67,000 transferred teachers full severance pay but also because it instituted economic incentives for the municipalities to encourage them to accept the transfer of the schools. The incentive was larger for those that accepted first: municipalities receiving schools in 1980 got the equivalent of 5 percent of their schools' wages and salaries; those receiving schools in 1981 got 4 percent; and those receiving them in 1982, 3 percent.

The effects of the 1982–1983 crisis.   The 1982 crisis not only led to the suspension of the school transfers and the loss of momentum of the reforms but also created other problems, such as the suspension of cost-of-living adjustments mandated for the per-student payment and salary increases. In response, between 1982 and 1985 the government had to introduce emergency measures, many of which contradicted the basic principles of the reforms and were later removed. Some of these measures were as follows.

In June 1982, the mandated adjustment in the per-student payments based on increases in the consumer price index (CPI) was suspended. Beginning on that date, the payments were to be adjusted based on the increase in wages and salaries of the public sector. Since inflation ran higher than the wage increases, the per-student payments fell about 20 percent in real value from 1982 to 1985. Soon, the municipalities faced deficits in administration costs (Table 2.1), a large part of which the Ministry of Education had to cover, with the balance falling to the municipalities themselves.

The new municipal teachers started to exert a great deal of pressure to receive the same salaries and tenure privileges as those teachers who were still public employees under the Ministry of Education. To meet these demands, the government provided a special appropriation (parallel to the per-student payment) to cover the supplementary salaries. This appropriation was a major setback for municipal autonomy vis-à-vis teachers, in that the central government became involved in municipal wage policy. Further, the transferred teachers had already received full severance pay and other benefits when they left the public employ.

The municipalities were not allowed to fire excess teachers. This measure also resulted from teachers' pressure and the dramatically high

TABLE 2.1 Municipal Deficit, 1982–1985 (millions of U.S.$)

Year	Deficit
1982	3.5
1983	5.7
1984	11.6
1985	10.6

SOURCE: ODEPLAN 1986a.

rate of unemployment (over 20 percent) in those years. This provision further limited the municipalities' ability to manage their own personnel and incentives, some of the basic themes of the decentralization reform.

A clause in the 1980 subvention law restricted the opening of new private schools providing free education that could apply for per-student payments. For a new school to be approved, the Ministry of Education had to declare that there was no excess supply in the area where the establishment was to be located.[5] The aim was to protect the municipalities from private-sector competition.

The financial problems of the rural municipalities were especially acute, because the per-student payment was calculated on the basis of an average of thirty students per teacher, a level difficult to obtain in rural areas. Moreover, attendance varied greatly because of migration and child labor during harvest time.

Resuming the transfers and corrective measures.   The government resumed and completed the transfers of schools to the municipalities from August to October 1986, although not without opposition by groups of teachers. It was also concluded that the deficits were primarily the result of the relatively low student-teacher ratios in municipal schools: in 1984 this ratio was twenty-four; in public schools that were not yet transferred, the ratio was twenty; but in the private subsidized schools, it was over forty, a level close to the forty-five permitted by the Ministry of Education. According to the National Planning Office (ODEPLAN), the low ratio in public schools was the primary reason why the costs per student in public and municipal schools were higher in 1985 than in private subsidized schools (ODEPLAN 1985a). In 1986 municipal schools had a student-teacher ratio of only sixteen, less than half the ratio of thirty-eight in private subsidized schools.

To address the deficit, the government introduced several measures: the Ministry of Education put a limit on the resources available to meet the deficit and programmed its gradual elimination by February 1988, and it lifted the restriction on municipalities' ability to fire teachers. As a result, the municipalities reduced the number of teachers considerably so as to increase the very low student-teacher ratios and thus compete with the private subsidized schools. The deficits have gradually been reduced.

Additional corrective measures included elimination of supplementary pay to municipalities for additional teacher salaries, with the readjustment instead of the per-student payment based on the adjustment given to public-sector employees (Decree Law 355), and implementation of a differentiated per-student payment scheme based on the number of students enrolled in schools more than five kilometers from urban areas (called rural establishments).

In 1987, the government further modified the subvention law by (1) introducing a permanent unit of account, the Unit for Subvention in Education (USE), for adjusting the per-student payments in keeping with the adjustment in the wages and salaries of public-sector employees; (2) modifying the payment structure to approximate more closely the costs per school grade; and (3) introducing special coefficients for allocating additional payments for more costly types of education (special, technical, and rural). As shown in Tables 2.2 and 2.3, these changes meant significant increases in the payments per student for all grades and types of education. For instance, the per-student payment for the eighth grade increased from U.S. $10.40 per month under the 1980 law to $12.50 under the new law. The payment for adult education increased from $3.00 per month to $3.60 per student.

Article 26 of the 1987 law provided supplement indexes to be used to increase the per-student payments for students with mental or physical disabilities who required specialized education (Table 2.3). The supplements were 150 percent for mentally retarded children or those with movement problems, and 100 percent for children with sight and hearing problems.

To help the municipalities deal with the school deficits caused by too few students and the highly variable attendance in rural establishments, the new law included a "rural factor" for increasing the base payments. This factor was higher the lower the number of students. For instance, when the number of students was below eleven, the factor was 2.0, and when it was as high as eighty-four, the factor was 1.05. A prerequisite for obtaining the additional payment was the absence of another school offering the same type of education within five kilometers, except when geographical conditions prevented easy access.

This additional payment was in addition to the hardship allowance (*asignación de zona*), which was retained from the 1980 law. Under this allowance, the payments were directly proportional to the distance between the province and the central zone of the country.

Article 25 of the modified law also included coefficients for determining additional per-student payments for technical/vocational education, with the amounts varying based on the type of training within a minimum and maximum value, as approved by the Ministry of Education. The values ranged from 1.0 to 2.0 for agricultural education, 0.6 to 1.2 for industrial education, and 0.0 to 0.3 for technical and commercial education.

TABLE 2.2 Payment per Student, 1980 (December 1987 pesos)

Type of education	UTM per student[a]	Pesos per student
Preschool	0.46	1,860.25
Primary		
Grades 1–2	0.46	1,860.25
Grades 3–5	0.52	2,102.90
Grades 6–8	0.56	2,264.67
Special education	1.17	4,731.51
Adult/primary	0.16	647.04
Secondary		
Scientific/humanistic, day	0.63	2,547.74
Scientific/humanistic, night	0.19	768.37
Technical/vocational		
Grades 1–2, day	0.37	1,496.30
Grades 3–5, day	0.63	2,547.74
All grades, evening and night	0.19	768.37

a. The value of the UTM in December 1987 was U.S. $18.40
SOURCE: "Ley de Subvenciones: D.L. No. 3,476" (Law of School Subsidies), *Diario Oficial* (Santiago), August 1980.

TABLE 2.3 Modified Payment per Student, 1987 (December 1987 pesos)

Type of education	USE per student[a]	Pesos per student
Preschool	0.909	2,254.50
Primary		
Grades 1–6	1.000	2,480.20
Grades 7–8	1.107	2,745.50
Adult education	0.316	783.70
Special education	1.000	2,480.20
Secondary		
Grades 1–4, day	1.245	3,087.80
All grades, evening and night	0.375	930.00

a. The value of the USE in December 1987 was U.S. $10.54.
SOURCE: Law 18,681, *Diario Oficial* (Santiago), December 1987.

Enrollment and coverage in 1986–1987

Preschool education. In 1986, preschool education for children under six years of age was provided by the Ministry of Education at public (untransferred) and municipal schools, by the National Board of Kindergartens (JUNJI), and by the Foundation for Community Aid (Fundación Nacional de Ayuda a la Comunidad, or FNAC), a private corporation directed by the president's wife that received a special subvention per student enrolled. These programs were targeted at poor children without the economic means to attend private for-pay schools. The public and municipal schools and private subsidized schools served only children between five and six years of age, while the JUNJI and FNAC programs focused on children between birth and five years, offering integrated health, nutrition, early stimulation, and educational programs.

JUNJI offers a regular program of eight-hour-per-day schooling eleven months of the year, a small part-time program, and some special programs, recently introduced, for very poor children at risk of undernourishment who are not enrolled in any other preschool. Under the regular program, JUNJI also provides food supplements at its 426 establishments, as does the National Board of School Assistance and Scholarships (JUNAEB), to be discussed later. Supplementary food provides up to 80 percent of the daily calories recommended by the World Health Organization/Food and Agriculture Organization. Children at high risk of undernourishment are given an additional 150 calories per day. To increase the coverage and introduce new, more cost-effective programs, the government initiated four new programs in 1985. The largest is the Program for Nutritional Intervention and Language Development (CADEL), directed at two- to five-year-old children in extreme poverty who are not enrolled in preschools. These children receive supplementary food of about 700 calories a day (about 50 percent of WHO's recommendation) and special education for language development.

The FNAC's program is designed for two- to six-year-old children in extreme poverty, with priority given to children at risk of undernourishment. The program provides free education and nutrition supplements, along with recreation, early childhood stimulation, and training on good health habits for children. Financing for the food supplements is provided by the Social Fund, administered by the president of the Republic, and by donation from a Baptist international assistance program (see Chapter 3) (ODEPLAN 1985a).

Drastic changes in total enrollment and in the structure of enrollment by type of establishment have occurred. Between 1980 and 1986, total enrollment rose by over 65 percent, greatly increasing the number of children with preschool education. The JUNJI and FNAC integrated programs have benefited more than 110,000 (mainly poor) children, an increase of over 55 percent since 1980. The public and municipal, private subsidized, and private for-pay schools together enrolled more than 216,000 in 1986, an increase of over 70 percent since 1980.

Most remarkable, however, has been the increase of over nine times in the number of children attending tuition-free private subsidized preschools between 1980 and 1986. This increase has been only marginally the result of the reduction in the number of private for-pay schools, which may have been caused by children switching to subsidized schools. Children in the private nonsubsidized schools decreased from 27,500 in 1980 to 23,500 in 1986 (Table 2.4).

As for the redistributive or targeting impact of public spending on these programs, the 1985 Living Standards Measurement Survey, CASEN, shows that over 45 percent of the preschool subsidies went to the poorest 30 percent of the population, another 35 percent to the next poorest 30 percent, and the remaining 20 percent to the richest 40 percent of the population.[6] While there is no similar data for the earlier years, it appears targeting of beneficiaries has improved in recent years. The 1985 data indicate, however, that the subsidies received by the richest 40 percent need to be reduced substantially. Further, there is a need to study the cost-effectiveness of JUNJI's programs with a view to reducing the costs and increasing the coverage of the new programs, particularly those giving greater emphasis to community participation.

Primary education.   Primary education today consists of an eight-year compulsory cycle for children between six and fourteen. It is provided by the Ministry of Education through the municipal schools and the public schools not yet transferred to the municipalities and by the private subsidized and unsubsidized schools. In 1987, about 2,007,300 children were enrolled (excluding special education), a figure 8.2 percent lower than that of 1980 (Table 2.5). This sharp reduction in students enrolled (Table 2.6) was the result to a large extent of declines in birth rates since the 1970s and a reduction in dropout and repetition rates, which reduced the proportion of students outside the six-to-fourteen age range in primary school.[7] Some reduction in coverage appears to have resulted, however, from the 1982–1983 crisis, when open unemployment skyrocketed to over 20 percent.

The distribution of enrollment by type of establishment has varied markedly since the initiation of the reforms in 1980. Enrollment in private subsidized schools almost doubled between 1980 and 1986, indicative of a rapid response by the private sector to the subvention law.

TABLE 2.4 Preschool Enrollment by Institution, 1980–1986
(thousands of children)

Year	JUNJI	FNAC	Public and municipal schools[a]	Private schools		Total
				Subsidized	Nonsubsidized	
1980	47.7	23.4	91.5	8.2	27.5	198.3
1983	45.6	36.1	89.2	37.1	20.0	228.0
1984	46.4	43.4	103.6	54.5	18.0	265.0
1985	57.7	42.1	114.2	67.8	20.2	302.0
1986	70.0	41.1	117.4	75.6	23.5	327.6

a. Public schools are those not yet transferred to municipalities.
SOURCE: ODEPLAN 1987a.

TABLE 2.5 Primary School Enrollment by Type of School, 1980–1987
(thousands of children)

Year	Public and municipal schools	Private schools		Total[a]
		Subsidized	Nonsubsidized	
1980	1,743.9	306.2	136.4	2,186.5
1983	1,524.3	448.5	112.3	2,085.1
1984	1,445.7	511.6	88.6	2,045.9
1985	1,406.8	549.2	106.4	2,062.3
1986	1,345.7	594.9	107.5	2,048.1
1987	1,299.3	592.3	115.7	2,007.3

a. Excludes special education.
SOURCE: Ministry of Education, cited in ODEPLAN 1987a.

TABLE 2.6 Primary School Coverage, 1980–1986

Year	Enrollment (thousands)	Population (ages 6–14)	Coverage (%)
1980	2,206.7	2,263.6	97.5
1983	2,109.5	2,218.9	95.1
1984	2,073.4	2,206.8	94.0
1985	2,083.3	2,202.4	95.0
1986	2,077.8	2,204.8	94.2
1987	2,038.6	2,207.2	93.0

NOTE: Enrollment figures include special education.
SOURCES: The enrollment figures are from the Ministry of Education; the population figures are from the National Institute of Statistics 1982.

Whereas private subsidized schools accounted for only about 14 percent of total enrollment in 1980, they increased their share to about 29 percent in 1986. This rise came at the expense of enrollment in the public and municipal schools, whose share decreased from 80 percent in 1980 to 65 percent in 1986. Since enrollment in the private for-pay schools also declined, it is possible that some of these schools subsequently switched to offering tuition-free education.

Special or differentiated education is given to children between six and fourteen who have any disability, with the aim of enabling them to receive normal primary education. In 1987, this special enrollment reached 31,300, an increase of over 55 percent relative to 1980. Almost all children attended establishments that received public contributions. Enrollment in the private subsidized schools increased spectacularly, from about 1,300 in 1980 to over 14,200 in 1987 (Table 2.7).

According to the 1985 CASEN survey, the redistributive impact of primary education (general and special) was quite positive: 47 percent of the subsidies were received by the poorest 30 percent of the population, 31 percent by the following 30 percent, and 22 percent by the richest 40 percent. Primary education, along with government-sponsored preschool education, has had the highest redistributive impact compared with other levels of education. There is room, however, for improved targeting (for instance, by reducing or eliminating the subsidy to private schools located in rich neighborhoods), since nearly 10 percent of subsidies have gone to 20 percent of the richest population. Poor children located in these areas could be bused to nearby municipal or private subsidized schools.

Secondary education. High school education involves a cycle of four years divided into two tracks: the scientific/humanistic curriculum

TABLE 2.7 Enrollment in Special (Differentiated) Education by Type of School, 1980–1987 (thousands of children)

| Year | Public and municipal schools | Private schools | | Total |
		Subsidized	Nonsubsidized	
1980	18.7	1.3	0.1	20.1
1983	18.0	6.1	0.3	24.4
1984	18.7	8.6	0.1	27.5
1985	18.3	12.6	0.1	31.0
1986	16.8	12.8	0.1	29.7
1987	16.9	14.2	0.2	31.3

SOURCE: Ministry of Education, cited in ODEPLAN 1987a.

28

(*científico/humanista*), which prepares students for college study, and technical/vocational (*técnico/profesional*), which prepares them for work. Total high school enrollment in 1987 reached 695,800 students (about 55.8 percent of population fifteen to twenty years old), a figure 28 percent higher than that of 1980. Over 83 percent of the students chose the scientific/humanistic curriculum in 1987. Enrollment in private subsidized schools increased about 4.7 times between 1980 and 1987.

Table 2.8 shows the marked shift in the number of students choosing the scientific/humanistic versus the technical/vocational track. This trend is, however, to a large extent a statistical illusion resulting from the curriculum changes made in 1982. These changes made the first two grades of technical education the same as those of the scientific/ humanistic track, so that students postponed for two years their decision to specialize in technical training. The preference for the scientific/ humanistic curriculum may have been affected by the laws enacted in 1980 and 1981, which opened up new alternatives in higher education.

As for redistributive impact of the subsidies for high school education, as shown in Table 2.9, a much lower percentage went to the poorest 30 percent of the population in both types of high school education than was the case with preschool and primary education. A large proportion of the subsidies went to the middle 30 percent and the highest 40 percent of the income distribution range. The reason is that children from poor families leave the school system earlier to start working, usually to help their families. Targeting this subsidy to the poorest is therefore complicated, since it requires attracting the poorest children to a type of education that they may find very expensive in direct and opportunity costs and not very useful, in that much of high school prepares students for college rather than for work.

Vocational training programs.   As noted, the government started transferring the vocational schools to private corporations in related trades in 1978. The Ministry of Education continued to finance this education on the basis of what the government actually spent before the transfers. When the transfers were resumed in 1985, the ministry introduced a voucher or subvention system.

There is little information on how these schools are doing in terms of enrollment, quality of education, and relevance to the work place. Early assessments of the agricultural schools, which were the first to be transferred, indicate that community participation in school administration is much greater than in the past, a change that has helped close the gap between what is needed and what is taught at school, so that the

TABLE 2.8 Enrollment in Secondary Education by Type of School, 1980–1987 (thousands of students)

Year	Public and municipal schools	Private schools			Total
		Subsidized	Nonsubsidized		
Scientific/humanistic track					
1980	284.4	38.2	49.1		371.7
1983	333.9	109.2	45.0		488.4
1984	342.7	139.6	42.7		525.0
1985	331.0	156.1	52.2		539.3
1986	327.0	174.3	51.8		553.1
1987	319.4	179.2	53.1		579.1
Technical/vocational track					
1980	122.0	47.8	0.2		170.0
1983	76.3	42.7	6.2		125.2
1984	58.2	44.6	9.4		112.2
1985	66.2	60.5	2.0		128.7
1986	67.1	59.6	0.3		127.0
1987	37.9	48.6	0.2		116.0[a]

a. Includes 29,300 students enrolled by the "corporations," which administered the transferred technical schools.
SOURCE: Ministry of Education, cited in ODEPLAN 1987a.

30

TABLE 2.9 Distribution of Subsidies to Secondary Education
by Income Group, 1985 (%)

Income group	Scientific/humanistic schools	Technical/vocational schools
Poorest 30%	36.6	37.2
Middle 30%	34.6	37.1
Richest 40%	28.8	25.7

SOURCE: Calculation based on the CASEN Survey, in Haindl and Weber 1986.

employment prospects of graduates have improved. Before 1980, no more than 10 percent of agricultural school graduates worked in the agricultural sector (Anderson 1984). The present school structure, with the involvement of local farmers, has been important in designing relevant curricula.

There were problems, however, including lack of incentives for schools to increase enrollment (even if needed). This occurred because the Ministry of Education was transferring a fixed payment, indexed to inflation, without regard to enrollment. Also, a dual and discriminatory system was in operation, under which some schools received a per-student payment (municipal and, principally, private subsidized schools), while others received a fixed payment.

The National Institute of Training and Employment (INACAP), a government institute created by the Industrial Development Corporation (CORFO) in 1966, also provides vocational training. Until 1976–1977, CORFO provided the financing. Since 1978, INACAP has had to generate its own funding, including external financing. Since 1983, INACAP has also been one of the many institutions providing technical assistance to farmers. It has also entered into lucrative postsecondary technical education in mining and industry, benefiting from the financing provided by those industries and using tax rebates from the government.

Since its creation in 1976, the Employment and Vocational Training Service (SENCE) has been a major force in promoting, coordinating, and supervising the vocational training programs offered by the different institutions. Two of SENCE's major functions are to review, approve, and supervise the training that firms provide their own workers, financed with a tax rebate of 1 percent of taxable wages paid; and to provide scholarships for training provided by private-sector institutions, including INACAP. The training under the "firms program" benefited more than 100,000 workers in 1984–1986, at an annual cost of over 2 billion pesos.

Recently, the government introduced some restrictions aimed at targeting training by firms to less skilled workers. Each firm now has to pay 30 percent of the cost of the training provided to workers earning more than twelve times the minimum wage. They also must pay 40 percent of the cost of courses taken abroad if SENCE approves the training. Small firms whose 1 percent tax rebate is less than three times the minimum wage can have a further rebate of up to that amount for training purposes.

SENCE's scholarship program is directed mainly at unemployed and self-employed poor workers. In 1986, more than 13,000 scholarships were awarded, mostly to workers in agriculture (38 percent), fisheries (37 percent), and mining (15 percent), with the balance going to industry, construction, and services (10 percent) (ODEPLAN 1985a). Unfortunately, there has been no evaluation of the impact and cost-effectiveness of these programs.

Primary and secondary education for adults.   Adults wishing to complete their primary and secondary education may do so through a tuition-free program offered by private subsidized establishments. In 1987, more than 86,500 students were enrolled, only about half the number in 1980. To some extent, this reduction is explained by the increased employment opportunities in 1987 compared with 1980.

In addition to this formal school program, there are two special adult education programs. The first, the Fundamental Education Program, was introduced in 1983 and is directed at people over fifteen years of age who have not attained four years of primary education and are in extreme poverty. Private subsidized schools provide this type of education free of charge. The curriculum contains general as well as fundamental technical education and includes recreational and cultural activities. The technical education differs by zone so as to capture local training needs as much as possible. In 1985, more than 5,900 people attended this program. There is a payment based on the number of classes effectively taught per student. The second program, Elementary Technical Education, was introduced in 1984 and directed at people in extreme poverty over eighteen years of age whose prior education ranged from not less than a fourth-grade education to not more than the second grade of secondary school. In 1986, more than 17,000 students were enrolled, including those in private subsidized schools.

Summary of enrollment by type of establishment

Figure 2.1 shows significant change in overall enrollment between the public and municipal schools and the private sector after the initiation

FIGURE 2.1 Enrollment Shares of Private and Public/Municipal Schools, 1980–1986

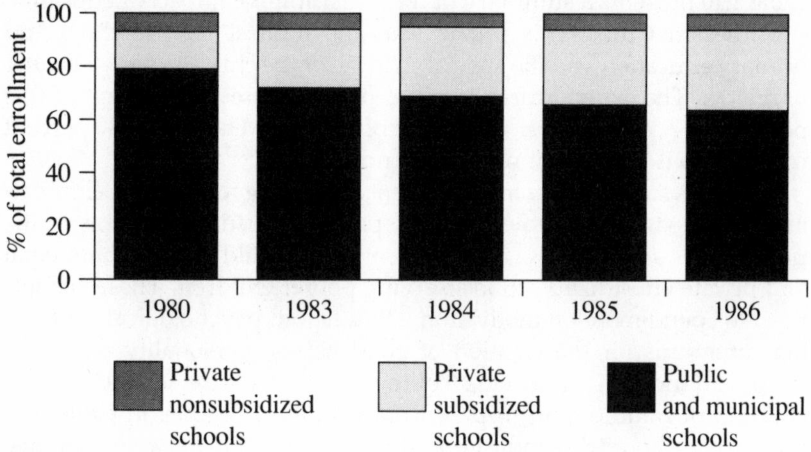

Private
nonsubsidized
schools

Private
subsidized
schools

Public
and municipal
schools

SOURCE: Table A2.1.

of the decentralization reforms of 1980. In 1986, more than 900,000 students (30 percent of the total) in preschool, secondary, and adult education were enrolled free of charge in private schools financed by the government through a per-student payment—more than double the figure in 1980. Enrollment in private subsidized schools increased the most in preschool and special differentiated primary education, followed by secondary education.

As a result of the adult education programs and advances in primary and secondary education, Chile reduced its illiteracy rate considerably, from about 11 percent in 1970 to 5.4 percent in 1985 (Central Bank of Chile 1987). According to the 1970 and 1982 population censuses, the average number of years of schooling (or schooling rate) of the Chilean population increased from 4.5 years in 1970 to 7.4 years in 1982. These figures give Chile the second lowest illiteracy rate in Latin America (after Argentina) and the highest schooling rate (UNESCO 1985). Most remarkable have been the advances in schooling achieved by the younger generation. For instance, the proportion of people fourteen to nineteen years old in the Greater Santiago area who had completed eight years of basic education increased from 59 percent in 1970 to 80 percent in 1983, while the proportion who had completed the four grades of secondary education rose from only about 12.4 percent in 1970 to 32 percent in 1983 (Castañeda 1984c).

The redistributive impact of education subsidies

Table 2.10 presents a summary of the redistributive impact of education subsidies in Chile. This impact was the highest for preschool and primary education and the special schools for the children with learning problems. The expenditures received by the poorest 30 percent of this population represent over 45 percent of the total. The richest 40 percent receive about 20 percent of the expenditures.

There is still room for improvement in terms of reducing or eliminating the per-student payments to the private subsidized schools in the richest areas and increasing the subvention per child going to municipal and private subsidized schools serving poorer children. These schools need to spend more on motivation, stimulation, psychological counseling, programs for the creation of good habits, personality reinforcement, and modern school aids (computers) than do the schools serving children of middle- and upper-income families. Studies in Chile and many other countries indicate a strong correlation between parents' education (especially the mother's) and their children's educational attainment.[8] Because of this factor, the poor municipalities need to spend considerably more than the richer municipalities to attain similar quality. With more resources, these municipalities would be able to attract and retain more high-quality teachers and school administrators.

School programs for feeding, scholarships, and textbook distribution

Created in the 1960s, JUNAEB administers the school feeding and scholarship programs. The major JUNAEB program is school feeding, which was reorganized in 1975 as part of the effort to target the National

TABLE 2.10 Redistributive Impact of Expenditures on Preschool, Primary, and Secondary Education, 1985 (%)

Type of education	Poorest 30%	Middle 30%	Richest 40%
Preschool	45.0	25.0	20.0
Primary	47.0	30.9	22.1
Secondary			
Scientific/humanistic track	36.6	34.6	28.8
Technical/vocational track	37.2	37.1	25.7
Special education	48.9	29.7	21.4
Adult education	36.0	33.8	30.2

SOURCE: University of Chile, ODEPLAN, results from the CASEN Survey, 1985.

Program of Food Supplementation (PNAC). The PNAC was to concentrate on serving children below six years of age through the distribution of food at health centers and posts, while JUNAEB was to distribute food supplements in schools (breakfast, lunch, and snacks). (More discussion of this follows in Chapter 3.)

The school feeding program provides up to 800 daily calories and 15 to 20 grams of protein in the public and municipal schools and the private subsidized schools during the school year. Food is provided to poor students belonging to levels 1 to 3 of the CAS Poverty Index, and to other students based on teacher recommendations and health records. This individual targeting has created some problems, since not all students in a given classroom received the food, notwithstanding the fact they were far away from home and also relatively poor. Recently, an approach using targeting by region has been followed. Production and distribution of food rations for school children is handled by private companies that bid competitively for specified supplies and geographic locations.

The scholarship programs include one directed especially at very poor children who reside in remote areas with no secondary schools and who have to move in order to get that level of education. JUNAEB's assistance includes room and board and school supplies. A second program provides scholarships for poor secondary school students. Others include vacation programs for very poor children and travel expenses for students living in remote areas.

Complementing JUNAEB's efforts is a major program of the Ministry of Education that distributes textbooks free of charge. In 1986, the ministry spent about U.S. $1 million to purchase and distribute about 3 million new books and redistribute over 3 million more, reaching more than 2.5 million students. Until 1983, textbooks were only given to primary school students, but since then some secondary courses have also been eligible. According to the CASEN survey, over 50 percent of the textbooks distributed were received by the poorest 30 percent of the population.

Student performance and the quality of education

To provide information about children's performance in school to administrators, parents, and students, the Ministry of Education administered the School Achievement Test to all students in the fourth and eighth grades of primary school in 1982, 1984, and 1987. The test aimed to measure affective and cognitive development through questions on reading and mathematics. Table 2.11, which is based on the 1984 test results, indicates that of the establishments financed by the state,

TABLE 2.11 Children Achieving Specified Objectives
in Spanish and Math by Type of Primary School, 1984 (%)

Type of school	Fourth grade		Eighth grade	
	Spanish	Math	Spanish	Math
Public	59.4	53.9	59.6	50.6
Municipal	59.6	53.4	54.4	49.9
Private subsidized	64.8	58.3	58.3	53.5
Private nonsubsidized	82.2	77.6	75.0	72.7

SOURCE: Ministry of Education, based on the School Achievement Test (PER) for 1984.

the private subsidized schools had the best scores. The differences in scores by type of school are statistically significant in econometric studies (controlling for socioeconomic background) using disaggregated information (Rodríguez-Grossi 1985). These scores, however, were far from those obtained by children in the private for-pay establishments, which include some of the best and most expensive schools in the country.

Econometric studies based on this same information have found that socioeconomic factors are the main determinants of school achievement in Chile, as has been found in many other countries (Himmel et al. 1985). The implication is a need for stronger compensatory actions capable of modifying variables at the school level; these actions include early stimulation, motivation, and personality building, which could be combined with typical school variables to improve student achievement. Little research has been carried out on specific and concrete ways to provide these compensatory measures.

Other measures of student performance and internal efficiency of the education system are provided by periodic information on promotion and dropout rates. These rates improved markedly in primary and secondary education in recent years (Table 2.12). For instance, the promotion rates in primary and secondary education increased by about 12 percent between 1973 and 1986. As a result, Chile's repetition rates are the lowest in Latin America.[9]

These indicators vary markedly by type of school, however. In 1986, promotion rates in private schools were higher than in public and municipal schools. The dropout rates were the lowest in private for-pay schools, which were generally of better quality and enrolled well-to-do students. The highest failure and dropout rates were experienced in the "corporation" schools, which were primarily technical schools transferred to corporations or foundations under the respective trade associations (see Figure 2.2).

TABLE 2.12 Promotion, Failure, and Dropout Rates
in Public and Municipal Schools, 1973–1986 (%)

Year	Promotion rate	Failure rate	Dropout rate
Primary			
1973[a]	79.8	14.0	6.2
1978	81.7	12.4	5.9
1981	86.7	8.4	4.6
1986	90.4	6.7	2.9
Secondary			
1973[a]	72.2	19.5	8.3
1978	78.3	13.8	7.9
1981	79.9	12.8	6.7
1986	81.1	10.9	8.0

a. Refers only to Ministry of Education schools.
SOURCE: Superintendency of Education, Ministry of Education.

FIGURE 2.2 Promotion, Failure, and Dropout Rates by Type of School, 1986

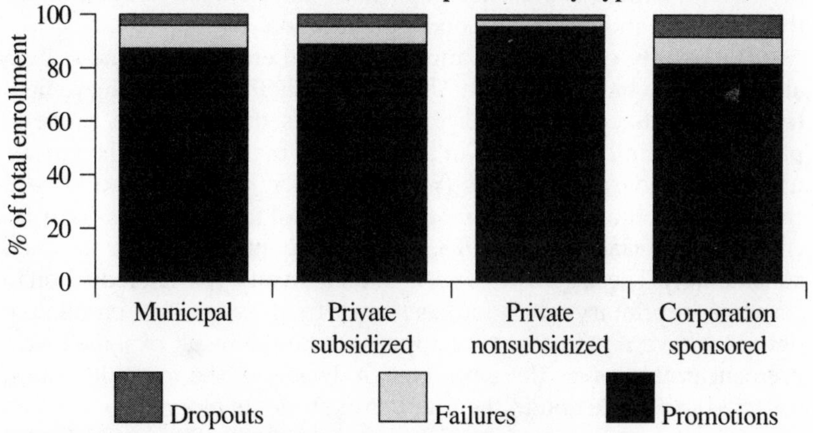

SOURCE: Superintendency of Education, Ministry of Education.

Summary and some further issues

As a result of the reforms initiated in 1980 and thereafter, Chile's preschool, primary, and secondary education system has become more competitive and decentralized. The reforms have consisted of the transferring of schools to the municipalities, which now have complete autonomy to administer the infrastructure, personnel, and procurement of goods and services, and the introduction of a financing mechanism by which fiscal resources are transferred on the basis of payments per student enrolled. The latter is equivalent to a voucher (or subsidy for demand) system that applies equally to private schools that want to provide free education in competition with municipal schools. The decentralization reforms applied to the technical schools as well, and they were transferred to private corporations or trade associations.

The figures for 1986 indicate a strong response by private schools, whose enrollment has more than doubled over the levels of 1980. This rise is a net increase in private-school enrollment, as enrollment in private for-pay schools has declined marginally, an indication that a few previously for-pay schools have switched to providing free education under government financing. Enrollment in private subsidized schools has risen the most in preschool, special or differentiated education for the disabled, and general secondary education.

The quality of education and the internal efficiency of the system also appear to have improved. The 1984 and 1987 national achievement tests found that students in private schools outperformed those in public and municipal schools in Spanish and mathematics when measured by standardized scores (with socioeconomic background held constant). Promotion rates in public and municipal schools have increased appreciably since 1973, while dropout rates have declined considerably. These indicators are at odds with an apparent reduction in coverage in primary education, as shown by the aggregate enrollment figures. However, the disparity appears to be the result of some measurement problems, as there has been a decline in the repetition rates, reflected in a reduction in the number of students older than fourteen years of age in primary school. However, some reduction in enrollment appears to have taken place during the 1982–1983 crisis, with the increase in open unemployment.

The CASEN survey of about 20,000 families nationwide, conducted in 1985, indicated that the government expenditures for preschool and primary education had a major redistributive or targeting impact. Over 45 percent of expenditures on these two levels were received by the poorest 30 percent of the population, with only about 20 percent received by the richest 40 percent. No similar data exist for earlier years, so comparisons are not possible, but it is highly likely that the distribution has not worsened in recent years as a result of the increased private-sector participation. The reason is simply that, as with the municipal schools, the private subsidized schools also provide free education.

The reforms have been difficult and costly to implement. A major problem was the transfer of teachers from the central government's payroll to those of the municipalities. The central government had to provide full severance pay and offer early retirement. In addition, it had to give economic incentives to the municipalities to accept the schools. The result was larger fiscal outlays for the Ministry of Education: expenditures increased by 6 percent between 1979 and 1980, 20 percent between 1980 and 1981, and 2.1 percent between 1981 and 1982, when the reforms were suspended because of budgetary constraints. The transfer, however, proceeded relatively smoothly and without major opposition at the beginning because of the severance pay and the fact that, during 1980 and 1981, the economy was growing and unemployment was decreasing rapidly.

Three issues deserve close attention in the future. First is the quality of education. Second is the targeting of subsidies for preschool, primary, and secondary education, so that more resources go to better education for poorer children. Third is the evaluation of school performance.

School quality has become a very important factor in determining upward mobility in the education system, and probably in the workplace, as Chile expands its modern competitive sector. Better-quality primary and secondary education is key to equalizing the university opportunities for poorer children. The quality of education for poorer children can be improved considerably by strengthening the financial and technical assistance to municipal and private subsidized schools. It is well documented in education studies that because socioeconomic background plays such a large role in determining the educational attainment of children, schools need to pay a larger compensatory role in the case of the children of lower socioeconomic background. Measures would include not only specialized (and costly) assistance in motivation, creation of good learning habits, and personality reinforcement, but also educational aids (such as computers) that poorer children lack at home.

More resources can be targeted to municipal and private subsidized schools through, for example, a financial factor that relies on regional targeting (giving higher per-student payments to schools serving children in a given area) or by using the CAS Poverty Index to single out students requiring a higher per-student payment. Regional targeting of students and schools would be relatively easy to implement and would facilitate monitoring quality improvements.

Two types of evaluating instruments are required. First is a periodic examination of students, as was done in 1982, 1984, and 1987 with the School Achievement Test (PER), to provide information to parents, school administrators, and the Ministry of Education on the achievement of students and the differences across schools. This information would guide parents' decisions on what school to send their children to and would help schools compete in attracting students. Second is periodic and more comprehensive sampling information to guide researchers on the best and cheapest ways to attain quality improvements and evaluate the impact of different technologies on school achievement. These two evaluation instruments and the studies derived from them could be conducted under contract by universities and research institutes in Chile.

Reform of the Higher Education System

Higher education before the reforms

Until 1980, the Chilean higher education system was composed solely of two public (University of Chile and State Technical University) and six private universities. In 1980, these eight universities had 116,962 students enrolled, or 7.2 percent of the population between eighteen and twenty-four years of age. The two public universities accounted for about 65 percent of the students at their main campus (*Casa Central*) in Santiago and numerous branches throughout the country. All universities, including the private ones, relied heavily on public financing, and there was no major difference between the public and private universities in terms of the proportion of expenditures financed by the state.[10] In 1980, the universities received 14.2 billion pesos, which accounted for more than 30 percent of total government expenditures on education. This percentage was even higher in 1974—47 percent—when university enrollment peaked as a result of the expansion after 1970 (Castañeda 1986b).

According to an assessment made by Chilean planning authorities, in 1980 the system had several problems. First, public and private subsidized universities offered a limited number of places vis-à-vis demand, but they could not expand because of public financing constraints. Second, high school graduates had no higher education alternatives other than the universities. Third, the public universities were administering their regional branches poorly from their main campuses in Santiago. Fourth, distribution of the subsidies for higher education was highly inequitable, in that a minority of university students coming primarily from middle- and upper-income families received a larger share. Finally, the transfer of resources to the universities based on historical allocations provided no incentives to increase enrollment, improve the quality of education, or offer more relevant studies (ODEPLAN 1981).

The reforms

Based on this assessment, the Chilean education authorities introduced several reforms. These reforms permitted the creation of new private universities; gave formal higher-education status to nonuniversity education alternatives requiring less time to complete than university studies; decentralized the two large public universities; increased the tuition at public universities and permitted increases at private subsidized universities; and introduced a new mechanism for funding the public and private subsidized universities whereby an increasing part of the funds would be allocated through per-student payments and student loans rather than through the unconditional, historically based budget allocations.

To expand and diversify the opportunities open to high school graduates, three types of higher education institutions were encouraged: private universities, "professional institutes," and centers for technical training. The universities were to provide twelve undergraduate degrees lasting from five to six years and the advanced degrees of master of arts and Ph.D.[11] The professional institutes were to provide programs of study of four or fewer years leading to degrees in a wide range of professional careers. They were to emphasize teaching (rather than research) and produce qualified professionals. The centers for technical training were to provide technical education through a large variety of short-term courses lasting no more than two years. They were expected to emphasize practical training so as to produce skilled workers (and even middle-level managers) in a short time.

The new private universities, professional institutes, and centers for technical training are free to set their tuition charges, but they have to submit their study programs for approval to the examining institutions. In the case of the new private universities and professional institutes, the examining institution is one of the existing universities. For the centers for technical training, the examining institution is the Ministry of Education itself, which uses private consultants to review study programs.

In addition, the examiners have the authority to give exams to students at the professional institutes in each course each semester for the first three graduating classes, and to university students during the first five graduating classes. The administration of the centers for technical training is also supervised to ensure that they have the minimum infrastructure and materials required to deliver education of an acceptable quality.

To decentralize the two public universities, the 1981 law stated that the regional branches had to be rearranged to form independent regional universities or professional institutes. They have their own presidents (appointed by the president of the Republic), their own budgets, and responsibility for managing their personnel and service deliveries. This decentralization was to promote better use of resources and move the universities closer to the community, to better match university studies and community needs.

Financing for the universities and professional institutes comes from three basic sources: tuition paid by students, loans (*crédito fiscal*) to needy students, and government transfers. The law included increases in university financing totaling 50 percent in real terms between 1980 and 1986 (Table 2.13), to come from student loans and public allocations based on projections of a rapid increase in GDP and government revenues. Major shifts were programmed to permit rapid growth in student loans to support the tuition increases and to raise the government transfers given on the basis of enrollment. In 1986, public university financing was to be composed of one-third direct, historically based transfers, one-third per-student transfers, and one-third student loans.

According to Article 8 of Decree Law 4, 1981, the tuition fees were to reflect the actual cost of the studies and were to be uniform for all students of a graduating class in the same field of study. The purpose of the tuition fees was to reduce the subsidies to the university students and the dependency of universities on government contributions. They were also aimed at reducing the inequity in education spending, since government spending in higher education benefits mostly students who come from middle- and upper-income families.

The student loans were to cover the tuition of students who could not afford it. Each university was to determine eligibility based on a student's family income, family size, number of students in the family, and place of permanent residence. Students were charged 1 percent annual real interest on the loan starting at the time the loan was made, with repayment to begin two years after completion of their studies or two years after dropping out. The term of repayment was ten years but could be extended to fifteen years when the annual payments over the ten-year term would exceed specified limits. Loans were not to be made available to students in the new private universities, professional institutes, and centers for technical training.

TABLE 2.13 Planned Government Transfers and Loans, 1980–1986

Year	Direct transfers Billions of 1982 pesos	Index (1980 = 100)	Indirect transfers Billions of 1982 pesos	Index (1980 = 100)	Loans Billions of 1982 pesos	Index (1980 = 100)	Total Billions of 1982 pesos	Index (1980 = 100)
1980	14.2	100					14.2	100
1982	12.7	90	1.4	10	2.1	15	16.2	115
1983	10.6	75	3.5	25	3.3	23	17.4	123
1984	8.5	60	5.7	40	4.2	30	18.4	130
1985	7.1	50	7.1	50	5.6	40	19.8	140
1986	7.1	50	7.1	50	7.1	50	21.3	150

Blank = not applicable.
NOTE: 1981 is not included because it was a transition year. The budget was similar to that of 1980.
SOURCE: Decree Law 4, 1981.

43

The government transfers were of two sorts: direct and indirect. The Ministry of Education was to make the direct transfers based on the proportion of government contributions each university received in 1980. These transfers were to decline in absolute and relative terms as a source of financing until they accounted for only one-third of the government financing in 1986. The indirect transfers consisted of a per-student payment given to each university and professional institute for every student recruited from among the 20,000 receiving the best scores in the Academic Aptitude Test.[12] The total transfer to be given under this arrangement was to be increased from 10 percent to 50 percent of the 1980 transfer amount until it accounted for one-third of the government financing, including student loans, in 1986 and thereafter.

Since the per-student payment was expected to cover primarily the costs of teaching (nonresearch costs), it was cost-differentiated by subject. Medicine and dentistry, for instance, were to receive 2.5 times more, and several engineering studies 1.8 times more, than the less expensive disciplines, such as the social sciences and humanities. This payment system was expected to induce universities to increase enrollment and improve the quality and relevance of education, since they would have to compete with each other to attract students and hence resources. Of the three sources of financing, only the direct transfers were guaranteed and not tied to competition and performance.

Originally, all universities, including the new ones, were to be eligible to receive the indirect transfers.[13] However, for political considerations, the final decree stated that the indirect transfers would go only to universities existing before the reform and to the newly created public universities derived from the decentralized universities.

Implementation of the reforms

Soon after Decree Law 4 was enacted in 1981, the private universities, professional institutes, and centers for technical training started to appear; the branches of the public universities were converted into new public universities; tuition was increased; and the new financing arrangements were initiated. In 1980, the twenty-one branches (*sedes*) of the two public universities were rearranged, and some merged to form eleven new independent regional universities and eight professional institutes. When the branches of the private universities that became independent are counted, the total number of public and private subsidized universities at the end of 1981 was twenty-nine.

The financing law of 1981 was the first university reform to suffer from the 1982–1983 financial crisis, when major changes were needed to accommodate the large decline in public-sector expenditures. Higher education was the hardest hit by the cuts as compared with the other levels of education and social sectors (Castañeda 1985b). Among the changes made in 1982 were the 2 percent reduction in each component of the government financing, including student loans; the reduction of 2,700 pesos in the per-student payment, to be deducted from the direct transfer; and the freezing of the government allocation at the levels mandated in 1982 in nominal terms, excluding student loans. The indirect transfers were increased by 10 percent, however, so the decline in fiscal allocations was less in this year than it might have been.

Further changes were made in 1983. The per-student payment was reduced from 75 UTM to 45 UTM, and the allocation system for the indirect transfer was modified in two main ways: the differentiated payment by field of study was changed to a uniform payment, and the allocation of resources according to the 20,000 best-scoring students was modified to cover all students (about 30,000) entering the universities. This new allocation system included a weighting scheme in which the highest scores received a larger number of points than the lower scores.

The reason for eliminating the differential payment by type of study was that many universities had substantially increased the number of places and the number of disciplines costing the most in order to obtain more resources. This behavior reflected the keen competition among the universities to attract students, but it fueled opposition by members of the expanding professions and by universities not able to offer the costly studies.[14] The reason for changing the 20,000-best-scores system was that it was perceived as benefiting primarily the older and more prestigious universities, which could easily attract the best students. The two changes meant, however, that the universities would receive relatively larger payments for the less expensive studies (that is, social sciences, law, and humanities) and that indirect transfers would not vary much among the universities, since they applied to all enrolled students.

Still other changes occurred in 1984. The direct government transfers were frozen at the 1983 level in nominal terms, with some adjustments to cover the salary increases of August 1983 (5 percent) and June 1984 (15 percent). The indirect government transfers were frozen at the 1983 level, and the modifications made to the distribution scheme in 1983 were implemented. The amount of the student loans mandated by the original law was increased by 400 million pesos. As will be seen, the student loan allocation suffered the least. In addition, the allocation of student loans was centralized in the Ministry of Education, which applied uniform criteria for the distribution of loans based on the socioeconomic background of students.

These changes were major departures from what was originally intended for the government allocations. The result was threefold: (1) increased uncertainty on the part of the universities, since they did not know in advance what they would get; (2) related difficulty in planning activities and investments for expanding enrollment and improving the quality of education; and (3) a sharp reduction in the salaries and wages of university professors and workers, which produced discontent and political agitation. To cope with the severity of the financial constraints, some universities tried to increase the resources they earned from providing services and consultation to private sector and government agencies. The government allocations and composition of the three components—direct and indirect transfers and student loans—planned and actual, are presented in Figure 2.3.

The government allocation to the universities decreased by about 40 percent in real terms between 1981 and 1986. In 1986, those allocations were only about 48 percent of what had been planned under the reform. This drastic decline resulted, as noted, in a sharp fall in the salaries and wages of university personnel. Reductions in personnel have not occurred, however, despite government requests to the universities that they adjust to the lower resources and reduce some of the inefficiencies that exist. The high unemployment rates since 1982, which have affected professional and low-level workers similarly, have inhibited layoffs.

Evolution of direct government transfers.   Except in 1983, the direct government transfers have followed closely what was planned under the financial law of 1981 (Figure 2.4). In absolute terms, the direct transfers declined from 14.2 billion pesos, which was the amount the universities received in 1980, to 6.7 billion pesos in 1986, only 0.4 billion less than was planned. Since the other two transfer items increased much less than was planned, the direct fiscal transfers remained the main source of financing, representing over 65 percent of fiscal resources in 1986 instead of the planned 33 percent.

Evolution of indirect government transfers.   The indirect government transfers in the form of per-student payments saw the largest departures from what was originally intended (Figure 2.5). In 1986, the amount allocated was only 14 percent of that planned and represented only 10 percent of total fiscal allocations instead of the intended 33 percent. The change in the allocation mechanism—from payments based on the 20,000 highest-scoring students to payments for all freshmen students—probably removed some of the incentive for universities to compete to attract the best students.

FIGURE 2.3 Planned and Actual Government Transfers to Higher
Education, 1980–1986

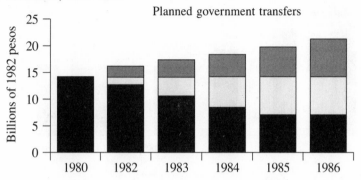

Planned government transfers

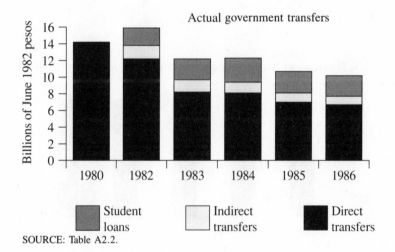

Actual government transfers

Student loans   Indirect transfers   Direct transfers

SOURCE: Table A2.2.

Evolution of student loans.   The level of student loans started to depart
appreciably from the planned amounts in 1983; by 1986 they were about
35 percent of what was planned for that year (Figure 2.6). They represented, however, about 25 percent of the total financing in 1986, compared with 13 percent in 1982. This financing source has consisted of
allocations determined each year and given to each university to distribute among applying students. Usually the amount requested by
students has been larger than the amount available, in which case the
Budget Directorate of the Ministry of Finance has applied across-the-
board cuts to all requests.

The universities have tended to spread these lesser resources across

FIGURE 2.4 Planned and Actual Direct Government Transfers, 1982–1987

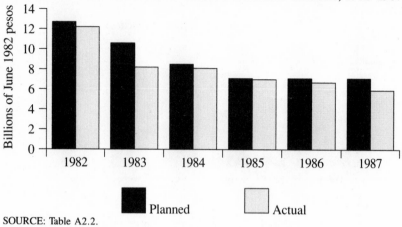

SOURCE: Table A2.2.

FIGURE 2.5 Planned and Actual Indirect Government Transfers, 1982–1987

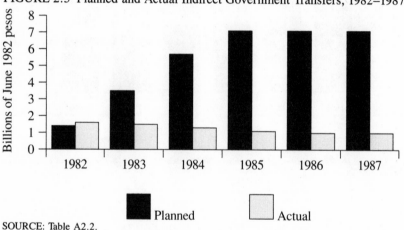

SOURCE: Table A2.2.

a larger number of students. As shown in Figure 2.7, while the proportion of students who received 100 percent of the requested amount declined from about 43 percent in 1984 to 26 percent in 1985 and 36 percent in 1986, the proportion of students receiving from 40 to 69 percent and the proportion receiving less than 40 percent of their requested amounts increased from 12 percent to 20 percent and 7 percent to 10 percent, respectively, between 1984 and 1986.

FIGURE 2.6 Planned and Actual Student Loan Amounts, 1982–1987

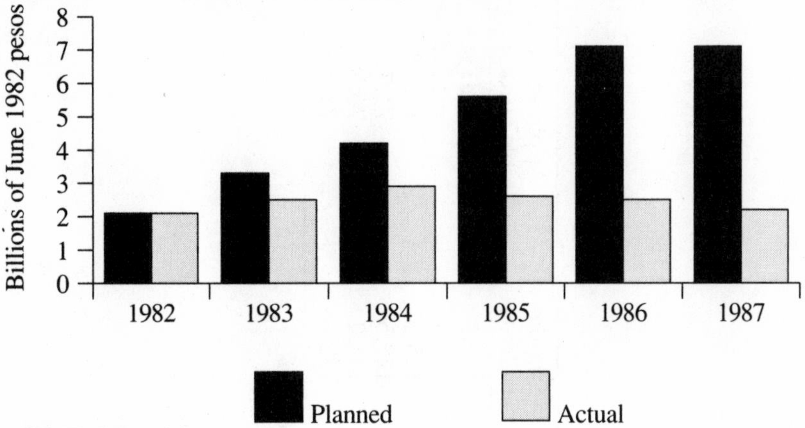

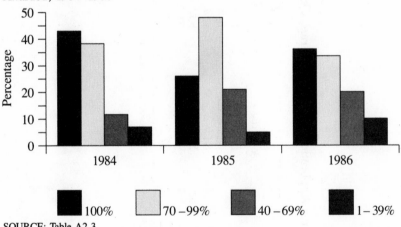

SOURCE: Table A2.2.

FIGURE 2.7 Student Loans: Percentage of Requested Amount That Was Awarded, 1984–1986

SOURCE: Table A2.3.

Targeting of loans to the students most in need also appears to have improved. This is indicated by the downward trend since 1985 in the proportion of students who applied for loans, which probably has resulted from a more stringent application of the criteria set by the Ministry of Education after 1984, when it started to administer the loans (see Table 2.14). In 1985, about 76 percent of eligible students applied for

TABLE 2.14 Student Loans: Applications and Beneficiaries, 1981–1986
(thousands of students)

Year	Applications	Awards	Awards to applications (%)	Eligible students[a]	Applications to eligible students (%)
1981	n.a.	55.6	n.a.	115.8	n.a.
1982	n.a.	68.7	n.a.	119.9	n.a.
1983	n.a.	84.7	n.a.	125.5	n.a.
1984	92.9	86.9	93.5	129.5	71.7
1985	100.0	91.3	91.3	131.2	76.2
1986	99.3	87.2	87.8	132.6	74.9

a. Eligible refers to total enrollment in universities and professional institutes that received government contributions.
n.a. = not available.
SOURCE: ODEPLAN 1985b and 1986a.

loans, of whom about 91 percent received them, compared with 1986, when about 75 percent applied and 88 percent received loans. Furthermore, the CASEN survey indicated that the distribution of student loans was much more equitable than that of the government transfers to universities by income group in 1985.

The proportion of students applying for loans in 1986 still appears, however, to have been very high (75 percent), given that, as shown by the CASEN survey, only about 27 percent of university students in 1985 came from the lowest 60 percent of the income distribution range. The proportion of applicants appears to have been even higher in 1980–1983, as a result of the recession and the fact that the universities, which were administering the student loan applications, encouraged applications as a way of guaranteeing prompt and timely payment of the increased tuition.

The size of the individual student loans has been modest; even in the case of those who got the full amount requested, the loan covered only tuition. No credit has been allocated for living expenses and materials, a gap that has had a considerable impact on middle-class and, in particular, poor students. It is well known that for these students, especially those from rural areas or provinces without universities, attending a university is very costly in terms of direct and opportunity costs.

Evolution of the tuition fees.   Although tuition at the subsidized universities increased in real terms between 1982 and 1984, it declined in real terms by over 18 percent between 1984 and 1986 (Table 2.15). This trend is most likely a reflection of the decline in the student loans, which fell by 14 percent in the same period. Loan payments by students also dropped (by 26 percent), to some extent the result of the depressed income of parents and the debts accumulated by students.[15] Tuition at the private unsubsidized universities has risen in real terms and is now considerably higher than at the subsidized universities. For instance, the tuition to study economics at one private university was 212,000 pesos in 1985 (U.S. $1,000), more than twice the tuition at the public and private subsidized universities (Castañeda 1986b). The fees at the professional institutes and centers for technical training were also high, ranging from one-fourth to one-half the tuition of the private universities.

Changes to the financing law in 1987.   In January 1987, the 1981 law was modified to create a student loan fund for each institution eligible for this program. The individual institutions were to administer this fund, rather than the Ministry of Education. An initial capital base was

TABLE 2.15 Tuition Fees, Student Loans, and Student Payments, 1984–1986
(billions of 1986 pesos)

Year	Tuition fees		Student loans		Student payments	
	Amount		Amount	% of tuition	Amount	% of tuition
1984	12.7		7.3	57.5	5.4	42.5
1985	10.9		6.7	61.5	4.2	38.5
1986	10.2		6.3	61.8	3.9	38.2
% change, 1986–1984	−18.7		−14.0		−26.0	

SOURCE: ODEPLAN 1987a.

52

established for each institution, which consisted of outstanding loans, except those due to mature in 1987, and Treasury bonds (called university bonds), denominated in local currency.

The distribution of bonds by institution was determined as a fixed proportion (based on past allocations) for a seven-year period. In case all the funds were not allocated to the students, the institutions could invest the balance in Treasury bills, Central Bank paper, or other instruments classified by the Risk Classification Commission for pension fund investment.[16] Each institution sets the criteria for distribution among students but can delegate administration of the funds to other specialized agencies.

Because resources are transferred to the institutions and not to the students directly under the 1987 law, debts between the students and institutions are regulated by the general credit rules that apply to the private sector. Students become debtors to the institutions, not the government or Treasury. If the institutions want to maintain their capital, they have to recover the loans. Some universities such as the Catholic University are starting to require collateral for their loans.

The decision to have the institutions administer the funds directly and to create the capital funds was motivated by the chaotic administration of past loans and high default rates, estimated at about 40 percent. The number of debtors increased from 8,400 in 1981 to 53,000 in 1987 and the accumulated debt from 62,800 UTM in 1981 to 120,000 UTM in 1987. The high default rate has been attributed to several factors. First, the students who were debtors to the government were to pay their loans to the general Treasury, which had no way to follow up and enforce recovery. Second, the economic crisis and high unemployment rate hindered repayment. Also, the high dropout and repetition rates resulting from poor screening and the difficult economic situation may have induced poorer students to drop out to help support their families.[17]

Although the new mechanism is simpler and clearer and provides incentives for payment, since the universities have to recover the loans so as not to decapitalize themselves, some problems may arise in the administration of the loans. The universities lack the infrastructure for loan administration, follow-up, and recovery. The requirements for collateral may affect poor students' access to the loans. In addition, the universities may try to attract students with higher socioeconomic background to avoid providing loans to poorer students.

A solution to the first concern would be for the universities to contract the administration of loans out to private financial institutions on the basis of percentage payments for the amounts recovered. This measure could, however, exacerbate the other concerns, since the poorer the students or the less adequate the guarantees involved, the higher the discount the university would have to pay.[18]

Chilean higher education in 1987

By 1987, the higher education institutions showed signs of financial and political stress. University professors and academicians were pressing for increased salaries, while the government was pointing to financial constraints. At the same time, the university's allocation of resources was inefficient and the staffing bloated. A government report indicated, for instance, that the student–full-time teacher ratio at the University of Chile, the biggest public university, was 5.5, compared with 8.8 at the Catholic University, one of the most prestigious and highest-quality universities. The ratio of students to administrative personnel at the University of Chile was 4.1, compared with 5.6 at the Catholic University. The average student-teacher ratio varies between 12 and 17, but in some cases reached more than 30, over all the universities. Another example of the inefficient allocation of resources is that of the Department of Physics and Mathematics of the University of Chile, where only about 13 percent of the full-time professors taught two to three courses per semester, while about 37 percent taught none.[19]

The regional universities appear to have been the most affected by financial constraints. As noted, they have been unable to attract the best students. Further, although there are no data on the subject, the reduction in student loans has affected them badly, since they appear to have a relatively higher proportion of poor students than do the more prestigious universities.[20] At the end of 1987, a proposal was made to create a special fund to finance research and development projects at the regional universities.[21]

Enrollment in higher education.   Despite the many problems faced by the universities and other higher education institutions, enrollment increased by over 43 percent between 1982 and 1987. This trend reflects the high demand for college education in Chile and the expansion of private-sector alternatives, especially the technical training centers, where enrollment more than doubled in those years. Enrollment also increased by over 5.3 times at the private universities and professional institutes that received no government grants. The lowest increase in enrollment, 9 percent, was at the institutions receiving public contributions (Table 2.16). In 1987, 25 universities were offering programs of five to six years, compared with 8 in 1980; there were 23 professional institutes with four-year programs and 122 centers for technical training

TABLE 2.16 Higher Education Enrollment by Type of Institution, 1982–1987 (thousands of students)

Institution	1982	1983	1984	1985	1986	1987
With public support						
Universities	105.1	107.4	110.4	113.1	122.1	119.4
Professional institutes	14.3	17.9	19.1	18.1	10.4	10.6
Without public support						
Universities	0.4	2.7	3.7	4.9	5.2	7.6
Professional institutes	3.8	7.5	11.1	14.6	18.7	19.0
Centers of technical training	32.8	39.7	45.4	50.4	57.8	67.6
Total by institution						
Universities	105.5	110.1	114.1	118.1	127.4	127.0
Professional institutes	18.1	25.4	30.1	32.6	29.2	29.7
Centers of technical training	32.8	39.7	45.4	50.4	57.8	67.6
Total	156.4	175.2	189.6	201.1	214.4	224.3

SOURCE: Ministry of Education.

with two-year programs. In spite of all the constraints, the development that has occurred and the new initiatives taking place are noteworthy.

Enrollment by subject of study shows that the new private institutions have made a wider range of subjects available. The new universities primarily offer courses of study in the social sciences, humanities, administration, and commerce, while the old universities emphasize technology (mainly engineering) and health. The professional institutes concentrate on technical training, education, administration, and commerce; the centers of technical training offer a large number of short-term courses, primarily in administration and commerce (secretarial, business administration, and accounting), technology (computer programming and motor repair) and education (preschool teaching) (Table 2.17).

Quality of education.   The quality of many of the private institutions appears to be low. Most private universities employ only part-time teachers who are not responsible for doing research, in contrast to the older public and private subsidized universities, which have large numbers of highly qualified teachers and researchers able to deliver quality education. An important drawback of some professional institutes and most centers for technical training is that they provide primarily classroom teaching and not much practical training. Problems with quality also appear to be present at the regional universities.

TABLE 2.17 Enrollment by Discipline in Institutions with and without Public Support, 1984 (%)

Discipline[a]	Universities		Professional institutes		Centers of technical training
	Support	No support	Support	No support	No support
Agriculture	6.3	0.0	3.0	1.4	1.8
Art and architecture	3.9	4.3	2.9	3.5	6.3
Basic sciences	4.5	0.0	2.0	0.0	0.5
Social sciences	8.1	29.7	3.3	10.4	3.1
Law	2.7	29.0	0.0	0.0	0.0
Humanities	4.6	14.3	1.3	1.5	2.8
Education	18.6	4.4	59.6	44.4	4.9
Technology	32.9	0.0	17.9	10.8	34.6
Health	12.3	0.0	1.0	0.0	40.1
Administration and commerce	6.0	18.2	9.0	28.0	5.8
Total	100.0	100.0	100.0	100.0	100.0

a. The classification follows UNESCO's guidelines, except for social sciences, which was changed to exclude administration and commerce (included separately in the table).
SOURCE: Lemaitre and Lavados 1985.

Although there is a strong demand for education—as seen by the very high number of applications at some of the best universities in Santiago and the large increases in private-sector enrollment—some of the new regional universities have not been able to fill their available places (Larraín 1985).

The quality and relevance to work of the training provided at the centers for technical training appears to have improved noticeably in recent years, however, as judged by the strong demand for this type of short-term education. By 1989, these centers were capturing about 60 percent of all students in higher education. The shares for the professional institutes and the traditional universities were 10 percent and 30 percent, respectively. In 1981, the share of traditional universities was over 60 percent. These changes also reflect the increase in employment opportunities for technical workers resulting from the dramatic increases in exports and competitiveness of the economy.[22]

Conclusions

The higher education reforms introduced in 1981 sought to increase the fiscal resources for the universities through a financing scheme that provided for incentives and competition among the universities. Two-thirds of the university financing from government funds was to be performance-related in 1986, when the reform was to be completed. The key elements of the financing scheme were a per-student government contribution to the universities, aimed at encouraging them to attract the best students, and loans that the students could use to pay the increased tuition. Participation by the private sector at the university level and lower technical levels would induce competition with the traditional universities and professional institutes, forcing them to improve their performance and quality.

The deep financial crisis in 1982–1983 severely curtailed funding for the universities and inflicted heavy damage on the financing structure that had been envisioned. The per-student payment allocations decreased after 1982 instead of increasing rapidly, as proposed in the reform, to constitute one-third of government financing. Instead, these allocations were only 13 percent of financing in 1986. The student loan allocations were also far from those planned, a gap that affected not only the universities' finances but also student enrollment, because the loans had to be spread over more students. As a result, only a few students, probably the poorest, could get enough funds to pay the full tuition. Students coming from middle-income families have probably suffered the most from smaller loans and the recession. As will be seen in the next section, university financing was cut back to protect the financing for the lower levels of education, which have higher social and private rates of return and redistributive impact. The universities adjusted to the fiscal crunch by reducing their salaries in real terms rather than by laying off staff. There was little reduction in staff in most of the public sector in these years, to a great extent because of unemployment rates of over 20 percent. The salary reductions caused discontent at most universities. This in turn resulted in a political crisis and public pressure by students and academicians. The government, aware of the situation, has insisted that financing is only part of the problem and has pointed to inefficiencies of university administration.

There have been benefits from the reform. Despite the acute financial crisis of these years, the private sector has responded by offering a variety of higher education alternatives for students and parents. As a result, there was an increase of over 1,800 percent in enrollment in private unsubsidized (and costly) universities and over 106 percent in two-year technical schools between 1982 and 1987. This increase shows the great demand for education that was not being satisfied by the traditional system. Although the issue of the low quality of education has led many scholars in Chile to propose greater government control, this is best left to parents and students, who will assess the value of the studies offered and choose accordingly.

Fiscal Expenditures for Education and Their Redistributive Impact

To a great extent, the sharp reduction in university financing resulted from government efforts to maintain and protect its expenditures for the lower levels of education, especially primary. As indicated, expenditures for primary and secondary education increased greatly in 1982, the worst year of the crisis, because of decentralization and the high expenditures it implied. Although expenditures for nonuniversity education fell in 1983–1985 relative to 1982, they held at the levels of 1980 (Figure 2.8). As a result, the ratio of government expenditures for nonuniversity spending to GDP increased considerably during the crisis, while the ratio for university spending decreased (Figure 2.9).

The strategy of protecting nonuniversity spending during the 1982–1983 crisis was justified in view of the greater redistributive impact this spending had and its much higher social and private rate of return compared with university spending. The CASEN survey of 1985 and an earlier study in 1983 indicate a higher progressivity for nonuniversity spending, especially for preschool and primary education.[23] The rates

FIGURE 2.8 Public Expenditures for University and Nonuniversity Education, 1980–1987

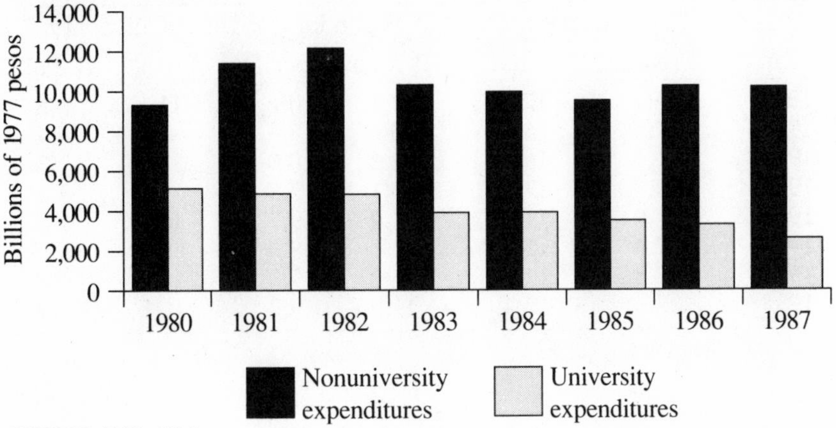

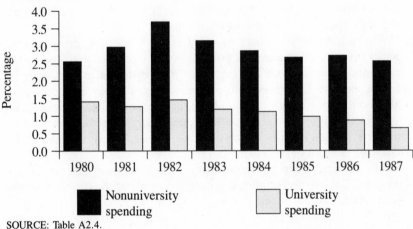

SOURCE: Table A2.4.

FIGURE 2.9 Share of University and Nonuniversity Spending for Education in GDP, 1980–1987

SOURCE: Table A2.4.

of return on primary education have shown a long-term decline since 1960, as expected, but they are still much higher than the social and private rates of secondary and university educations (Table 2.18).

Although the private rates of return on primary education were still over 25 percent in 1985, the social rates were less than half that, and were only about three percentage points higher than for secondary

TABLE 2.18 Private and Social Rates of Return on Primary, Secondary, and University Education, 1960–1985 (%)

Year	Primary		Secondary		University	
	Private	Social	Private	Social	Private	Social
1960	33.1	17.2	12.5	10.6	11.6	6.8
1965	27.9	15.7	10.6	8.8	8.4	4.4
1968	31.6	16.4	12.3	10.0	11.3	7.3
1972	27.7	12.4	10.1	7.7	8.9	4.2
1976	27.9	11.5	12.2	9.7	10.4	6.9
1978	27.4	11.9	11.1	8.8	9.9	6.7
1982	27.8	12.1	11.2	9.0	10.1	6.8
1985	27.6	12.4	11.0	9.2	10.3	6.9

SOURCE: Riveros 1989.

and five points higher than those for university education. The largest gap between the private and social rates (or subsidization) was in primary education, where public spending benefited poor children proportionally more. If the rapid modernization of the Chilean economy continues, the rates of return on investment in the quality of all levels of education will most likely increase.

The redistributive impact was highest for preschool, primary, and special primary education for poor disabled children, and lowest for university education. Of the expenditures for the latter, less than 25 percent went to the poorest 60 percent of the population, compared with about 80 percent at the lower levels of education. The student loans were better targeted to the poorer groups than were the government university transfers, but even in this case, about 50 percent went to the richest 40 percent of the students (Table 2.19).

The redistribution of expenditures across levels of education, together with the differential redistributive impact of the different levels of education, has produced a strong reallocation absolutely and proportionately in the overall education subsidies going to the poorest population. One way to illustrate this phenomenon is to combine Tables 2.19 and 2.20 to calculate the percentages of overall expenditures going to the different income groups. This calculation assumes that the distribution of the subsidies by education level in 1985 has been the same since 1974. However, targeting may have been better because of the decrease in dropout and repetition rates, which typically affect poor children more.[24]

Table 2.21 indicates that the proportion of all subsidies in education received by the poorest 30 percent of the population may have increased

TABLE 2.19 Redistributive Impact of Expenditures on Preschool, Primary, and Secondary Education, 1985 (%)

Type of education	Poorest 30%	Middle 30%	Richest 40%
Preschool	45.0	35.0	20.0
Primary	47.0	30.9	22.1
Special education	48.9	29.7	21.4
Adult education	36.0	33.8	30.2
Secondary			
Scientific/humanistic	36.6	34.6	28.8
Technical/vocational	37.2	37.1	25.7
University education	11.1	15.6	73.3
Government university transfers	9.9	14.6	75.5
Student loans	22.3	29.1	48.6

SOURCE: University of Chile, ODEPLAN, results from the CASEN Survey, 1985.

TABLE 2.20 Distribution of Public Spending by Education Level, 1974–1986 (%)

Year	Preschool	Primary	Secondary	University	Total
1974	1.0	37.6	14.0	47.4	100.0
1980	2.6	45.7	18.1	33.6	100.0
1983	3.8	50.2	16.4	29.6	100.0
1986	6.3	51.1	18.8	23.8	100.0

SOURCE: The data for 1974–1983 are from Castañeda 1984a. The data for 1986 are from ODEPLAN 1987a.

from about 29 percent in 1974 to 38 percent in 1986, while the proportion received by the richest 40 percent of the population decreased from 47 percent in 1974 to about 35 percent in 1986. The proportion received by the 30 percent middle-income group increased modestly from 24 percent to 28 percent during the same period. These figures, while showing good progress in targeting the education subsidies to the poorest population, indicate that further improvements are still needed in targeting subsidies at all levels of education, particularly university and secondary.

The targeting of the subsidies for preschool, primary, and secondary education can be improved by increasing the expenditures through higher per-student payments to the schools serving poorer children and by reducing the payments to schools in richer neighborhoods serving middle- and upper-income children. With increased resources, the

TABLE 2.21 Likely Distribution of Overall Spending on Education by Income Group, 1974–1986 (%)

Year	Poorest 30%	Middle 30%	Richest 40%
1974	28.6	24.1	47.3
1980	33.1	26.4	40.5
1983	34.8	26.8	38.4
1986	37.5	28.0	34.5

NOTE: The calculations were made by multiplying the appropriate columns and rows of Tables 2.19 and 2.20. For secondary education, the figures for scientific/humanistic education were used. SOURCE: Tables 2.19 and 2.20.

schools serving poorer children could increase the availability of specialized personnel and equipment, which could compensate for the disadvantages poor children bring from home and improve the overall quality of education. The subsidized schools serving middle- and upper-income students would be allowed to charge a fee, part of which would be paid by the government through the subvention system, similar to that of the National Health Fund (FONASA) system for curative health care (see Chapter 3).[25]

Given the relatively small number of poorer students attending universities, the potential for targeting subsidies at this level is limited. The potential for targeting overall education subsidies by shifting more resources from higher education to other lower levels may also be limited because of pressure by the universities and students for more resources. Within these constraints, targeting of the subsidies may be improved by combining a strong student-loan program for low- and middle-income students to cover not only tuition but also living expenses, and emphasizing scholarships for the poorest students. In the absence of a scholarship program, student loans tend to benefit primarily the poorer students, leaving middle-income parents and students with large payments they will find hard to meet and resulting in increased opposition to adequate tuition increases and rationalization reforms.

Scholarships for poorer high-performing students are essential because many of them may be afraid to take out unsubsidized loans, based on their more uncertain prospects of finding good jobs in the labor market, given their few connections and poor family backgrounds. The scholarship program could be funded with the indirect transfer mechanism (per-student payment) by providing funds on the basis of the number of poor students enrolled, rather than on the basis of all students, as is currently done.

Summary and Conclusions

The purpose of the education reforms was to increase the efficiency of public education and to expand educational opportunities by encouraging the private sector to offer more programs. Efficiency was to be pursued by decentralizing the provision of public education and changing the way in which the central government transferred resources to the providers of services. The government moved from the old system of giving money to schools and universities based on historical government allocations for teacher salaries and other costs to a new system of channeling resources based on attendance. Under this new system, if public education institutions want more resources, they have to increase their enrollment or reduce the number of dropouts and, therefore, compete with the private sector. Although the reforms introduced no user charges for public primary and secondary schools, they raised the tuitions at the university level, but at the same time they provided loans for needy students.

Implementing the reforms has been difficult. The primary reason was the 1982–1983 recession, which occurred just as the reforms were about to be fully implemented. In 1982, the transfer of responsibility for schools to the municipalities had to be suspended for budgetary reasons, leaving about 20 percent of the schools and teachers still under the Ministry of Education and most of the ministry's bureaucracy untouched. Furthermore, this bureaucracy could not be reduced, despite the reduction in the number of schools under the ministry, because open unemployment had soared to more than 20 percent. Another difficulty was that the wage hikes the central government gave to public employees went to the municipalized teachers as well, not only during the recession, when the raises were to be initiated, but also thereafter. These wage increases, coupled with several measures that precluded dismissing teachers, restrained municipal mayors from restructuring their staffs as students moved from one school to another.

In addition to these problems, the system of transferring funds on a per-student basis has not worked well at the university level. Here the system is differentiated (albeit imperfectly) by the degrees offered, an approach that has encouraged the universities to expand the "best-paid" areas of study, an unintended outcome. At the same time, many of the expanding professions and universities unable to offer the best-paid studies have opposed the reform. This situation has caused a substantial setback in this form of financing of universities, which was expected to increase over time. In contrast, the system has promoted competition among primary and secondary schools and appears to face no opposition there.

Although student loans have increased substantially since they were introduced and now constitute more than one-fourth of university financing, several problems remain. Subsidization is high, and students in private universities and professional institutes who may be as poor as some of those in the public and private subsidized universities are excluded. Moreover, initially the universities were to administer the loans, so that they were encouraging their students to ask for loans to ensure payment of the tuition. In 1989, a new system by which universities are given initial loan capital to allocate to students and are responsible for recovering the loans was introduced. Collections should increase, since the universities have an incentive to recover the loans to avoid decapitalization. The universities will have to introduce a scholarship program for the poorest students, as they may resist acquiring debts, given their perceived inferior prospects in the labor market and lack of collateral as required by the universities.

There has also been a sharp reduction in university financing until recently, the result to some extent of the government's efforts to maintain and protect its expenditures for the lower levels of education, especially primary. Expenditures for primary and secondary education increased greatly in 1982, the worst year of the crisis, because of the high cost of the decentralization reform. At the same time, although expenditures for nonuniversity education declined in 1983–1985 compared with 1982, they did remain at the 1980 level. As a result, the ratio of government expenditures for nonuniversity education to GDP rose considerably during the crisis, and the ratio for university education decreased.

The strategy of protecting nonuniversity spending during the 1982–1983 crisis was seen as appropriate in view of its greater redistributive impact, as compared with university spending, and its much higher social and private rates of return. The extensive household survey (CASEN) of 1985 and an earlier study in 1982 indicated greater progressivity for nonuniversity spending, especially for preschool and primary education.

The redistribution of expenditures across the levels of education, together with the differential redistributive impact of the different levels of education, has produced a strong reallocation, both absolutely and proportionately, of the overall education subsidies going to the poorest population. While a major effort has been made to target the poorest population, nonetheless much more is needed to target subsidies at all education levels, particularly at the university and secondary levels.

Appendix

TABLE A2.1 Total Enrollment in Nonuniversity Education and
Respective Shares by Type of School, 1980–1986
(thousands)

	Public and municipal schools	Private subsidized schools	Private nonsubsidized schools	Total
Enrollment[a]				
1980	2,308.2	401.7	213.3	2,923.2
1983	2,087.3	643.9	163.8	2,895.0
1984	2,015.3	758.9	140.0	2,914.2
1985	1,994.2	846.2	180.7	3,021.1
1986	1,994.0	917.2	177.7	3,088.9
Relative share (%)				
1980	79	14	7	100
1983	72	22	6	100
1984	69	26	5	100
1985	66	28	6	100
1986	64	30	6	100

a. Public/municipal includes JUNJI in preschool; private subsidized includes preschool children
   enrolled in FNAC, a private foundation receiving subsidies.
SOURCE: Calculations based on figures from ODEPLAN 1987a.

TABLE A2.2 Planned and Actual Government Transfers to Universities,
1980–1987 (billions of June 1982 pesos)

Year	Direct		Indirect		Loans		Ratio of total actual to total planned
	Planned	Actual	Planned	Actual	Planned	Actual	
1980	14.2	14.2	n.a.	n.a.	n.a.	n.a.	1.00
1982	12.7	12.2	1.4	1.6	2.1	2.1	0.98
1983	10.6	8.2	3.5	1.5	3.3	2.5	0.71
1984	8.5	8.1	5.7	1.3	4.2	2.9	0.67
1985	7.1	7.0	7.1	1.1	5.6	2.6	0.54
1986	7.1	6.7	7.1	1.0	7.1	2.5	0.48
1987[a]	7.1	5.9	7.1	1.0	7.1	2.2	0.43

n.a. = not applicable.
a. The planned figures for 1987 are assumed to be the same in real terms as those for 1986. The original law did
   not preclude increases in indirect transfers and student loans, in real terms.
SOURCE: Decree Law 4, 1981, Ministry of Education, and Budget Directorate.

TABLE A2.3 Student Loans: Percentage of Requested Amount That Was Awarded, 1984–1986 (%)

Percentage of amount awarded	1984	1985	1986
100	43.0	26.0	36.2
70–99	38.3	48.0	33.6
40–69	11.7	21.0	20.1
1–39	7.0	5.0	10.1
Total	100.0	100.0	100.0

SOURCE: Ministry of Education, Higher Education Division.

TABLE A2.4 Government Expenditures for Nonuniversity and University Education, 1980–1987 (millions of 1977 pesos)

Year	Nonuniversity[a]		University		Total	
	Amount	Share of GDP[b] (%)	Amount	Share of GDP (%)	Amount	Share of GDP (%)
1980	9,319	2.56	5,122	1.41	14,441	3.97
1981	11,397	2.97	4,859	1.27	16,256	4.24
1982	12,152	3.69	4,825	1.46	16,977	5.15
1983	10,304	3.15	3,895	1.19	14,199	4.34
1984	9,950	2.86	3,904	1.12	13,854	3.98
1985	9,511	2.67	3,501	0.98	13,012	3.65
1986	10,238	2.72	3,284	0.87	13,521	3.59
1987	10,186	2.56	2,599	0.65	12,785	3.21

a. Nonuniversity education includes preschool, primary, secondary, and technical education.
b. The GDP ratios were calculated based on GDP in real 1977 pesos; the government expenditures were deflated by the CPI.
SOURCE: The data on expenditures are from the Budget Directorate, Ministry of Finance; the data on GDP are published by the Central Bank of Chile.

CHAPTER 3

Reforms of Health and Nutrition Programs and Delivery Systems

The Chilean government's reforms of the health-care system had two main objectives: to improve the targeting of health services and food supplements to the needy and to increase the efficiency of the system itself. To upgrade the targeting, the government expanded and improved primary health care, with emphasis on the mothers and young children living in rural areas where ODEPLAN's map of extreme poverty showed the most deficient health indicators.[1] To improve efficiency, the government undertook major institutional and financial reforms of the health-care system, principally of the Ministry of Health (MOH) and the National Health System (NHS).

This chapter reviews policies and reforms of the Chilean health sector since 1975. Following a brief summary of the situation in 1974–1975, before the major reforms, it examines the main policy changes after 1975, including those related to the targeting of health and nutrition programs and the restructuring of the health-care delivery system started in 1979. Other topics of discussion include how the restructuring was implemented; aggregate public-health-sector revenues and expenditures since 1974; and reasons for the dramatic improvement in Chile's health indicators during recent years.

As the detailed review in this chapter will show, the reforms have not been easy and have required considerable negotiation, trial and error, and correction. There has been disagreement with the government's decision to concentrate resources on primary health care and to reduce the emphasis on building and rehabilitation of hospitals, especially during the 1982–1983 crisis. In 1989, a program for hospital investment and equipment began. The targeting of health and nutrition interventions has also been difficult, requiring the development of good information systems at the central and municipal levels, extensive coordination among programs, and substantial reform of the health-care delivery system to enable it to concentrate on the poorest population.

The reforms have transformed Chile's health-care system from a centralized public-operated one to a decentralized one allowing for private sector participation. In this system, the private sector offers competitive health insurance alternatives for those who can pay, allowing the public sector to concentrate its resources on those who need state assistance and who, for the most part, will be served free of charge. This strategy, which appears to be an effective way of targeting health expenditures to the poorest, needs to be accompanied, however, by a commitment to provide the poor with good-quality services and to protect expenditures for them.

The Public Health System in 1974–1975

The Chilean public health system had long been known for its well-organized services delivered to a large proportion of the population. In 1974–1975 (and until 1979), the system was composed of the NHS, serving blue-collar workers and the indigent, and the National Medical Service for Employees (SERMENA), the preferred provider system for financing health services for white-collar workers and their dependents. Blue-collar workers and the indigent received free services, including medicine; white-collar workers had to pay part of the cost of ambulatory and hospital care and the entire cost of medicine. In all, the NHS covered about 60 percent of the population and SERMENA about 25 percent. The health-care system of the armed forces covered about 5 percent of the population. The private sector handled the rest, consisting of independent workers and their dependents, most of whom had high incomes.

Payroll contributions by blue-collar workers and direct government contributions from the national budget financed the NHS. Payroll contributions and out-of-pocket payments by users for vouchers (bonos) for medical services financed SERMENA. The MOH allocated the budgets for the hospitals and other public health providers on the basis of historic budgetary allocations related to the "assigned" population but unrelated to the volume, quality, or type of services rendered. The government planned investments centrally in Santiago, emphasizing architectural design and specifying technical norms without much regard for cost-benefit or cost-effectiveness analysis. Goods and services were purchased by the Central Warehouse (Central de Abastecimientos), which had to follow complex bureaucratic procedures for even minor supplies.

The NHS, which owned more than 90 percent of all hospital infrastructure, provided services at its numerous rural and urban health posts, public clinics, and hospitals. It employed over two-thirds of all the physicians (a great number on a part-time basis) and other health professionals in the country. The SERMENA paid on a fee-for-services basis for the services of the private medical centers, clinics, and hospitals and of the establishments of the NHS with which it had working agreements. The armed forces had their own clinics and hospitals. Private patients used private and NHS facilities. In fact, because of the predominant role of the public relative to the private infrastructure and the very low prices charged for using the public infrastructure, private practice in public hospitals and clinics was common and crowded out the legitimate beneficiaries of the public health system.

The NHS board of directors made policies for the health sector. The Chilean Medical Association had a strong influence with the board and was a main actor in policy making. The MOH had only a minor supervisory role. As a result of this structure of responsibilities and the highly specialized nature of physician education in Chilean medical schools, there was excessive emphasis on curative medicine as opposed to the less expensive primary and preventive health care that typically requires less sophisticated health professionals.

Policy Changes after 1974–1975

The policy changes after 1974–1975 consisted of

- shifting the emphasis to primary health care, especially in poor rural areas where mortality rates were highest

- targeting health-care and nutrition interventions to the poorest population

- making the system more responsive to regional and local needs and promoting a more efficient use of resources

- tying the financing of the service provider to the volume and type of services rendered rather than to a fixed budgetary allocation

- introducing user charges proportional to the economic capacity of patients, a change that eliminated the distinction between white- and blue-collar workers in terms of their access to services and out-of-pocket expenditures

- promoting the participation of the private sector in the provision of services and the health insurance market, which had not been open to this sector previously

The emphasis on primary health care was aimed at treating the more widespread simple sickness and providing preventive health services (for example, vaccinations, pre- and postnatal care, and well-baby care) to the poorest population, especially in the rural areas.

The mechanisms for achieving the policy objectives included (1) a program of investments in outpatient clinics, begun in 1978, aimed at building a large number of rural health centers and posts, with financing from the Inter-American Development Bank (IDB); (2) a significant increase in the training and hiring of nurses, midwives, paramedical, and other auxiliary personnel to staff those centers;[2] (3) a strengthening of policy-making and normative roles of the MOH after 1974–1975; and (4) in 1979, a radical restructuring of the MOH and the NHS, which included the assignment of new functions and roles, decentralization, transfer of primary health care to the municipalities, and permission to the private sector to create insurance companies to offer prepaid health insurance plans to affiliates.

In 1987, the government introduced a new health strategy that shifted emphasis to the prevention and treatment of chronic illnesses, in response to dramatic changes in biomedical indicators of the Chilean population since 1970. The new strategy and priorities included procedures and financing of treatment for chronic diseases; increased equipment and drugs for the detection and treatment of cancer; norms and procedures for the treatment of hypertension, epilepsy, and diabetes; and increased and improved basic and specialized medical equipment.

Targeting of Health and Nutrition Intervention

Chile has had a long history of combined health and nutrition programs. The three major programs have been the National Program of Food Supplementation (PNAC), the School Feeding Program (SFP), and the preschool programs of the National Board of Kindergartens (JUNJI), which offer food supplementation. Other programs have included recuperation centers for severely undernourished children and day care for the children of poor families, developed by a private foundation (financed on a per-student payment basis by the government). The PNAC and the SFP have experienced several changes since the mid-1970s as a result of the government's effort to improve the targeting of food to the most needy and those at risk of undernutrition and to increase the efficiency of food distribution. Table 3.1 summarizes the principal programs and their main features and coverage in 1987.

The National Program of Food Supplementation

The national feeding programs that gave birth to the PNAC started as early as 1936 with the distribution of fresh and powdered milk to all children less than two years old attending the primary health-care centers of the NHS. Originally, the government distributed the milk only to nursing children (zero to two years old), but in 1954 it extended the coverage to preschoolers (two to five years old) and in 1971 to all children under fifteen. Since 1974, however, the PNAC has been available only to children under six and to pregnant and nursing mothers. The general objective of the program since its beginning has been to reduce malnutrition in children and mothers. The government has introduced major changes in the targeting mechanisms and administration since 1974, as will be described.

Targeting mechanisms. By law, the PNAC is to be available to any person within the beneficiary groups designated by the MOH who demands food. To improve targeting of the poorest and neediest populations by encouraging self-selection and greater participation, in 1974 the government began to institute major changes in the PNAC. In 1974, the program was restricted to children zero to six years of age, with school-aged children (six to fourteen years old) to be served by the SFP under selection criteria specified for that program. There was also a reduction and gradual elimination of the distribution of food at the work place and increased distribution through the health-care system, accompanied by monitoring of well-baby care and nutrition. In 1974–1975, a change was instituted in the caloric content of the distributed food and special food was provided for infants below one year of age and children one to six years old. Better food presentation was emphasized to induce greater public acceptance. Improvement in the monitoring of growth of children and nutritional vigilance information systems permitted identification of groups at risk and facilitated the design of appropriate

TABLE 3.1 Main Nutrition Programs, 1987

Program	Cost (millions of U.S.$)[a]	Target group	Type of food	% of WHO requirements	Targeting mechanism	Number attended (thousands)	Coverage
National Program of Food Supplementation (PNAC)	44	0–23 months old	Milk with 26% fat	Depends on nutrition status	Health checkups in MOH	1,200.0	80% of children and mothers
		2–5 years old; pregnant or nursing women	Milk/cereal	Depends on nutrition status	Health checkups in MOH		
Corporation for Infantile Nutrition (CONIN)	n.a.	Undernourished children	All meals	100	Severe under-nutrition	3.2 (1983)	Near 100%
School Feeding Program (SFP)	34	6–14 years old	Breakfast Lunch All meals	33 33 100	Needs as established by school[b]	523.0 490.0 27.0	35% of children in 1985
National Board of Kindergartens (JUNJI)	18	0–2 years old 2–5 years old Half-day CADEL[c] All-day	All meals 2 meals 1 meal All meals	80 56 48 75	CAS/MOH[b] CAS/MOH[b]	4.0 10.0 10.0 43.6	38% of children in extreme poverty
Foundation for Community Aid (FNAC)	n.a.	Poor preschool children	All meals	100	CAS/MOH[b]	44.0	

n.a. = not available.
a. The 1987 peso figures were divided by the average exchange rate (219.4 pesos/U.S. dollar).
b. Indicates that the CAS Index is used, with additional information on nutrition provided by the MOH.
c. Program for Nutritional Intervention and Language Development.
SOURCE: Table prepared on the basis of information from the Secretaría de Desarrollo y Asistencia Social 1989.

measures to deal with them. Information on the nutritional status of children was gathered at the health center or post, which had standards for the desirable weight-for-age and weight-for-height. Information on nutrition for pregnant and lactating mothers was based on weight-for-height and pregnancy elapsed-time tables adopted by the MOH.

In 1980, the program was financed by general tax revenues rather than contributions by workers. This system made it easier for the government to justify the reduction and gradual elimination of the distribution of food in the work place. In 1982, as a way to improve the targeting of food subsidies, distribution of food was carried out entirely through the primary health-care system, eliminating other channels such as the "welfare offices" of public and private enterprises, through which middle- and upper-income groups had been able to get food.[3] The last major change came in 1985, when the program was separated into two parts: a basic preventive program directed at the entire eligible population attending the health and nutrition facilities and a reinforcement program directed at the eligible population at risk of undernutrition.

Administration and financing.   The PNAC program is administered and operated by the Central Warehouse, which purchases, stores, and distributes the food to the health service facilities nationwide. No major changes were made in administration and financing until 1987, when the government began a program of administrative and financial decentralization. Under this program, the regional health services receive a budget account (at the Central Warehouse), allocated on the basis of the target population and health and nutrition indicators to be attained. The health facilities draw from that account to pay for food as needed. The MOH retains a supervisory, normative, and evaluative role with respect to the achievement of specified indicators. Purchases continue to be made by the Central Warehouse. The health-care facilities can use the savings from the program for other priorities.

The School Feeding Program

The SFP goes back to 1964, when the National Board of School Assistance and Scholarships (JUNAEB) was created and charged with administering the program.[4] The objectives of the SFP are to provide nutritional support for low-income children attending primary school, so that they are alert and do better in school, and to reduce the dropout and increase the school attendance rates. In 1987, the program provided breakfast, lunch, and snacks, with each ration equal to 700 calories and 20 grams of protein a day, or an average of 33 percent of the Food and

Agriculture Organization (FAO)/World Health Organization (WHO) requirement for school children. JUNAEB administers a smaller room-and-board program that provides complete rations (four meals) with a total of 2,500 calories a day.

Targeting mechanisms.   From the beginning of the program until 1980, the distribution of supplies among the localities and schools was based on historic allocations. The teacher was responsible for selecting the students to receive the benefits. Since 1980, the Committee for Social Action (CAS) Index system, administered by the municipalities, has been used to select the beneficiaries, along with the teacher's assessment of the urgency of need.[5]

The government has made several changes in this program to improve targeting. Beginning in 1984, data from the CAS Index and information on child nutrition, the need for food supplementation as assessed by teachers, age of children, family income, and distance from the school were gathered for all children in the schools in which the program was available. The intention was to select individual students rather than schools as the basis for distributing the food rations. This system could not be implemented because of the administrative complexity and the lack of up-to-date information. In 1986, based on the information collected, a first prioritization of the about 320 communities (*comunas*) was made for purposes of distributing the food. The information used included the percentage of children less than nine years old whose height was less than 90 percent of the WHO standard for their age, as revealed in the 1984 survey; the percentage of children born with low birth weight, as recorded in the civil registrar records in 1984; and the promotion rates in primary school, as reported by the Ministry of Education. More recent efforts to improve the targeting of the SFP include implementation of a new method for better and more equitable distribution of the benefits. This method assigns a point score by school, community, and region to each of the following variables: nutritional deficit (height-for-age), need as assessed by the teacher, educational level of the parents, repetition rates, age-for-grade deficit, and school achievement as revealed in the School Achievement Test (PER) scores of 1984. These point scores are used as the basis for establishing distribution priorities.

Administration and financing.   Until 1976, JUNAEB operated the program directly, buying the food, warehousing it in its own facilities, and distributing it to the schools. The main problems with this were (1) the complex procedures for acquiring and managing the food and the storage and distribution infrastructure; (2) lack of adequate quality control over the inputs and food, which made it difficult to establish the nutritional content; (3) losses of food because of inadequate warehouse controls, contamination, and poor administration; and (4) uncertainty that food would be supplied in a timely manner to the schools.

To address these problems, the government initiated major administrative reforms to pass the distribution of school lunches to private companies progressively during 1976–1980. In 1976, a pilot program delegated the production and distribution of food supplies to private companies. In 1977–1978, through competitive bidding, the distribution of food by the private sector was extended to the farthest regions in the north and south and to 50 percent of the metropolitan region of Santiago. By 1980, production and distribution of all food to the school children was handled by the private sector. The distribution responsibilities included delivering the food to children in the schools and providing needed utensils.

JUNAEB was assigned responsibility after 1980 for payment for each unit of food distributed,[6] establishment of technical norms and nutrition content, determination of the beneficiary populations by region, contracting of services with private companies, and supervision and control to enforce norms and regulations. Supervision by JUNAEB involves visits to the processing plants to verify the nutritional content and quality of food by random sampling.

According to JUNAEB, the new system has had several benefits. Among these are substantial savings in administrative costs; timely distribution to the schools; quality control and verification of the nutritional content; and savings in teacher time (in the past teachers not only distributed the rations themselves but in some cases helped prepare them).

The JUNJI's preschool programs

The JUNJI was created in 1970, its principal objective being to provide day-care services for the children of working mothers. Its preschool programs are very important in terms of food supplementation and are closely coordinated with the MOH and the CAS system for purposes of targeting.

Program objectives and beneficiaries.   Beginning in 1974, the main objective of the JUNJI program was to support preschool children from poor families by providing them with food supplements to improve their nutrition and better prepare them to enter the primary school system.

JUNJI has two traditional programs: child care (*sala cuna*) for children under two years, and the preschool program, which has two elements, part-time and full-time.

In 1985, the Program for Nutritional Intervention and Language Development (CADEL) was established to help children from families in extreme poverty who were undernourished or at risk of undernutrition and were not using the traditional programs. The CADEL program provides part-time child care and food supplementation that amounts to about 48 percent of the daily requirement. The program is operated by auxiliary personnel supported by JUNJI and mothers who help care for the children. Among the program's objectives is to train mothers in the early stimulation and nutrition of children.

Financing of JUNJI and costs of the programs. Financing is provided through direct budget allocations. The cost per child per year is estimated at U.S. $504 for child care, $418 for full-time attendance in preschool, and $124 for the CADEL program. These costs appear high: the child-care costs are only 15 percent lower than the cost of treating a severely undernourished child in a rehabilitation center (as will soon be discussed). This high cost prevents an increase in coverage and indicates a need for a thorough evaluation of the cost-effectiveness of these programs. More emphasis should be given to community participation, as is being done in pilot programs developed by some Regional Services in the Santiago area. The reasons the costs of the CADEL program are lower are community participation, the cooperation of the municipalities in providing facilities for children, and JUNAEB's contributions of food and personnel.

Targeting mechanism. In 1980, JUNJI began using the CAS Index as the selection criterion to target its programs better. In 1985, it also obtained information on undernutrition from the health posts and centers of the MOH. This information was used to select beneficiaries in the CADEL program in particular.

Rehabilitation centers for undernourished children

In 1975 the government set up a pilot program of special rehabilitation centers to house and feed severely undernourished children until their complete recuperation. According to studies, about 80 percent of these children were less than six months old and had about an 85 percent chance of dying before reaching one year. The program included food, physical and mental stimulation of the child, and education of the mother. The pilot program was very successful in that no deaths occurred, compared with the 25 percent death rate for similar children treated in hospitals.

The Corporation for Infantile Nutrition (CONIN), a private non-profit foundation, was set up by the Nutrition and Food Technology Institute (INTA) of the University of Chile to extend this successful pilot project nationwide, financed to a great extent by the health services of the MOH. Each center (of the thirty created between 1976 and 1983) consisted of forty to sixty beds and a kitchen, laundry, and medical facilities. Because of the rapid decline in severe undernutrition, there is now excess capacity in the CONIN centers.

Financing and costs. About 80 percent of the financing for this program is provided by the National Health Service System (SNSS, which replaced the NHS) and 20 percent comes from CONIN's own funds, which in turn come from donations and public collections. In 1987, the cost per day per bed was estimated at U.S. $6.50, and the cost of total rehabilitation of a severely undernourished child at $600. This is high, but it is probably lower than what would be incurred in a hospital (where maternal education would not be offered).

The Foundation for Community Aid

The FNAC program is designed for two- to six-year-old children in extreme poverty, with priority given to children at risk of undernourishment. The program provides education and nutrition supplements, along with recreation, early childhood stimulation, and emphasis on developing good health habits in children. The FNAC is a private nonprofit foundation run by women volunteers, directed by the president's wife. Financing is on a per-student basis, and the food supplements are provided by the Social Fund, administered by the presidency, and donations from a Baptist international assistance program (OFASA).

Summary of programs and expenditures, 1970–1987

As indicated in Table 3.1, in 1987 Chile expended over U.S. $100 million (about 0.6 percent of GDP) on nutrition programs. The amount has not varied much since the mid-1970s (Table 3.2), but it appears that the reforms have improved beneficiary targeting and efficiency considerably. Recent changes in the emphasis and money spent on the different programs have favored the programs directed toward mothers and

TABLE 3.2 Expenditures on the PNAC, SFP, and JUNJI, 1978–1988 (millions of 1987 pesos)

Year	PNAC[a]	SFP	JUNJI	Total
1978	8,099.7	7,851.3	4,207.1	20,158.1
1980	6,428.5	8,490.4	3,762.6	18,681.5
1982	8,310.5	9,428.8	3,917.7	21,657.0
1983	6,523.1	9,615.5	3,698.1	19,836.7
1988	9,379.1	6,911.9	4,335.4	20,626.4

a. The PNAC figures include the money value of donations by the U.S. Agency for International Development (USAID).
SOURCE: The figures have been produced by the Secretaría de Desarrollo y Asistencia Social based on information provided by the Ministry of Health for PNAC and the JUNAEB for the SFP and the JUNJI.

children and, to a lesser extent, the school feeding program (Tables 3.2 and 3.3). While the PNAC and preschool education nutrition programs have more than doubled the distribution of food, the school lunch program has been reduced. The coverage of the children in school declined to 37 percent in 1987. There is no information on the impact of these changes on the nutritional status of children. However, it appears that the school feeding program has increasingly been concentrated on the poorest children. In 1985, for instance, it was found that, although the total coverage of school children nationwide was only 35 percent,

TABLE 3.3 Food Distribution Interventions by the PNAC and School Feeding Programs, 1975–1987

Year	PNAC (millions of kg.)	School breakfasts (thousands of rations)	School lunches (thousands of rations)	Three meals per day (thousands of rations)
1975	23.6	746	594	10
1980	29.2	760	295	25
1982	30.3	690	333	22
1983	22.0	673	323	22
1984	27.8	675	425	20
1987	30.0	529	491	28

SOURCE: Ministry of Health and JUNAEB.

over 90 percent of the food distributed went to the poorest three deciles of the income distribution in urban areas and about 80 percent in rural areas (ODEPLAN 1987a). An assessment of the impact on children in need of assistance and nutrition is needed to determine whether the program should be expanded by drawing some resources from a better targeted PNAC.

Unlike many other directed food programs in Latin America, in which participation by the beneficiaries is low, the PNAC program covers most of the intended population, including higher-income people. Of the children one to five served by the SNSS, over 90 percent of the participants request the milk cereal offered, 80 percent of them regularly. The participation rates are lower for children from the upper four deciles of the income distribution, but they are still about 70 percent. In the lower two income deciles, the milk cereal ration distributed per child was found to be very important in providing the required daily calorie intake (Muchnik and Vial 1988).

The reasons for the high rates of participation include (1) the long history of the program and the wide knowledge and acceptance of it; (2) easy access by most people to the health centers and posts, which are located even in remote areas and in the poorest areas in cities; (3) acceptability of the food distributed, which is similar to that sold in the commercial market; (4) the continued education of mothers by health personnel; and (5) the "apolitical" nature of the programs. From the beginning, the nutrition programs were viewed as instruments for reducing malnutrition and not as belonging to any political party or platform (Vial, Muchnik, and Kain 1988a).

Although targeting has improved recently, significant subsidies are still being given to other than the poorest 30 percent of the population, which is the government's target. In the first socioeconomic survey (CASEN), carried out in 1985, it was found that about 40 percent of the food subsidies were provided to the wealthiest 60 percent of the population. The universal nature of the PNAC has limited its targeting of the poorest population: any one beneficiary who uses a health facility of the SNSS can ask for and receive food supplementation.

Restructuring of the Health-Care Delivery System

The restructuring of the health system, which began in 1979, consisted of reorganizing the MOH and the NHS, transferring responsibility for primary health care to the municipalities (initiated in 1981), and permitting the private sector to offer prepaid health insurance plans to affiliates of the public system and workers in general, to be financed by payroll deductions.

The reorganization of the MOH and the NHS involved the creation or redefinition of five institutions, which were given separate roles. The MOH is the normative, policy-making, and evaluative body. The National Health Fund (FONASA) is the financial center of the system, charged with distributing resources to public providers and administering the SERMENA preferred provider system. The SNSS, which is the old NHS divided into twenty-six autonomous Regional Services (plus one for environmental protection), is charged with actually providing health care. The Central Warehouse purchases, warehouses, and distributes drugs, supplies, and some equipment for the SNSS. The Institute of Public Health acts as a national reference laboratory and quality-control agency, which manufactures vaccines and other biological products.

The changes were made after intense negotiations with the Chilean Medical Association (Colegio Médico) and other organizations of health professionals regarding the staff structure of the new services. The new labor code introduced in 1979 had already weakened the role of those health-professional organizations. Whereas the law once required professionals to affiliate themselves with the Colegio as a prerequisite for practice, they no longer had to do so, and the new "association of professionals" was to be concerned only with the work demands of their members, and not with political or policy-making practices.

Transfer of the responsibility for primary health care to the municipalities included transfer of the health centers and posts and all the personnel working in them. The FONASA was to provide the funds to finance the full cost of services.

Following is a description of the operations and financing of the SNSS, the health centers transferred to the municipalities, FONASA's preferred provider system, and the private-sector companies providing health insurance (instituciones de salud previsional, or ISAPREs).

The National Health Service System

The SNSS is composed of twenty-six autonomous Regional Services, each with the infrastructure to deliver any level of health care from primary to the more complex tertiary or specialized care, plus one service responsible for environmental protection. A referral mechanism seeks to ensure that patients in each Regional Service enter the system through the municipal primary health-care center, which, for purposes of referral and supervision, continues to be attached to the corresponding Regional Service. Each Regional Service is administered by a director, who can be a physician or other specialized professional and is appointed by the president of the Republic. The director is responsible for administering all infrastructure and human resources previously administered by the NHS in Santiago. The MOH retains normative, evaluative, and supervisory roles through its thirteen Regional Secretariats.

Although the director of each service is autonomous with regard to personnel, he cannot change the pay scale or the structure by profession of personnel hired. In fact, as a result of intense negotiations between the MOH and the health sector unions, each service was given a fixed number of vacancies by profession and specialization to be filled with permanent workers, who could be dismissed only for very extreme offenses. This provision limits the director's ability to allocate human resources according to needs and hampers the FONASA's efforts to transfer resources according to the services rendered as a way of increasing the coverage and improving the quality of health care.

Another of each director's duties is to apply the MOH's regulations regarding private practice in public hospitals. According to government authorities, private practice was affecting the number and quality of services provided to beneficiaries of the public system. A director can authorize, on a selective basis, private practice outside normal hospital hours only in regions where private infrastructure is lacking, and can charge physicians increased prices to use the hospital and auxiliary personnel. Because the health professional organizations had proposed the prices charged before the reform, these tended to be very low in relation to the cost of similar services in the private sector.

In addition to providing curative health care to the beneficiary populations, each Regional Service is charged with delivering preventive health measures (for example, vaccinations and quality control of food and drugs) to the entire population and with distributing vitamins, dairy products, and other enriched food to target groups (pregnant women, nursing women, and poor children under six years of age) under the PNAC program. The latter activity, which is carried out primarily through the rural and urban municipal primary health-care posts, is accompanied by prenatal care for pregnant women and well-baby care for children up to six years of age.

Financing of the SNSS. The FONASA provides the financing for the SNSS, with the funds coming from the national budget and payroll contributions of workers and retired people not affiliated with the private-sector ISAPREs. The funds are allocated based on the number of personnel working in each service and a fee-for-service mechanism taking into account the amount and type of services rendered; selected biomedical performance and financial indicators are also applied. The system of billing for services rendered (FAP) is based on a comprehensive list of prices for medical services and is used to reimburse services for part of their expenditures. The aim of the FAP system is to increase the amount and quality of services.

The MOH carries out investments with budgeted funds under its normal investment program or under the National Fund for Regional Development (FNDR) upon the recommendation of the National Planning Office (ODEPLAN), which is charged with performing or ensuring that economic analysis is applied to all public-sector projects in Chile. ODEPLAN reviews all health projects coming from different sources, such as the MOH, regional governments, and municipalities, and advises the budget directorate or the FNDR on the inclusion of approved projects in their financing program. Projects costing less than the equivalent of 70 million pesos (U.S. $330,000 in 1987) are approved at the regional level. Given the difficulty of applying cost-benefit analysis to health projects, a simple method for determining project priorities is used that gives more weight to the expansion and improvement of the primary health-care system, rehabilitation of infrastructure, and repair of equipment.

User fees in the SNSS. The health law enacted in 1986 eliminated the distinction between blue- and white-collar workers in terms of access to the public health system and introduced user fees for patients on the basis of economic capacity. These fees vary according to four income categories and the type of services provided (Table 3.4).

Patients in groups C and D can choose private providers, but if they do so group C patients have to pay 50 percent (instead of 25 percent) of the level 1 prices. Patients are also free to use private providers for some types of medial needs and public providers (that is, establishments of the SNSS) for others. To facilitate payments, patients are eligible for loans from the FONASA. The loans are indexed to inflation but earn no real interest and are repayable over a variable period, since the monthly payments are not to exceed 10 percent of monthly income.

Municipal primary health-care services

In 1981, the government started transferring primary health-care centers and posts to the municipalities. The main objectives of the transfer were further decentralization of health-care services, designed to involve communities; provision of adequate services relative to community needs; channeling of municipal resources to health-care activities;

TABLE 3.4 Required Copayment at Facilities of the SNSS
(% of level 1 prices)

Type of worker and service	Income group			
	A[a]	B[b]	C[c]	D[d]
Blue-collar workers				
Medical services				
1986	0	0	10	10
1987	0	0	15	25
1988	0	0	20	35
1989	0	0	25	50
Dialysis	0	0	7	13
Maternity care	0	0	25	25
Prosthesis	0	0	25	0
Dental care				
In primary health-care centers	0	40	60	90
For children under six years and pregnant women	0	0	0	0
Drugs				
In primary health-care centers	0	0	0	0
In specialized outpatient centers	0	0	25	50
In hospitals	0	0	50	75
White-collar workers				
All items above starting in 1986	0	0	25	50

a. Group A as classified by each service. These people are the indigent population not contributing to any social security system, benefiting from assistance pensions (PASIS), or receiving the family subsidy (SUF).
b. Group B: Monthly income below 16,288 pesos (about the minimum wage) in December 1987.
c. Group C: Monthly income between 16,228 and 25,450 pesos in December 1987.
d. Group D: Monthly income greater than 25,450 pesos in December 1987. These limits are adjusted periodically for the increase in wages and salaries.
SOURCE: Ministry of Health.

and greater integration of the social services sector administered by the municipalities.

The transfer mechanisms included an agreement between the SNSS and the municipalities under which the latter would receive all the infrastructure in *comodato* for five years, with an automatic renewal if both parties agreed to it, and a list of personnel transferred to them, who would become municipal employees, governed by the labor code applicable to the private sector. These employees (physicians, nurses, midwives, and auxiliary personnel) would be taken off the payroll of the respective health service; they would then provide all the required health care at the transferred centers and all the complementary health-care initiatives mandated by the MOH, such as vaccinations and delivering food under the PNAC program. Each respective service would be responsible for giving supervision, control, evaluation, and assistance to the municipalities and for caring for patients referred by the municipal services.

Financing mechanism for the municipal health-care centers.   Financing for the municipal health-care services is based on the amount and type of services rendered under a scheme called billing for services rendered by municipalities (FAPEM). The FAPEM is a prospective-payment-reimbursement scheme with fifteen categories of primary health-care services, each priced at a level aimed at covering the goods and services, personnel, and maintenance expenditures. Capital investments are financed by municipalities with their own funds, augmented by the FNDR. To help control overall expenditures (that is, to avoid the excessive billing for services rendered that had occurred when the scheme was first introduced), an expenditure ceiling has been established for each municipality, based on similar per capita expenditures on primary health care in all regions.

Investment in infrastructure and equipment is a municipal responsibility. The municipalities can apply for investment funds from the FNDR, administered by the Ministry of the Interior and ODEPLAN, or to the Social Fund administered by the office of the president, or may use their own funds.

User fees at municipal health-care centers.   Services and medicines prescribed at the health care centers and posts are provided free of charge. The only exception is dental care, for which copayment is required for patients in the three highest income brackets, as specified in Table 3.4

FONASA's Preferred Provider System

The government introduced the Preferred Provider System (PPS) in 1968 for white-collar workers and their dependents as a way of unifying the health services offered by a great number of independent employee social security institutions (Cajas). In 1984, employees (active and retired) and their families numbered about 2.8 million, or about one-quarter of the population. Until 1980, the PPS could be used only by white-collar workers (*empleados*). Since then, it has been opened to any worker contributing to FONASA. When a person desires medical services, he has to buy a voucher from FONASA (called a *bono* FONASA), which he then uses to pay the provider.

List of prices.   Each medical service and hospital procedure has been given a price that providers must honor. Until 1983–1984, the list of medical services was limited, covering principally outpatient care, and the prices were very low compared with private practice. These factors, combined with poor supervision and control, motivated multiple billing for the same services.[7] The government then extended the list of medical procedures, and in 1985 over 2,500 were covered. Prices were also brought more in line with private practice.

The current price list is based on a "relative-value scale" that assigns every medical procedure a monetary value when multiplied by a unit value expressed in pesos (*unidad arancelaria*). FONASA has not explained the basis for the relative-value scale, but it is believed to be derived from studies and interviews with a number of physicians on the relative costs of providing specified services.[8] The PPS has no ceilings or caps on the amount it pays providers as a way of controlling costs, as was proposed recently in the United States for Medicare payments to physicians. Instead, cost containment is sought through the differentiated copayments that users make, as will be explained.[9]

Providers can charge three different prices for their services (outpatient and inpatient). The low price, called level 1, is the base price specified by FONASA in the list of medical procedures; the medium price, or level 2, is the level 1 price increased by 30 percent (or 50 percent in the case of medical consultations); and the high price, or level 3, is the level 1 price increased by 60 percent (or 100 percent for medical consultations). FONASA's reimbursement is limited to 50 percent of level 1 prices, so that patients desiring to use more expensive providers have to pay more out of their pockets. These rules mean that copayments at levels 2 and 3 for medical services are 61 percent and 69 percent, which are high by international standards.

Each provider (physician, nurse, midwife, and hospital) must choose a price level to charge when registering with FONASA, and must maintain that level for all patients for at least six months before changing to another level. The aim of this differentiated price system was to motivate high-quality providers to enter the system, while retaining low-cost options for users and providers. Providers are strictly prohibited from charging other than the authorized prices or asking for more vouchers than are authorized, and they are closely monitored by the MOH, which also reviews inpatient treatment. The only price that is unregulated is that for hospital beds. To ensure the availability of a low-cost alternative for patients, all establishments in the SNSS, which are spread throughout Chile, are registered at level 1.

Financing of the PPS.   FONASA's funds for reimbursing the providers of services come from workers' contributions for health (7 percent of wages and salaries), direct government allocations, and the proceeds of the sale of vouchers. Reimbursement is made at the numerous FONASA offices nationwide and by commercial banks with which it has entered into agreements.

The private health insurance companies

The private sector was permitted to enter into the health insurance business in 1981 when private institutions (ISAPREs) were allowed to operate and collect the 7 percent payroll contributions of enrollees. In return, they offered a wide variety of insurance plans.[10] ISAPREs are easily created: the basic requirements include minimum capital of 2,000 UF (about U.S. $61,000 in 1981); the provision of health insurance directly or through a third party; and the approval of FONASA, the supervising agent. To guarantee fulfillment of these obligations, FONASA requires all ISAPREs to deposit one month's contributions.

The rules of affiliation are very flexible, with ample room left for private negotiations between ISAPREs and their clients regarding payments beyond the compulsory 7 percent contribution, service coverage (beyond the required), and deductibles. To promote competition among ISAPREs and ensure that the contracts are met, the affiliates can terminate their contracts and move from one institution to another or return to the public health system with only thirty days' advance notice. ISAPREs cannot, however, terminate the annual contracts unilaterally, except when the affiliates are not meeting their payment obligations.

Summary of health-care options for workers in 1987

In summary, any worker has the following options for health insurance: he can enroll in FONASA or any ISAPRE of his choice and ask his employer to send the payroll contribution there. If the worker enrolls in FONASA, he has two alternatives for medical attention: he may seek services at the facilities of the SNSS or municipal health centers and posts, paying the copayments specified in Table 3.4, or he may seek services with any private provider, paying copayments that depend on the provider's price level with the FONASA. Indigent people and those who are eligible for the Family Subsidy (SUF) or Assistance Pensions

(PASIS) are served free of charge at the SNSS facilities. Independent workers can enroll in the FONASA or the ISAPREs.

Implementation of Institutional Changes and Financing Schemes

The SNSS

Implementation of these changes has not been easy, both because of inherent difficulties in the design of good financing schemes and because of the sharp economic decline in 1982–1983, which affected the amount of resources that could be transferred to the SNSS system. These factors may have affected the quality, although not the quantity, of the curative services provided.

Financing schemes.   FONASA pays directly all wages and salaries, investments, and other fixed costs of the Regional Services, and any services provided by third parties. In addition, it reimburses providers for services on the basis of the FAP schedules to cover some of the expenditures for goods and services. FONASA started to apply the FAP schedules around 1979–1980. After 1985, it began to apply the list of procedures and the price schedules used in the PPS system for reimbursement under the FAP.

Because FONASA pays all personnel, investments, and costs of services directly, the reimbursed FAP amount is a percentage of the PPS level 1 prices. This percentage varies by type of service, with higher percentages for more complicated procedures. For instance, the reimbursement for medical consultations is 60 percent of the level 1 PPS schedules, for heart surgery 70 percent, and for brain surgery 80 percent. This differentiation was instituted in 1988 to respond to criticisms about deficient inpatient services. In addition to these incentives, a system of biomedical and financial performance indicators has been designed to give additional FAP monies to the Regional Services.[11] The proportion of the FAP reimbursed by FONASA has increased recently, giving greater weight to the amounts transferred under the incentive schemes.[12]

Financial resources for the SNSS, 1980–1987.   Overall, the funds for the SNSS declined sharply from 1981 to 1985, largely because of the 1982–1983 economic crisis. They recovered in 1986–1988 (Figure 3.1). The greatest reduction was in operating income (about 50 percent), which includes revenues from user fees and other income from operations.

FIGURE 3.1 Sources of Funds of the SNSS, 1981–1988

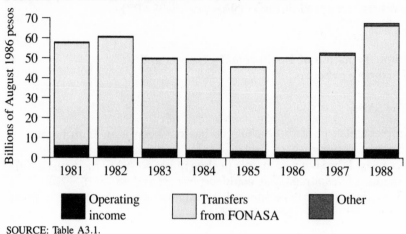

SOURCE: Table A3.1.

This decline can be attributed to the economic crisis and high level of unemployment, which reduced people's economic capacity, and to the expected reduction in the use of public services by wealthier patients, who used the PPS more and transferred to the private health insurance market. Transfers from FONASA declined by 10 percent between 1981 and 1985 but increased recently, especially in 1988, in part as a result of the decentralization of the PNAC budget (which had been under the Central Warehouse) to the Regional Services.

User fees have made up a minimal proportion of the revenues of the SNSS. The reasons include the fact that the Regional Services have attended primarily to blue-collar workers who made payroll contributions and to the indigent population. White-collar workers have primarily used FONASA's Preferred Provider System, although they could use the SNSS after the 1986 health law. This law has not been easy to implement and has required much work by FONASA to classify workers according to income levels. Over 90 percent of the medical services provided under the SNSS are free of charge (to people classified in the A and B income brackets), a reflection of the problems with the income reporting and selection process. There is no simple solution to this problem other than improving the controls and income information.[13]

Expenditures in the SNSS, 1980–1987.   Expenditures have declined much less than revenues (generating a deficit in some years) and fell much less than did GDP during the 1982–1983 crisis. As noted later, the result has been countercyclical behavior in the health expenditures that has helped maintain the precrisis level of services. The sharpest declines between 1981 and 1985 occurred in cash benefits (55 percent), which are mainly sick-leave payments under the public health system, including the PPS; in the wage bill (20 percent); and in investments (8 percent). Expenditures for goods and services increased by 8 percent in real terms during the same period (Table 3.5).

The reduction in expenditures appears to have affected the quality of certain services, especially inpatient health care. Primary health care appears not to have been affected, because it is relatively more labor-intensive than is inpatient health care, which requires more infrastructure, working equipment, and supplies of medicines and other goods and services. The decline in investments and maintenance has resulted in the deterioration of the infrastructure and equipment, aggravated by the earthquake of 1985, which damaged several hospitals in Santiago and neighboring areas. In 1989, the government introduced a program for hospital rehabilitation and equipment.

Resource use in the SNSS.   One objective of the decentralization was to improve resource use and accountability in the public health system. Although direct measures are not available, there are indications that resource use has improved in recent years. The number of medical visits per capita per year increased from 1.08 in 1970 to 1.65 in 1986, despite decreased expenditures; the number of medical visits per child per year increased from 1.01 to 1.70; the total number of medical visits by mothers increased from 513,000 to 1,209,000 (Table 3.6); and the average stay in a hospital fell by about two days (the implication being that with a relatively unchanged hospital infrastructure and occupancy rate of about 75 percent over the period, a substantial increase in the number of beds available has taken place).

Table 3.6 also shows a significant change since 1975 in the use of resources in the health sector, with a shift toward mother and child care. This shift is indicated by the increase in the proportion of hospital beds devoted to obstetric and pediatric care from 29 percent in 1970 to 37 percent in 1986. There also has been a rise in the share of nurses, midwives, and nutritionists hired, from 6.5 percent of all personnel hired by the SNSS in 1970 to 8.5 percent in 1986.

Issues for the future.   Despite these improvements and the better incentive structure for hospitals and other providers introduced with the FAP system, and despite the biomedical and financial performance

TABLE 3.5 Expenditures of the SNSS, 1981–1988
(millions of August 1986 pesos)

	1981	1982	1983	1984	1985	1986	1987	1988
Personnel	33,409	33,849	28,296	28,052	26,794	27,914	27,657	30,572
Supplies	15,315	18,573	17,725	17,515	16,529	16,866	18,811	24,164
Cash benefits	5,848	5,936	3,468	3,127	2,608	2,842	2,779	3,558
Investment	2,376	2,206	606	1,105	2,184	828	1,155	2,124
Other	2,289	1,866	1,897	2,081	937	1,075	2,137	7,049
Total	59,237	62,430	51,992	51,880	49,052	49,525	52,540	67,466

SOURCE: FONASA, Annual Report.

TABLE 3.6 Selected Indicators of Health-Care Resource Use and
Efficiency, 1970–1986

Resources	1970	1975	1980	1983	1986
Medical visits per capita	1.08	0.88	1.44	1.73	1.65
Medical visits per infant	1.01	1.01	1.30	1.60	1.70
Medical visits by mothers[a]	513	680	928	1,201	1,209
Delivery by professionals (%)	81.0	87.0	91.0	95.0	98.0
Hospital beds (per thousand persons)	n.a.	3.2	3.1	2.9	2.7
Discharges (per thousand persons)	n.a.	89	89	94	85
Average stay (days)	11.6	11.2	9.7	8.8	8.5
Hospital occupancy (%)	n.a.	77.0	76.0	76.0	75.0
Beds for obstetrics and pediatrics per total (%)	29.0	34.0	36.0	37.0	37.0
Physicians employed as % of total personnel	9.0	8.0	7.0	8.8	9.4
Nurses, nutritionists, and midwives employed as % of total of personnel	6.5	6.6	8.4	8.6	8.5

a. Thousands.
n.a. = not available.
SOURCE: Ministry of Health.

indicators, further improvements are still needed. These include such
areas as the administration of SNSS personnel and overall resources and
the incentive structure, which must induce providers to improve the
quality of their services.

The centralized payment by FONASA and the fixed structure of
personnel in the health services limit the efficient allocation of public
health resources. The staff with permanent appointments comprise
about 70 percent of the total, and their number and qualifications are
fixed by Law 2,763, enacted as part of the reforms of the health system
in 1980. Permanent staff cannot be removed except for very serious
offenses. Of the temporary staff, 30 percent have their contracts re-
newed every year almost automatically. Although the director of the
SNSS has the authority not to renew the contract of a temporary
employee and can hire a different person and interchange personnel
categories, the total number of posts and the pay scales are fixed. As a
result, only a limited amount of financial resources can be transferred
on the basis of the performance indicators, so that efforts for cost
containment through the incentive schemes are hampered. Services

need to be more autonomous and have more control over their resources.

The incentive schemes introduced through the FAP and the performance indicators still need to offer more inducement to hospitals to increase their own revenues from the provision of services. For instance, hospitals recover little from insurance companies for treating patients hurt in car accidents, who are covered by a compulsory law enacted in 1984. Further, improvements in the incentive structure could be made if ceilings were established by the FAP for each health service, as is currently done for sick leave. The services could then retain and freely use any savings. Some FAP funds could also be given as a matching grant for hospital operating income.

The hospital information system (SIGMO) now in place has the potential to generate measures of productivity, performance, and unit costs. Full implementation of the system would make it possible to introduce cost and utilization controls, billing and collections for services provided to private users of public facilities, and potential revisions of the FAP schedules. Hospitals are currently poorly managed, and, partly as a result, many of them have large debts with providers.

The municipal primary health-care services

The government began to transfer the health centers and posts to the municipalities in rural areas in 1981; after a suspension, the process was concluded in 1987. Among the reasons for the suspension (besides the 1982–1983 economic crisis) were the cap on FAPEM expenditures, which discouraged the municipalities from asking for transfers; some opposition by the medical profession, which did not want health professionals to become municipal employees under the contracting rules of the private sector; and some hesitancy by the MOH, which wanted to proceed cautiously after evaluating the experience of the first centers that were transferred.

Evaluation studies. There have been two recent evaluations of the municipal experience. The first was a study made in 1986 using a random sample of thirty municipalities that had received health centers and posts in 1981 (Secretaría de Desarrollo y Asistencia Social 1988). The second study, conducted in 1988, was based on a number of interviews and visits to health posts in the Santiago metropolitan area (Jiménez and Gili 1988).

The 1986 study showed the following results:

- The municipalities have expanded the health post infrastructure, in terms of square meters and number of examination rooms built by 45 percent and 38 percent respectively, excluding repairs, renovations, and reconstruction of existing health centers and posts.

- They have increased the availability of basic equipment and basic services. For instance, dental equipment rose by 85 percent, and laboratory equipment, which was lacking in all centers, increased to seven units. Other equipment that was added included beds, refrigerators, furniture, and scales. Basic services of potable water, electricity, gas and heating, and telephone and radio services increased appreciably, especially in rural areas.

- They have expanded the number of service hours offered per beneficiary population by over 80 percent in rural areas for physicians and dentists, and by over 45 percent for paramedical personnel. The reason for this is sharp increases in the number of people hired by the municipalities. The slower growth in paramedical personnel in rural areas appears to be because these centers already had many paramedics, while physicians and dentists covered the rural areas on rounds from the health services in the regional capitals.

- They have expanded the number of services provided over and above those at similar establishments still under the SNSS. The increase, however, was greater in urban than in rural areas, and greater in dental services than in medical. The number of medical consultations per hour reached 3.8 in municipal establishments, compared with 2.8 in similar establishments in the SNSS and the standard of 5.0 set by the MOH.

The 1988 study concluded, on the positive side, that there was a high degree of compliance with the standards (over 80 percent) at most health centers (*consultorios generales*) and rural health posts in terms of the extensive list of elements necessary to provide the required services. These elements included infrastructure and equipment, human resources, supplies, administration, and health education. On the negative side, cited as problems were difficulties with budgets, the low salaries paid by the municipalities, and an inadequate level of compliance with the human resource and supervision norms for rural health posts. (Supervision is the responsibility of the health service that transferred the health center to the municipality.)

Financial situation of the municipalities in the health program.   Most municipalities appear to be running deficits in their health-care programs, apparently because of the ceiling put on FAPEM expenditures in 1982. This ceiling has been only partially adjusted for price increases and the cost of medicines, which rose rapidly after the devaluations in 1982 and the following years.[14] The FAPEM mechanism was supposed to cover the total cost of providing services, so as to allow all municipalities (poor and rich) to provide a specified minimum level of services. The deficits are more likely to affect the poorer municipalities, which may find it harder to finance health expenditures from their own budgets financed through the revenue-sharing system (FCM) and a few other sources (see Chapter 6). Increasing FAPEM expenditures is probably a better, less distortionary solution than increasing the progressivity of the revenue-sharing system to transfer more resources to the poorer municipalities in order to finance the deficits in health services.[15]

Personnel at the health centers have complained about the salary levels and adjustment they have received. They feel discriminated against by FONASA for several reasons: they do not get an adjustment similar to that of the personnel of the SNSS, but rather receive the adjustment mandated by their municipalities; they have more unstable jobs and cannot pursue a career; and they do not have a seniority system. A positive note is that they appear to be very enthusiastic about working closer to the community, about their autonomy, and about the possibility of tighter team work and greater chances for training (Jiménez and Gili 1988).

Issues for the future.   The FAPEM system is good but needs to be improved in these areas: meeting the full cost of the minimum services to be provided by all municipalities irrespective of their other revenue sources; adjusting the price system to account for the differences in the costs of home visits and other services in rural areas (home visits in rural areas are more costly the farther the distance to the health center); and providing incentives for increases not just in the quantity but also in the quality of services, with an improved financing scheme that provides incentives for cost containment.

There are two ways to improve the financing scheme. One is to combine grant financing with an improved FAPEM system. The system could operate as follows. FONASA would allocate a given amount to each municipality per month or year for health services. Each medical service billed under FAPEM prices would be paid from that fund and from FONASA revenue on a matching basis until the municipal grant was exhausted. The percentages to be matched would need to be established and carefully explained to the municipalities. When the grant for matching purposes was exhausted, FONASA would not provide additional funds, and the municipalities would have to finance further services with their own funds. If the grant were not exhausted, the funds would be given to the municipality, as long as the municipality met the biomedical targets and indicators.

The other alternative, which is more radical, is to provide health insurance money to the municipalities for public health services for the beneficiary populations. The municipalities could act as health-care insurers or health maintenance organizations. In this case, financing the municipalities on a per capita (or per beneficiary) basis would probably be better than on the FAPEM basis. The municipalities could refer patients for inpatient care to the SNSS or the private sector (whichever provided the best and cheapest service). This mechanism would help improve the referral mechanism, which appears not to be working because the SNSS has little incentive to enforce the referral rules. The SNSS is reimbursed the same amount irrespective of whether the patient was referred from a lower level.

FONASA's Preferred Provider System

After the numerous improvements, the PPS appears to be working expeditiously and has great acceptance by providers and users. No major irregularities or fraud have been detected. Expenditures by FONASA and users of the PPS increased by over 3.6 times in real terms between 1974 and 1986 (Figure 3.2). The share of payments of the PPS in the total expenditures of the public health system went from 6 percent in 1974 to 25 percent in 1983, the peak year, and to 21 percent in 1986 (Figure 3.3). These shares are even bigger if the expenditures for sick leave in the PPS (which cannot be separated out from other sick-leave payments) are included. The decline in PPS expenditures after 1983 reflects lower payments by FONASA, as the copayments by users and the transfer of people to the ISAPREs increased.

Several criticisms have arisen in connection with the transfer of people from the PPS to ISAPREs. One is that the PPS was cross-subsidizing the public system, since the contributions were a percentage of salaries, and people with higher incomes did not use the public health system. The cross-subsidization may not have been as great as suggested by critics, however. First, on the contributions side, the government set a cap on the salary for contribution purposes, and there were also marked differences between total salaries and taxable salaries, especially for public employees. Second, on the expenditure side, it appears, as indicated by the ISAPRE figures, that people with higher incomes demand more and costlier services. For instance, in 1987, the

FIGURE 3.2 FONASA and User Payments in the Preferred Provider System, 1974–1988

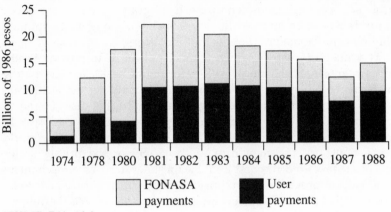

SOURCE: Table A3.2.

FIGURE 3.3 Percentage of PPS Expenditures in Total Public Health Expenditures, 1974–1986

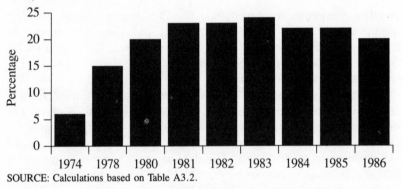

SOURCE: Calculations based on Table A3.2.

consultations per ISAPRE affiliate were 3.1, as compared with 1.7 for the whole population.

Some significant advantages of the ISAPRE system are that firms can save on the costs of the welfare offices and outpatient services, which they had previously offered their workers in addition to making payroll contributions to the public system, and can speed up services and avoid the paperwork required by the public health system.[16]

User payments in the PPS. Direct user payments or copayments increased in the aggregate from about 45 percent of the cost of medical attentions in the period 1975–1982 to about 60 percent in 1988 (Figure 3.4).

FIGURE 3.4 User Payments as Percentage of Expenditures in the PPS,
1974–1988

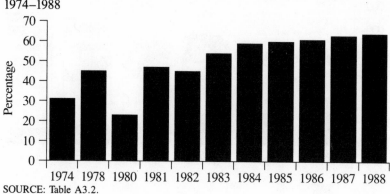

SOURCE: Table A3.2.

Two main reasons are the increased copayment requirements and the
use of more costly providers by patients. For instance, the use of level 3
providers for medical consultations and laboratory exams went from 10
percent in 1984 to 30 percent in 1987. Similar increases occurred in the
use of level 3 providers of hospital care—from 11 percent in 1984 to 30
percent in 1987 (FONASA 1985 and 1988).

The shift toward more expensive providers reflects both supply and
demand. On the supply side, there has been a marked shift by providers, including physicians, nurses, midwives, and health technicians, to levels 2 and 3. On the demand side, there has been an increase
in income and a reduction in unemployment since 1985.

The supply side.   The level at which providers enroll has changed
appreciably since 1983 when the differentiated price system began
(Figure 3.5). For instance, in 1983, 49 percent of the physicians enrolled
in level 1, 34 percent in level 2, and 17 percent in level 3. In 1988, the
percentage of physicians enrolling in level 1 decreased to 12 percent and
increased in level 3 to 57 percent. Other registered professionals and
health-care institutions (laboratories, hospitals, and clinics) have also
increased their enrollment in level 3. For instance, while in 1984 only 15
percent of health institutions were in level 3, by 1987 the percentage was
33 percent. It is also interesting to note the sharp increase in the overall
enrollment of professionals and health institutions: over 90 percent of all
physicians have joined the system, and the number of private health-
care institutions rose from about 700 in 1984 to about 1,100 in 1988.

The demand side.   The number of inpatient and outpatient services
provided under the PPS has decreased in recent years, a reflection of the

FIGURE 3.5 Physicians Enrolled in the PPS by Price Level, 1983–1988

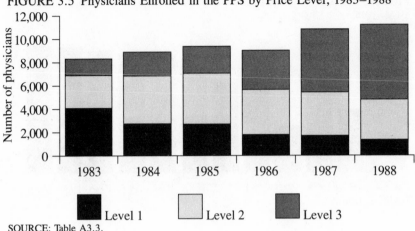

SOURCE: Table A3.3.

transfer of affiliates to ISAPREs rather than of the increased price of services. The "supply" price for consultations (an average of the three price levels, weighted by the number of physicians by level each year) has, in fact, risen much less than have real wages and salaries (Figure 3.6).[17]

Loans to patients.   Patient loans have increased rapidly since their introduction in 1986. At the end of that year, the number of credits approved reached over 41,000, for 736 million pesos (about U.S. $3.6 million), of which 95 percent went to PPS users and the rest to SNSS users. Loans in 1988 amounted to 930 million pesos (U.S. $3.7 million). Payments on outstanding loans increased from 500 million pesos in 1987 to 583 million pesos in 1988. Most payments have been made through a bank with which FONASA has entered into a working agreement for collection. There is no limit on the amount that can be borrowed by an individual, and credits accumulate. However, it appears that so far, late payments have accounted for only about 15 percent of the total outstanding loans.[18]

Issues for the future.   Three issues in the PPS require close attention. First, continued updating and revision of the level 1 prices is needed to avoid a concentration of providers at the higher price levels. Although more price levels could be allowed, a large number is harder to monitor and enforce. Second, continued tight control is necessary to prevent fraudulent use of the system. Third, the growth in health-care loans may require alternative administration arrangements. In the few years the loan system has been operating, FONASA has made over 100,000

FIGURE 3.6 Supply Price and Wage Indexes in Real Terms, 1983–1988

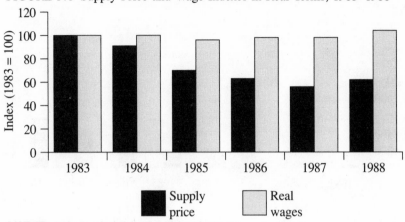

SOURCE: Author's calculations as explained in the text.

loans, and rapid growth is expected because the monthly payments are low and patients can ask for as many loans they need. FONASA has been successfully administering these loans, but it may find it hard and outside the range of its normal operations to administer a large portfolio.

The private sector (ISAPRES)

The growth of the ISAPREs has been impressive since they were allowed to operate in 1981 (Figure 3.7). In 1988, the number of affiliates and their families amounted to over 1.4 million people (12 percent of the population), and the trend is toward increased enrollment.

Types of ISAPREs.   Two types of ISAPREs have emerged: closed and open. Closed ISAPREs enroll only workers of a given company and are not open to other workers. Open ISAPREs, by contrast, are available to all workers and usually are very aggressive in recruiting affiliates. Since 1981 the number of ISAPREs has grown rapidly to thirty-one (eleven closed and twenty open). The open variety has grown the most, accounting for over 90 percent of affiliates in December 1988.

Because ISAPREs can refuse to renew annual contracts, they have a tendency to prefer "good risks," leaving the "bad risks" (such as the elderly, the frequently sick, and those diagnosed with serious illness) to the public health system. This practice could increase the financial burden on the public system. Correcting this situation would likely

FIGURE 3.7 Enrollees and Total Beneficiary Population in the ISAPREs, 1981–1988

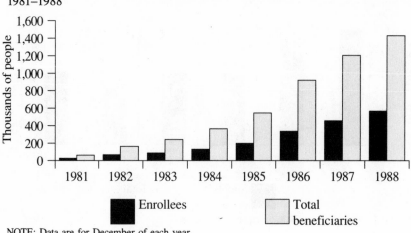

NOTE: Data are for December of each year.
SOURCE: Table A3.4.

result in higher premiums in the private sector and the establishment of long-term contracts between ISAPREs and affiliates.[19] Recently, some ISAPREs have started offering long-term contracts.

Parallel to the rapid increase in enrollment in the ISAPREs has been a rapid increase in infrastructure, including hospital beds, equipment, and laboratories provided by the private sector. Hospital beds in the private system have more than doubled, from 3,855 beds in 1981 to 9,185 beds in 1987.

Enrollment in the ISAPREs.   Although the ISAPREs have concentrated on the higher-income groups, the trend is toward increased enrollment of middle-income affiliates, as a result of the increased competition among ISAPREs and the expansion of group plans and agreements covering the entire work force of a given enterprise. A recent measure allows a tax of 2 percent, paid by the employer, to be devoted to increased ISAPRE contributions by workers earning about half the minimum wage. However, the estimated average income of recent affiliates was still about four times the minimum wage in 1988.

Figure 3.8 indicates that the proportion of enrollees with higher incomes is larger in the closed than in the open ISAPREs. The reason is that, to date, the closed ISAPREs are in the biggest state enterprises where workers earn high incomes, such as the copper company, the electricity company, and the State Bank (Banco del Estado).

FIGURE 3.8 Distribution of Affiliates by Monthly Income by Type of ISAPRE, 1988

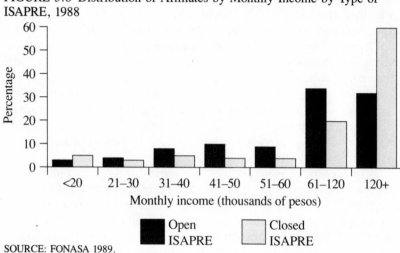

SOURCE: FONASA 1989.

Health plans and benefits. The health plans of all ISAPREs range from those in which the affiliates are restricted to certain providers that charge controlled prices (in some cases, the providers belong to the ISAPRE itself) to the more unrestricted plans in which ISAPREs reimburse any provider an established percentage. Further, although most ISAPREs do not cover dental services or eyeglasses, most have entered into agreements with providers whereby affiliates receive preferential prices. Only where private infrastructure is lacking can ISAPREs provide, under previously arranged agreements, services in the public facilities of the SNSS.

To eliminate the discrimination against the enrollment of women of child-bearing age, since 1986 the Sole Fund for Family Welfare (Fondo Unico de Prestaciones Familiares) has paid generous maternal leave benefits, which include maternal leave, pre- and postpartum care, and leave from work to care for sick children under one year old. The ISAPRE covers all hospital maternity charges and all doctors' fees as contracted with the affiliate.

ISAPREs are required to pay for policy holders' sick leave and to offer the basic preventive health care provided by the public health system (in other words, a free annual physical examination). The sick-leave payments and other cash benefits paid by ISAPREs in 1988 came to 29 percent of operating expenditures (FONASA 1985 and 1988).

Financial structure of ISAPREs. The revenue structure of ISAPREs differs by their type. In 1988, the closed ISAPREs derived about 97 percent
of their revenues from mandatory contributions (7 percent of wages),
about 2 percent from additional contributions, and 1 percent from other
sources. By contrast, the open ISAPREs derived 90 percent from mandatory contributions, 9 percent from additional contributions, and 1
percent from other sources. One reason for the higher share of mandatory contributions in the closed ISAPREs is that they have been formed
by the workers of public enterprises who, judged by the amount of the
average payroll tax paid, received wages about 1.6 times higher than the
workers affiliated with the open ISAPREs.

The structure of expenditures also varies by type of ISAPRE. In
1988, operating costs were about 85 percent in the closed ISAPREs, as
opposed to 73 percent in the open; and administrative and sales and
promotion expenses were 15 percent in the closed and 27 percent in the
open. The difference is primarily that while the closed ISAPREs do not
need to spend money on advertising and promotion (they have a cap-
tive market, even though the workers can choose any ISAPRE), open
ISAPREs have been very active in recruiting affiliates.

Average operating expenditures are substantially higher in the
closed ISAPREs, an indication of the marked differences in the amount
(and possibly cost) of services and the number of other benefits (for
example, sick leave). In 1988, all service indicators listed in Table 3.7
were higher in the closed than in the open ISAPREs. For instance, the

TABLE 3.7 Service Differences by Type of ISAPRE, 1988
(per 1,000 beneficiaries)

Type of service	Open ISAPRE	Closed ISAPRE	Total
Medical consultations	2,985	4,123	3,128
Diagnostic exams	1,854	3,248	2,026
Clinical support and therapy	1,014	1,984	1,134
Surgery	127	90	122
Caesarean partum	19.8	5.7	18.1
Beds used per day	197	416	224
Preventive exams	18	300	4.4
Pap smear	3.1	60	10
Other preventive measures	1	7	1.6
Total clinical support	7	99	18

SOURCE: FONASA 1989.

number of medical visits per beneficiary was 4.1 in the closed ISAPREs and 3 in the open. The number of medical interventions was much lower in the closed ISAPREs, but the number of bed-days utilized was substantially greater, indicative of longer hospital stays. Additionally, the number of diagnostic exams (including the annual health preventive exams and Pap smears for women) was considerably larger in the closed ISAPREs.

There is no information that permits an assessment of the reasons for these differences. Possible supply factors include easier access, because the services are located in the work place in the closed ISAPREs, and active promotion, especially of health prevention and laboratory exams. The demand factors may include lower or no copayments and more lenient practices with respect to reimbursement, sick-leave pay, and maternity leave, which induce greater demand by affiliates and their dependents. Additionally, higher-income people (the affiliates of the closed ISAPREs) demand a larger number of more expensive services. A study of why the differences occur is essential for assessing the appropriateness of the level of services, cost-containment measures, and the balance between curative and preventive services.

Financial situation of the ISAPREs.   According to FONASA figures, the ISAPREs as a whole made an annual profit (after-tax earnings divided by capital and reserves) of about 20 percent between 1984 and 1988. The returns, however, varied widely across the ISAPREs. While the open types had profits higher than 30 percent on average, the closed types' profits were below 10 percent—a reflection, to a large extent, of the greater level of services provided. Only one ISAPRE had to close during this period because of operational and financial problems, and the beneficiaries were transferred to FONASA.

Improving the ISAPREs.   The functioning of the ISAPREs can be improved in two ways: by changing the rules governing the cancellation of contracts for both the ISAPREs and their affiliates to encourage multi-year contracts on behalf of the insurance companies and longer time periods for notices of nonrenewal by the contributor; and by allowing SNSS facilities to contract with the ISAPREs to provide health services to their enrollees. The latter is now limited to emergency services and a limited number of public hospital beds (*pensionados*). If ISAPREs continue to expand as rapidly as they have done recently, a more aggressive policy of allowing contracting with SNSS facilities will be beneficial, since it will increase the use of public infrastructure and the resources of the public hospitals and clinics.

FIGURE 3.9 Revenues of the Health Sector, 1974–1986

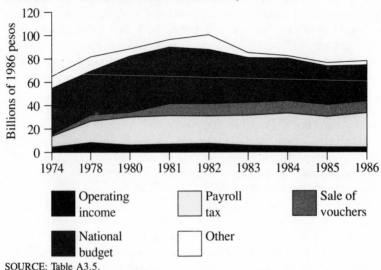

SOURCE: Table A3.5.

Revenues of and Expenditures on Public Health Services

Revenues

As shown in Figure 3.9, there was a major change in the evolution of revenues in real terms between 1974 and 1986. They increased steadily from 1974 to 1982 and then declined in 1983 as a result of the 1982–1983 recession and budget adjustment. The health sector, however, has gradually become less dependent on the national budget, a trend that means a significant change in the structure of revenues of the public health sector. In 1974, budget allocations represented over 60 percent of health-sector revenues, compared with 39 percent in 1986 (Table 3.8). By contrast, the share of payroll contributions went from 14 percent in 1974 to 38 percent in 1986, the result of increased contribution rates and better controls. The sale of vouchers went from a minimum of 0.02 percent in 1974 to 13 percent in 1986.

Expenditures

Overall expenditures on the public health sector have mirrored the behavior of revenues but have also shown a remarkable countercyclical trend since 1974. The share of health expenditures in GDP increased considerably during the acute recessions of 1975 and 1982–1983 (Figure 3.10), an indication that health expenditures declined much less than

TABLE 3.8 Structure of Health Sector Revenues,
1974, 1981, and 1986 (%)

Revenue source	1974	1981	1986
Operating income	7	7	5
Payroll contributions	14	25	38
Sale of vouchers	2	11	13
National budget	61	50	39
Other	16	7	5

SOURCE: Calculations from Table A3.5.

FIGURE 3.10 Share of Health Sector Expenditures in GDP, 1974–1987

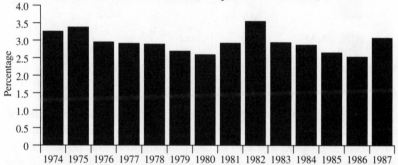

SOURCE: Expenditures are from Table A3.6; GDP is from the Central Bank of Chile (in constant 1977 pesos).

GDP during these years. This relative stability in expenditures during the recessions may have been the result of their short duration and rapid adjustment in other sectors of the economy, which had no major effects on employment in the MOH and a relatively small effect on wages and salaries. The PNAC program, however, suffered during the 1982–1983 recession. The major adjustment in 1982–1983 took place in "other expenses," which include subsidies, monetary benefits such as sick leave, and investments (Figure 3.11).

The primary reason for the decline in both revenues and expenditures in the public health system after 1984, however, has been the rapid increase in the transfer of people from the public system to the ISAPREs. Had this transfer not occurred, expenditures in the public health system in 1988 could have been over 27 percent higher than they were in 1980, when there was no ISAPRE system. With no ISAPRE system, all workers would have been required to affiliate with the public system.

FIGURE 3.11 Structure of Expenditures on Health, 1974–1986

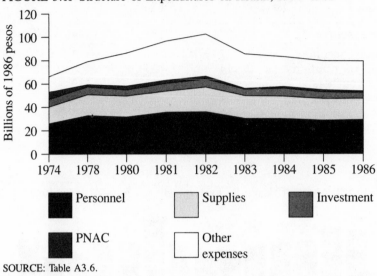

SOURCE: Table A3.6.

As indicated, one issue that has been raised in connection with the transfer of affiliates is the possible loss of cross-subsidization opportunity from high-paid workers to low-paid workers and noncontributing patients. Although data are not available, it is not clear that the cross-subsidization in the old system (when there were no ISAPREs) was a significant amount. This is because people with higher incomes contribute more but also demand more and costlier services. In addition, in unified public services with no private health insurance alternatives (such as the old system in Chile), people with higher incomes get preferential treatment through influence and friends. Poor people are relegated to queues and offered poorer services.

An important consideration arguing against cross-subsidization using the payroll contribution system for health care is that it drives up payroll deduction rates. This has a negative effect on the labor market, as it often signifies contribution rates much higher than those needed to finance health care of contributing workers. The ideal way is for the government to pay for health-care expenses of those uninsured using general taxpayers' funds.[20]

Evolution of Health Indicators

Chile's health status indicators have improved remarkably since 1965. Infant and child mortality, maternal mortality, and malnutrition have declined to record levels compared with other developing countries in Latin America and elsewhere (Table 3.9). For instance, the infant mortality rate in Chile, which was higher than the average for Latin America in 1965, was the second lowest in 1986, at half the average for Latin America. Although the trend toward improvement in these indicators has been occurring since the 1960s, a considerable acceleration has been observed since the mid-1970s (Table 3.10). This acceleration is evident in infant mortality, as observed in Figure 3.12, which shows the evolution expressed in logarithmic terms. The arrow indicates that the trend of the 1960s and early 1970s persisted in recent years. The rate of infant mortality from diarrhea and bronchopneumonia declined by 95 percent and 90 percent, respectively, between 1970 and 1986.

The main reasons for the decline in mortality indicators appear to have been the drastic shift in policies toward services for mothers and children and the health and nutrition interventions in the areas with the highest mortality rates. In 1974–1975, the government began targeting public spending on the poorest population and most vulnerable groups. While the long tradition and extensive coverage of Chile's public health care is an important factor in the reduction of mortality indicators, it is unlikely that the nation would have been able to achieve the recent results by continuing the policies and delivery systems of the 1960s and early 1970s, without major increases in social spending. Targeting was absent in policy and practice, and major inefficiencies affected the public health delivery system.[21]

The greatest reduction in infant and maternal mortality has taken place in the poorer rural areas, where mortality rates were more than double those in urban areas such as Santiago (Table 3.11). The decline

TABLE 3.9 Infant Mortality Rates in Selected Countries and Groups of Countries, 1965 and 1986
(deaths per 1,000 live births)

Countries	1965	1986	% change
Chile	107.0	19.4	−82.0
Costa Rica	72.0	17.0	−76.0
Latin America	96.0	48.0	−50.0
Asia	114.0	63.0	−45.0
Middle-income countries	107.0	62.0	−42.0
Low-income countries	122.0	92.0	−22.0
Highly indebted countries	105.0	61.0	−42.0

SOURCE: World Bank 1989.

TABLE 3.10 Selected Health Indicators, 1960–1986

Indicator	1960	1965	1970	1975	1980	1986
Population (millions)	7.7	n.a.	9.4	n.a.	n.a.	12.3
Birth rate[a]	37.8	n.a.	26.8	24.6	22.2	21.7
Death rate[a]	n.a.	n.a.	8.1	7.2	6.6	5.9
Infant mortality[b]	120.3	95.4	79.3	55.4	31.8	19.4
Neonatal mortality[b]	35.2	33.5	31.3	24.8	16.3	9.7
Postneonatal mortality[b]	n.a.	n.a.	38.3	30.6	15.5	9.4
Maternal mortality[b]	2.99	2.79	1.68	1.31	0.73	0.47
Diarrhea mortality[b]	n.a.	n.a.	14.6	7.1	1.9	0.7
Bronchopneumonia mortality[b]	n.a.	n.a.	23.6	11.3	3.8	2.6

a. Per 1,000 population.
b. Per 1,000 live births.
n.a. = not available.
SOURCES: Ministry of Health, *Indicadores Biodemográficos* (Biodemographic Indicators) and Central Bank of Chile 1989.

FIGURE 3.12 Infant Mortality Rates, 1960–1986

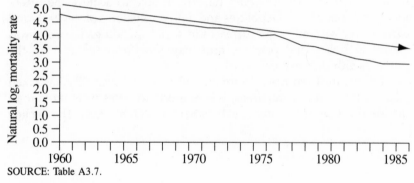

SOURCE: Table A3.7.

TABLE 3.11 Minimum and Maximum Values for
Infant Mortality Rates, 1975–1986

Value	1975	1980	1982	1986
Minimum (Santiago)	34.3	23.3	17.1	15.1
Maximum (IX Region)	93.3	60.0	37.9	24.9
Difference (maximum less minimum)	59.0	36.7	20.8	9.8
National average	55.4	31.8	23.6	19.4

SOURCE: Ministry of Health.

was achieved by reducing the differences in access to basic services such as potable water and sewerage (see Chapter 4) and in the amount and quality of social services provided to mothers and children. More access was possible because of the great emphasis on investments in health posts and low-technology medical facilities in the late 1970s, which permitted a considerable expansion of health services in remote areas by well-trained community auxiliary personnel. This personnel also actively promoted other health-related measures, such as the construction of latrines, improvements in the disposal of refuse, and better nutrition. The rapid elimination of the regional differences in services for mothers and children is responsible more than any other factor for the leveling of the differences in mortality rates across the regions (Castañeda 1985a).

Other factors accounting for the decline in mortality rates are the increase in growth monitoring and checkups for children and pregnant women, together with nutritional intervention, which helped drastically reduce the malnutrition of children under six years of age. Children under the growth-monitoring program in the SNSS comprised over 80 percent of the population up to six years old in 1975, the first year for which systematic nutrition information was collected. This high coverage of children has permitted rapid detection and treatment at rehabilitation centers of the worst cases, and preventive measures for pregnant mothers and children at risk. The population covered by the SNSS has declined recently, apparently because of the rapid expansion of the ISAPREs. As shown in Table 3.12, undernutrition has declined drastically in Chile since 1975.

Evaluations of the PNAC program have documented its great impact in reducing malnutrition both directly, through food supplementation for poor families, and indirectly, through the program of growth

TABLE 3.12 Malnutrition Rates (Weight for Age), 1975–1988 (%)

Year	Total	Mild	Moderate	Serious
1975	15.5	12.1	2.7	0.7
1980	11.5	10.0	1.4	0.2
1982	8.8	7.9	0.9	0.1
1983	9.8	8.6	1.0	0.1
1984	8.4	7.6	0.8	0.1
1988	8.6	7.7	0.8	0.1

SOURCE: Ministry of Health, using the French SEMPE scale.

monitoring for mothers and children (Harbert and Scandizo 1985; Torche 1985; Vial, Muchnick, and Kain 1988b). The direct benefits include increased birth weight, reduction in infant mortality and morbidity, improvements in school performance and future productivity, and increased productivity of parents because of fewer family problems. Calculation of the present value of these benefits indicates that they far exceed the cost for low-income children, but the benefit value is not as great for high-income children (Torche 1985).

It has puzzled some researchers that although the fiscal expenditures for health care did not grow much, unemployment was very high until 1985, and GDP declined sharply in 1975 and 1982–1983, still mortality rates continued declining at a constant rapid pace. To explain this paradox, econometric studies based on aggregate data have been conducted (Hojman 1989). These arrived at rather unusual (and sometimes implausible) results that attributed the decline in mortality to factors such as cheap energy for poor households, the high level of unemployment, and the increased participation of middle- and upper-class women in the labor market during the economic expansion. Others have emphasized the tradition in public health care.

Summary and Conclusions

The reforms of the Chilean health system represent a serious attempt to improve both the targeting of health services and food supplements to needy populations and the efficiency of the public health system. Targeting was strengthened by substantially expanding and upgrading preventive and primary health-care services, with a focus on the most vulnerable groups: mothers and young children. Efficiency has been improved by decentralizing the public health system, modifying the incentive structure for the public providers of health services (hospitals and primary health-care centers), and enhancing the role of the private sector in the provision of services.

The major emphasis in primary health care has been to link maternal and child programs with growth monitoring and food supplementation measures, with special attention to the groups at risk. The substantial amount of money that Chile spent on food subsidies was gradually targeted to needy groups through a variety of means, including restricting the distribution of food supplementation to health posts and centers (where it was conditional on well-baby care and maternal checkups), rehabilitation centers for the undernourished, preschool programs for poor children, and the school feeding program. These interventions, coupled with significant increases in the coverage of potable water and sewerage, produced record declines in infant mortality and morbidity, undernutrition, and maternal mortality.

The main factor behind the improvements in the efficiency of the public health services has been the decentralization of health services to twenty-six Regional Services, which are autonomous entities charged with delivering preventive and curative health services to the beneficiary populations in their jurisdictions. The further transfer of responsibility for primary health care to the municipalities, which was completed in 1988, has also contributed to better use of resources and expanded services.

The decentralization reforms have been accompanied by significant changes in budgeting and the financing arrangements within the health system. The regional health services and municipalities have been financed increasingly through fee-for-service systems (FAP and FAPEM), a significant change from the traditional, historically based budgeting method of financing the hospitals and primary health-care centers. Introduction of these new financing mechanisms has been a slow trial-and-error process that has improved in the past few years as the list of procedures and relative costs have been refined and introduced for public and private providers. Better incentives are still needed to induce providers to improve the quality of services and to improve financing of the cost of the basic health services provided by the municipalities.

The administration of the SNSS hospitals continues to have problems, mainly because the service directors have only limited control over the large personnel budget, which accounts for about 53 percent of total expenses. The personnel structure is fixed by law, and a large share entails permanent positions. The part of the budget derived from fee-for-services is a smaller proportion. Given the inflexibility of the personnel structure, a reduction in the allocations for goods and services on the fee-for-service basis tends to be reflected in lower-quality services rather than in reductions in other expenditures, such as personnel. Much more autonomy needs to be given to the Regional Services.

The private sector participates in the provision of health services in two ways: by providing services through the PPS administered by FONASA and by offering prepaid health insurance plans through ISAPREs, which began operating in 1981. These companies can collect the compulsory 7 percent payroll tax (the 1988 rate) previously collected solely by the public system.

The PPS system, after several improvements in its reimbursement schemes and controls, has become an expeditious program that is highly popular with both patients and the suppliers of services. Nevertheless, the growth of the ISAPREs has been impressive: over 1.4 million people, or about 12 percent of the population, were enrolled in thirty-one ISAPREs in 1988. Future expansion of the ISAPREs is expected as more group plans are offered to firms in the private and public sectors. In addition, recent changes allow an existing tax paid by employers to be used for additional payments to the ISAPREs for lower-income workers, and measures have been introduced to increase taxable income of public employees.

As the detailed history in this chapter shows, the reforms have not been easy to implement and have required much time for negotiation, trial and error, and amendment. Targeting of health and nutrition interventions to the poorest populations, which still needs improvement, has necessitated the development of information systems at the central and local levels, constant work by health personnel and municipal workers, and institutional changes. There has been criticism of the government's decision to concentrate resources on primary health care and to reduce the emphasis on hospital building, rehabilitation, and equipment, especially during the 1982–1983 financial crisis and following years. Labor unrest by health workers has been manifest at the municipal level, where workers have complained about their new status as municipal employees, whereby they do not enjoy the salary adjustments and pay scales of the SNSS employees.

Issues for the future

The dramatic change in Chile's mortality and morbidity rates poses new challenges to the health authorities. The main causes of death and morbidity are now cardiovascular diseases, cancer, hepatic cirrhosis, and illnesses of old age. This pattern requires a change in investment priorities away from the most simple preventive and primary health-care measures to more costly curative health care, and especially toward measures that can change behavior and affect the prevalence of several diseases. Examples are education campaigns to reduce smoking and alcohol consumption and to induce improved dietary practices aimed at reducing cardiovascular problems.

Financing this new health strategy may be more difficult and costly than financing the primary health-care strategy. It requires investment in infrastructure, equipment, and diagnostic exams performed not only by the regional SNSS but also by the municipal health centers. The FAP and FAPEM reimbursement schedules will have to be revised to include the new, more expensive preventive and curative inpatient and outpatient procedures, so that services have the incentive and ability to meet these new needs.

A major challenge for future governments is to consolidate and continue improving the financing mechanism, incentive structures, and institutional arrangements made during the past fifteen years. The private sector plays a large role, offering competitive health insurance alternatives for those who can pay so that the public sector can concentrate and target its resources on those who need state assistance and will, for the most part, be served free of charge. This strategy, which appears to be a good way to target health expenditures to the poorest, must be accompanied by a commitment to provide quality services and to protect expenditures so that the poor are not discriminated against through low-quality services.

Appendix

TABLE A3.1 Revenues of the SNSS, 1981–1988
(millions of August 1986 pesos)

	1981	1982	1983	1984	1985	1986	1987	1988
Operating income	6,004	5,791	4,224	3,772	3,321	2,955	3,427	4,235
Transfers from FONASA	51,401	54,461	45,223	45,441	42,079	46,883	47,999	61,838
Other	468	502	438	320	233	−313	1,114	1,394
Total	57,873	60,754	49,885	49,533	45,633	49,525	52,540	67,466

SOURCE: FONASA, Annual Report.

TABLE A3.2 FONASA and User Payments in the PPS, 1974–1988 (millions of 1986 pesos and %)

	1974	1978	1980	1981	1982	1983	1984	1985	1986	1987	1988
User payments	1,350	5,500	4,101	10,389	10,606	11,055	10,616	10,242	9,492	7,656	9,435
FONASA payments	2,937	6,749	13,476	11,867	12,802	9,284	7,495	6,912	6,073	4,540	5,336
Total	4,287	12,249	17,577	22,256	23,408	20,339	18,111	17,154	15,565	12,196	14,771
% User payments	31	45	23	47	45	54	59	60	61	63	64
% FONASA payments	69	55	77	53	55	46	41	40	39	37	36

SOURCE: FONASA, Annual Report.

TABLE A3.3 Physicians Enrolled in the PPS by
Price Level, 1983–1988

Year	Level 1	Level 2	Level 3	Total
1983	4,077	2,819	1,417	8,313
1984	2,738	4,116	2,035	8,889
1985	2,704	4,368	2,297	9,369
1986	1,785	3,876	3,351	9,012
1987	1,696	3,733	5,395	10,824
1988	1,342	3,446	6,425	11,213

SOURCE: FONASA, Annual Report.

TABLE A3.4 Enrollees and Total Beneficiary Population in
the ISAPREs, 1981–1988
(thousands of people in December of each year)

Year	Enrollees	Total beneficiaries	Beneficiaries/ enrollees
1981	26.4	61.6	2.33
1982	66.8	164.3	2.46
1983	88.8	242.6	2.73
1984	131.6	365.3	2.78
1985	198.8	545.6	2.74
1986	336.3	921.3	2.74
1987	457.1	1,205.1	2.64
1988	567.6	1,430.2	2.52

SOURCE: FONASA, Annual Report.

TABLE A3.5 Revenues of the Health Sector, 1974–1986
(billions of 1986 pesos)

	1974	1978	1980	1981	1982	1983	1984	1985	1986
Operating income	4.500	8.292	6.180	6.959	7.405	5.674	5.005	4.185	4.026
Payroll tax	9.226	18.150	23.810	24.206	23.403	25.708	28.191	26.059	29.401
Sale vouchers	1.350	5.500	4.101	10.389	10.606	11.055	10.616	10.242	10.156
National budget	39.828	37.521	48.200	48.382	46.459	38.398	36.445	33.141	30.768
Other	10.126	12.214	6.110	6.455	12.598	4.256	2.188	2.791	3.636
Total	65.030	81.677	88.401	96.391	100.471	85.091	82.445	76.418	77.987

SOURCE: FONASA, Annual Report.

TABLE A3.6 Structure of Expenditures on Health, 1974–1986
(billions of 1986 pesos)

	1974	1978	1980	1981	1982	1983	1984	1985	1986
Personnel	25.930	32.770	31.572	35.653	35.916	30.121	29.892	28.529	29.026
Supplies	14.305	17.926	17.928	18.121	21.225	19.634	19.340	18.507	18.295
Redemption vouchers	4.287	12.249	17.577	22.256	23.408	20.339	18.111	17.154	16.671
Subsidies	6.371	4.499	5.836	6.587	6.095	3.563	3.212	2.673	2.842
PNAC	6.401	6.761	5.366	6.655	6.937	5.445	6.777	5.728	5.035
Investment	6.313	1.910	3.272	2.635	2.385	.707	1.421	1.819	1.261
Other expenses	2.661	2.943	4.784	4.646	6.452	5.584	4.220	5.091	6.129
Total	66.268	79.058	86.335	96.553	102.418	85.393	82.973	79.501	79.259

SOURCE: FONASA, Annual Report.

TABLE A3.7 Infant Mortality Rates, 1960–1986
(per 1,000 live births)

Year	Infant mortality rate	Natural logarithm	Year	Infant mortality rate	Natural logarithm
1960	120.3	4.79	1974	65.2	4.18
1961	106.4	4.67	1975	55.4	4.01
1962	109.2	4.69	1976	56.6	4.04
1963	100.3	4.61	1977	47.5	3.86
1964	103.7	4.64	1978	38.7	3.65
1965	95.4	4.56	1979	36.6	3.60
1966	98.5	4.59	1980	31.8	3.46
1967	94.7	4.55	1981	27.2	3.30
1968	87.0	4.46	1982	23.6	3.16
1969	83.1	4.42	1983	21.9	3.09
1970	79.3	4.37	1984	19.6	2.97
1971	73.9	4.30	1985	19.5	2.97
1972	72.7	4.29	1986	19.4	2.96
1973	65.8	4.19			

SOURCE: Ministry of Health.

CHAPTER 4

Reforms in the Housing Sector

This chapter reviews the major policy changes and structural reforms that have taken place in Chile's housing sector since 1974, against the background of prior policies. It begins by examining the policies pursued before 1974, which emphasized government participation in the housing market as regulator, land developer, builder, and financial agent. Next, new policies and related structural changes are reviewed, and the impact of the housing subsidy programs targeted to help the poorest population is assessed, as well as the impact of housing programs on the overall housing situation in Chile.

A major policy change begun in 1975 targeted subsidies to some of the poorer population through programs tailored to their needs and economic capacity. Direct upfront subsidies for down payments (vouchers) were introduced to replace indirect subsidies provided through lower interest rates or reduced-price housing units. The role of the public sector was limited to financing and screening the beneficiaries of subsidies and establishing the norms and regulations, functions handled by the Ministry of Housing and Urban Affairs (MINVU) and by the municipalities. The private sector was responsible for land development, seeking connections to urban services such as water and sewerage, construction, and financial intermediation. A private mortgage market was also created to provide financing for housing for middle- and upper-income families.

Targeting the subsidies has not been easy. Initially, programs directed to the poor benefited primarily middle-income people because of excessive requirements for prior savings, poor means testing of applicants, and excessive valuation of the houses being applied for. These conditions created an incentive for relatively well-off people to apply for the subsidies. Moreover, because of a lack of information on the economic capacity of prospective target groups, the subsidies appear to have been excessive. Targeting improved considerably when the massive programs of urban rehabilitation and slum upgrading started in the early 1980s, following a concerted program to regularize land titles in the slums and peripheral areas that had been illegally occupied for numerous years.

Housing Policies before 1974

Long before the MINVU was established in 1965, the government had launched important initiatives to address Chile's housing problems. They ranged from the establishment of agencies directly involved in planning and building housing projects (for example, the Corporation for Reconstruction and Assistance, created in 1939) to the granting of incentives to the private sector to build (the so-called Pereira Law).

The administration of President Jorge Alessandri (1958–1964) gave special emphasis to the housing problem, working on three fronts: (1) eradication of spontaneously built slums and relocation of residents to land improved at low cost; (2) construction of low-cost housing through the Housing Corporation (CORVI, created in 1953); and (3) financing of housing units through the National Savings and Loan System (SINAP).

In 1959, CORVI was authorized to manage the surplus funds of the different social security systems. It used these funds to build housing units that it assigned, with an implicit interest rate subsidy, to families on a housing list. Location on the list depended on the applicant's savings and was influenced to a high degree by favoritism. In general, those able to get the subsidies were higher-income white-collar families. Blue-collar or manual workers belonging to the Caja of the Social Security Service (SSS) were not even eligible for housing credits (see Chapter 5).

SINAP, created in 1960, was formed by a number of savings and loan associations whose assets consisted of savings deposits and, especially at the beginning, loans from international agencies. These associations granted mortgage loans to medium- and high-income groups. Although a subsidy was not part of its initial objectives, SINAP eventually subsidized borrowers by not adjusting the loans fully for inflation and by offering below-market interest rates. The subsidy was provided in part by savers, who at times received negative real interest rates, and by the government through the Central Savings and Loan Fund, the inspection agency for the savings and loan associations. It has been estimated that in 1959 the Central Fund provided more than one-fourth of the subsidy (Arellano 1976). In terms of the financial resources it managed, SINAP was of great importance until 1975 (when it suffered a terminal crisis, following a great boom), because at times it was the only agency providing at least partial protection from inflation.

MINVU was established in 1965, during the administration of President Eduardo Frei (1964–1970), to assign the many functions of CORVI to several new agencies: the Urban Improvements Corporation (CORMU), responsible for the refurbishing of houses and land purchase; the Housing Services Corporation (CORHABIT), responsible for taking deposits and administering and distributing CORVI-built housing; and the Urban Works Corporation (COU), responsible for building the sidewalks and water and sewer systems at CORVI housing projects. CORVI was left with primary responsibility for construction work.

CORVI not only did building for programs administered by CORHABIT under the popular savings plans but also executed projects for the beneficiaries of the Cajas with surpluses that these funds transferred to it. The social security funds granted subsidies to beneficiaries (as CORHABIT did) participating in their programs, and gave loans to members so that they could meet the minimum savings required to apply for SINAP loans for more expensive houses.

During this period, the Operation Site (*operación sitio*) Program was initiated as a continuation of the previous administration's program of relocating inhabitants of slums. Under this program, selected families received a site, in most cases without basic services of potable water and sewerage. From 1965 to 1970, this program benefited over 120,000 families.

Finally, during the administration of socialist President Salvador Allende (1970–1973), while no institutional changes were made, the great economic difficulties of the country—especially the hyperinflation and measures taken by the government to avoid indexing debts—wreaked heavy damage on the housing sector. The economic problems had a tremendous impact on the financial situation of CORHABIT and SINAP. Further, extensive illegal occupation of municipal and private lands and of unfinished buildings took place during this time. It was estimated that by the end of 1973, over 100,000 families lived in recently occupied slums without any water, sewerage, or electricity.

Targeting of Housing Subsidies in 1969

A study made in 1976 provides information on the distribution of subsidies by income groups for the housing and Operation Site Programs in 1969 (Arellano 1976). The data pertained to the actual subsidies granted, including both direct and indirect ones (the latter again involving below-market interest rates). An assumption of the study was that beneficiaries paid the amounts owed on time, consistent with their obligations, and that no additional subsidies resulted either from a failure to pay in full or from less than full indexation of the debts. The programs covered were those of CORVI, CORHABIT, CORMU, and SINAP. The results, based on the income distribution brackets in the employment and unemployment surveys of the Department of Economics of the University of Chile, indicate the programs had a very low redistributive impact.[1] In fact, the poorest groups received only about 22 percent of all subsidies combined, while the middle 30 percent received 37 percent and the richest 40 percent, the remaining 41 percent.

Housing Policies after 1974

Policy principles and main measures

Housing policies since 1974 have followed three general principles: first, target government subsidies only to those people who cannot afford decent housing on their own; second, provide subsidies using direct, transparent mechanisms such as vouchers so that the amounts of the subsidies can be known, rather than using below-market interest rates; and third, limit the public-sector role to financing, setting of rules and regulations, and supervision rather than construction and execution of projects, which were seen as activities appropriate to the private sector. The private sector, through the development of financial instruments, was also to be responsible for meeting the financing needs of middle- and upper-income families, so that the public sector could concentrate on the lowest income groups.

A number of major policy measures to liberalize and rationalize the housing market have taken place since 1974. First, the indexation of housing debt was restored in 1974 in order to return to health the mortgage portfolio of CORHABIT, which had become very weak under the preceding government, and to reduce the subsidies to middle- and upper-income families. Second, interest rates were liberalized, a measure that caused SINAP serious financial problems when people withdrew large quantities of funds held in SINAP paper (*valores hipotecarios reajustables*) in search of higher interest rates. This situation meant SINAP's virtual termination in 1975.[2]

Third, the rental market for properties went through initial liberalization in 1975. Complete liberalization of higher-value properties and commercial properties occurred in 1982. The previous legislation specifying fixed rents had provoked enormous distortions in rent values and in incentives for construction for the rental market in the face of the substantial inflation. A law enacted in 1971, during the socialist government, enabling judges to suspend eviction procedures for noncompliance of rent contracts for up to a year, was derogated, and special procedures for these cases were established, along with time limits for the restitution of property.

The fourth measure involved the introduction in 1974 of several laws to facilitate massive titling and regularization of the tenancy. About 370,000 titles were issued between 1978 and 1984. Emergency laws were enacted in 1978–1979 for the titling of properties that had been illegally occupied before the government took power (September 11, 1973) and which were still occupied in 1979. The current occupants were to pay the previous owners the commercial value, using any of the subsidized programs described subsequently.

In 1977, the fifth reform measure reduced the stamp tax on the turnover of property from 8 to 4 percent (currently, the tax is 0.5 percent). The sixth measure liberalized the real estate agency market to permit participation of any agent, subject to only a few requirements (this market had been highly regulated and monopolistic, restricted to only a few authorized firms).

Finally, in 1977 the seventh reform measure introduced mortgage bonds (*letras de crédito hipotecarias*) to finance housing for middle- and high-income people who had been served previously by SINAP. Any commercial bank and other financial institution could issue the bonds in amounts equal to the credit given for housing. The maturities were to be no less than a year, and credit backed by mortgage bonds could be no more than 75 percent of the property value. The Central Bank of Chile set the rules and regulations, while the Superintendency of Banking Institutions handled the supervision.

At the time the mortgage bonds were to be implemented, most deposits were in certificates of less than 90 days. Prospects for the bonds were dim, since the government had frozen the previous mortgage instruments of SINAP. To induce more acceptance, the Central Bank became a major purchaser of the bonds through open-market operations in 1980. It introduced several conditions for the bonds, including a maximum maturity of twelve years, a maximum commission of 4 percent, and an interest rate of no more than 8 percent a year (after inflation, since the bonds were denominated in constant value units known as UF)[3] for credits of less than 620 UF and a total mortgage value of less than 1,000 UF. Beginning in 1979, the total mortgage value was raised to 1,500 UF. However, the Central Bank purchased only those bonds for credits less than 620 UF, according to the previous conditions regarding interest rates—a practice that boosted the interest rates for credits of higher amounts substantially (16 percent net of commissions) (Institute of Economics 1986). This situation induced banks to sell those assets in the capital market.

Recently, the government introduced endorsable mortgage bonds (*letras hipotecarias endosables*), which are expected to increase the attractiveness of mortgage bonds as financial instruments. The pension fund administration companies (AFPs) and the Central Bank are both large holders of the *letras*. There is ample room for expanding the mortgage bond market through investments by the pension funds, which are expected to increase rapidly in the coming years to about 35–40 percent of GDP in the year 2000 and to 80–90 percent of GDP in the year 2035.[4]

A final reform measure was the introduction in 1978 of an innovative mechanism, the *subsidio habitacional*, which is a voucher system, to give direct subsidies to the target population. It consists of an upfront subsidy in a voucher certificate that allows beneficiaries to buy specified housing units. Under this system, the beneficiary pools his own savings, money borrowed from the capital market, and the subsidy from the public sector, which is equivalent to the balance of the financing needed for the housing unit. This mechanism has since been refined with a view to improving subsidy targeting and has recently been applied to most programs.

Institutional arrangements and responsibilities

Community Housing Committees.   The creation of Community Housing Committees (CHCs) in 1975 was one of the first institutional changes the government made for housing. Decree Law 1,088 established the CHCs as independent agencies with their own legal structure and assets. The purpose was to decentralize public-sector efforts by transferring direct responsibility for housing to the communities—for example, to correct problems in slums (*marginalidad habitacional*) through improvements appropriate to permanent settlement or by relocation. The CHCs had to be organized by a community council and mayor. Their broad power permitted them to expropriate, sell, rent, and build real estate, provide loans, and enter into a great variety of legal agreements. The Regional Housing and Urban Affairs Services (SERVIUs) of

MINVU (there was one for each region) were to provide technical assistance and supervision and be responsible for the selection of people or communities to be served.

The target population comprised two groups. The first, group A, consisted of those people currently living in camps and slums whose current sites could be improved (that is, the land was suitable for housing and the property-rights problems could be solved). The second, group B, were those people who had to be moved elsewhere. The CHCs financed and built sites and services units (*casetas sanitarias*) and social housing units (*vivienda social*) until 1979. In that year, the CHCs were eliminated and their functions, assets, and responsibilities transferred to MINVU.

The Ministry of Housing and Urban Affairs.   MINVU underwent its main institutional changes in 1976 when it was reorganized to conform to the decentralization of the whole government. The operating agencies (CORVI, CORHABIT, CORMU, and COU) were eliminated and replaced by the SERVIUs. These changes, and the major role given to the private sector, meant a reduction in employees from about 45,000 in all government agencies involved in housing activities in 1973–1974 to about 3,000 in 1988.

The thirteen SERVIUs were charged initially with preparing housing plans and performing construction tasks (purchasing land, planning construction, and improving urban services), although these responsibilities were quickly reduced; administering the allocation of existing housing units under the applicants system and preparing lists for later assignment;[5] and administering funds, primarily those assigned either by the central ministry or under the National Fund for Regional Development (FNDR).

A high-level representative from MINVU (the Regional Ministerial Secretariat, or SEREMI) supervised the SERVIUs to ensure that they followed norms and regulations. The SEREMI also advised the regional superintendent (the governor) on housing policy and regulations. The SERVIUs were, nonetheless, autonomous, and as will be seen, they have become key players in regional development and construction plans and in the mortgage market for low-income beneficiaries of government subsidy programs.

Municipalities.   The municipalities have had a crucial role in executing housing policies since 1975, including the regulation of land use and supply of urban services, principally water and sewerage, in their jurisdictions. For example, before a plot is subdivided for housing and put up for sale, it is required (subject to legal sanctions) to have water and sewerage connections. The municipalities can execute these directly or go through the SERVIUs or some housing programs, such as the Social Housing, Basic Housing, and Sites and Services Programs (to be described later). Municipalities organize the demand for housing subsidies in their areas, serving as crucial agents for identifying beneficiaries through the CAS Index.[6] Since municipalities use the CAS to distribute many other subsidies, they have become the focal point for identifying needs and providing support through the social safety net. The Sites and Services Program has been very successful, playing a key role in eliminating the slums in major cities such as Santiago.

The private sector. The private sector plays an important role in executing Chile's housing policies. It is entirely responsible for construction, either through direct contracts with MINVU or the municipalities for a specified product under competitive bidding or through construction of units for sale directly to beneficiaries of the numerous subsidized housing programs. Cooperatives and nongovernment organizations (NGOs) can participate as builders or by organizing groups of people seeking to obtain government subsidies.

MINVU began to withdraw from construction in 1975, when a large number of the roughly 50,000 unfinished housing units begun by the previous government were given to private companies to finish under "delegated administration," whereby the government reimbursed them for all construction costs. In 1976–1977, the government introduced a new system to pay for finished housing (*llave en mano*), based on competitive bidding. Although this mechanism is still used with some programs, the bulk now operate under a system in which private contractors find the land, design and finance the project, and look for customers under the government subsidized programs, competing with one another in terms of location, price, and other amenities. Over 70 percent of housing construction is prompted by the government's subsidy programs. The enlarged market and great consistency of government policies toward the private sector have resulted in rapid specialization and increased the efficiency of the construction industry for low-cost housing, an activity to which the private sector had not traditionally been attracted.

Given the effectiveness of the private sector, even for very low-cost housing, including sites and services, the government has not considered the state-sponsored self-help programs and "materials banks" common in Chile in the 1960s and early 1970s and in most Latin American countries today. Under these programs, housing takes a long time to complete, is costly, and requires, if communities or NGOs are not involved, significant state participation in administration, delivery, and financing.

The private sector also participates in the financing of subsidized housing units through the financial sector. Beginning in 1975 with the Social Housing Program (SHP), the first program for the poorest, the government intended that private banks would provide commercial credit to complement its subsidies, but it soon found the banks were unwilling to do so for poor beneficiaries. Still, the government has gradually introduced incentives for more private-sector participation. These include state guarantees of between 70 and 90 percent of the loss on defaulting loans, once the lender has exhausted all legal steps for recovering the loan, and direct payment of the higher risk and transaction costs of low-cost housing mortgages. Moreover, MINVU, through its SERVIUs, continues to be a lender of last resort for the poorest population.

Housing programs and targeting the poorest population

One of the salient features of the Chilean experience has been the targeting of subsidies through different housing programs and solutions tailored to various groups of people based on their economic capacity. A great deal of experimentation has taken place since 1975, with programs being eliminated or consolidated. To reduce the pressure on the programs designed for the poor, the government introduced new programs for middle- and upper-income people. The targeting of the poorest population, although not successful at first, has improved considerably with the introduction of better programs and improvements in the screening and control of applicants. A description of some of the programs introduced since 1975 follows, indicating the targeting mechanisms used and the redistributive impact obtained.

Applicants System Program.   The Applicants System Program (ASP) began in 1975 as a successor to those run by CORHABIT and was, in fact, a transition program from the old to the new regime, aimed at providing an instrument for increasing savings for housing. It provided for the development of a registration list in each SERVIU. Applicants were classified as group A or B. Under group A, they had to have minimum savings of at least 600 saving "quotas" (about 25 UF or U.S. $319.70) and a family income of less than five minimum wages, while group B applicants had to show minimum savings of 1,000 quotas (about 40 UF or U.S. $511.60) and a family income in excess of five minimum wages.[7] Later, group B applicants were required to have a minimum of 1,600 savings quotas. Group A could opt for a unit valued up to 15,000 savings quotas (about 600 UF or U.S. $7,672.80), with a construction area of 50–60 square meters. The maximum value for group B was about 25,000 savings quotas (about 1,000 UF or U.S. $12,788) and an area of 50–80 square meters.

Houses were assigned in each community in order of priority based on the following factors: savings quotas (five points for each 100); each year of seniority in the program (five points); and family dependents (spouse, children under eighteen years of age, and a few other eligible dependents, at five points each). The transfer value of a housing unit was the appraised value expressed in indexed units,[8] which rose with the wage and salary index (ISS) or CPI, whichever was lower. Later, the debts were expressed in "housing savings quotas" (Decree Law 1,506 of 1976).

The government changed the applicants system several times before it halted new additions to the lists in 1978. A 200 UF subsidy (about U.S. $3,787.70) was granted to those beneficiaries who chose to pay the total value of the house with credit and cash (Supreme Decree 1,170 of November 1977). In 1978, the SERVIUs were authorized to extend additional UF credit for a period of twelve years at an annual real interest rate of 12 percent. The subsidy, however, was not to exceed 75 percent of the value of the house. Between 1976 and 1982, over 53,000 houses were built and assigned under this program.

While initially the private sector built the housing under the "delegate administration" system, the government switched quickly, in 1976, to a system of contracting based on a fixed price per finished product. Under this system, the construction company had the advantage of a guaranteed demand for its houses but ran the risk that the cost could be higher than the agreed price. Payment was made when the housing was finished, and MINVU reserved the right not to purchase it if it did not meet established standards. The construction company was responsible for providing the site and service connections to water and sewerage, along with other urbanization expenses.

Targeting under this program was deficient because of the high savings requirements and cut-off point at five minimum wages, which was also high. Group B applicants, who received about 30 percent of the housing units, belonged to the highest four deciles of the income distribution (the richest 40 percent), while only about half the group A beneficiaries may have belonged to the middle 30 percent of the income distribution. None of the applicants belonged to the poorest 30 percent of the population.[9] From 1978, when this program was ended, until 1981, the government continued to process the applications and award subsidies.[10]

Social Housing Program.   The SHP, initiated in 1975, was one of the first government efforts to target subsidies to the poorest population. It was initially run by the communities through the CHCs, with subsidies provided by selling houses below cost or by renting them on very favorable terms. It covered low-cost housing units of 35–45 square meters, a standard that was later lowered to 28–35 square meters for the poorest population. The CHCs were to finance the units through a 5 percent housing tax they administered and collected, along with other resources such as municipal contributions and donations.

The CHCs could either sell the housing units, by offering long-term credit without interest, or rent them. The regulations established that monthly payments (for rent or mortgage) could not exceed 15 percent of monthly family income. The value of the house for those purchasing was the appraised value, increased by 10 percent for administrative expenses (expressed in Indexed Units adjusted according to the ISS). In practice, the CHCs rented almost all the housing units they built.

The SHP covered two types of beneficiaries and housing units. Group A consisted of people living in slums that, according to MINVU, were suitable for permanent housing units. These people received primarily basic infrastructure (potable water, sewerage, and electricity) but not necessarily a finished house. Group B consisted of people who had to be moved from the site because it was not suitable for housing. These people received a house at a new site.

The SERVIUs arranged for the construction of the great majority of the housing units under competitive bidding by the private sector. Two methods of contracting were used: a minimum-cost project, which had to include the cost of the site and urbanization expenses, and *llave en mano*. Payment was made upon termination and acceptance of the work. Initially, around 1978, the National Construction Chamber was not enthusiastic about the methods and the type of work offered in public housing programs, and its members made a concerted attempt not to participate in the bidding. One firm, however, did not enter into this agreement and was awarded the entire contract. Its participation, and the threat that the government might use international competitive bidding, ended the resistance of the construction industry.

When the CHCs went out of existence in 1979, the SERVIUs inherited their assets, functions, and obligations.[11] To clarify the financial and tenancy situation of the CHCs and house owners and tenants, all rented housing units were sold to their tenants at a price that included a subsidy of 200 UF when paid for in cash. The total price of the units, which averaged 48 square meters in size, was about 320 UF. Additionally, in 1981 MINVU introduced major changes in the program by extending the regulations of the newly created Variable Housing Subsidy Program (VHSP). This step led to the Basic Housing Program (BHP).

The targeting of social housing units was not successful. Only about 24 percent of the subsidies went to the poorest 30 percent of the population. The not-so-poor 30 percent in the middle-income bracket obtained most of the subsidies (about 64 percent). The reasons included the relatively high standard of the housing, which may have attracted middle-income groups, and the poor screening of beneficiaries (Castañeda and Quiroz 1984).

Basic Housing Program. The BHP gave direct state assistance, on a one-time basis, to people living in extremely marginal housing (squatter camps, shunts, and other slum-type housing). It entailed a system of variable subsidies. The maximum subsidy was 200 UF for a housing unit whose appraised value or selling price was less than 266 UF and whose minimum floor space was 25 square meters on a site of no less than 100 square meters. Minimum requirements included basic living quarters and sanitation and an approved plan for expanding into a social housing unit whose market price was not to exceed 400 UF. That is, the basic house was envisioned as the first stage of a social housing unit.

The following point system was used to establish the priority of applicants: one point was given for each UF of difference between the 200 UF and the subsidy requested, twenty points for each year the person had been on the list without having received a subsidy, and four points for each family dependent. People living in camps (*campamentos*) and marginal slum areas were not required to show savings.

The SERVIUs granted a certificate (voucher) to selected applicants who could then choose either a direct or an applied subsidy. Under the direct subsidy option, the beneficiary bought the house on his own and paid for it with the certificate, his savings, and a credit from a SERVIU. Under the applied subsidy option, the SERVIU built the unit under contract with the private sector and then sold it to the applicant, with the cost of the certificate included in the selling price. In this case, the beneficiary could receive additional credit from the SERVIU. The monthly payment for the credit had to be less than 20 percent of family income.

In practice, almost all the basic housing units assigned between 1983 and mid-1984 received a 200 UF subsidy. This was because the beneficiaries were people who had to be moved from their present sites and relocated to other areas. People who could remain on their current sites were given title to the land and services under MINVU's slum rehabilitation program or the municipalities' sites and services unit and low-cost housing unit programs (described later).

Construction under the BHP was done by the private sector under the *llave en mano* mechanism. Until 1982, payment was made when construction was finished. Then, because of the 1982–1983 financial crisis, MINVU started to make advances and periodic payments based on progress to facilitate the entrance of small construction companies into the market. The current (1988) system entails two payments: an advance, and the balance payable when the work is complete. It is noteworthy that the direct subsidy option (in which the beneficiary got the voucher and looked for housing in the private sector) did not work as expected, apparently because it was not profitable for the construction industry to produce low-cost housing units except under large-scale operations and with assured demand.[12]

In 1984, the government made several modifications in the basic housing alternative to help those who had previously been left out, such as the *allegados*, or poor people living with relatives in slums or other conditions. Up to 1983, the basic houses had gone to people living under conditions of extreme urban poverty (slums and camps), which were easily identifiable geographically on MINVU and municipality plans. This system left out the *allegados*, the not easily identifiable families who lived with close relatives such as parents in tenements or other slum housing (including some scattered operation-site beneficiaries who had received no basic services).

The SERVIUs opened a new permanent listing system (*nuevo sistema de postulación*) that included the CAS Index poverty classification. In turn, the point system used in the application process depended on savings, number of dependents, and the CAS Index, with larger weight given to the CAS Index.

The basic housing units assigned through this new system were eligible for a subsidy equivalent to 75 percent of the value of the housing unit, not to exceed 180 UF. In 1985, 170,000 applicants had registered in the new system. (Changes made in 1988 to this program are discussed under the modified basic housing program).

The BHP has proven effective in targeting subsidies to the needy. Over 60 percent of the subsidies have gone to the poorest 30 percent of the population, and another 36 percent to the next 30 percent. It is estimated that only 12 percent have gone to people in the highest 40 percent of the income distribution. Key to the success of this program is the fact that it has emphasized families who have had to be relocated from slums not suitable for housing. In such cases, sites and services units were not adequate solutions because, upon relocation, the people needed shelter right away.[13] As will be seen later in this chapter, the rapid expansion of the Basic Housing Program from the 10,000 units built in 1981 to nearly 30,000 units in 1986 has been a key to improving the overall redistributive impact of Chile's housing programs.

Cooperatives program. During 1976–1979, the government initiated a program with a loan for U.S. $55 million from American banks guaranteed by the U.S. Agency for International Development (USAID). The objective of the loan was to finance housing units built by urban cooperatives. Under the terms of the loan, members of these cooperatives had to have a monthly income of less than U.S. $134. About 8,800 houses were built, at an average cost of over U.S. $6,200 each. Given the average cost, this program appears to have benefited people primarily in the middle 30 percent and upper 40 percent income brackets, similar to the Applicants System Program. While the program ended in 1980, the cooperatives have remained important players among the groups applying for the different housing subsidies offered by MINVU.

Housing Subsidy Program. The Housing Subsidy Program (HSP) was created in 1978 to "direct state assistance granted on a one-time basis to persons who are heads of families, with no obligation of repayment by the beneficiary" (Supreme Decree, March 1978). The subsidy was for heads of households, whether husband or wife, who neither owned a housing unit nor had acquired a unit at any time through institutions such as the social security funds, SINAP, CORVI, or other agencies in which the state participated. The amount of the subsidy varied depending on the appraised value of the housing unit (Table 4.1). The number of subsidies awarded on each year's call (*llamado,* or the number of subsidies awarded each time) was 55 percent, 30 percent, and 15 percent for the first, second, and third brackets, respectively. Selection was based on accumulated points, with four points given for each family dependent and one point for each UF in savings, including the value of a site that the applicant owned with a legal title and with no mortgage. In

TABLE 4.1 Housing Subsidy by Value of House (UF)

Bracket	Value of house	Subsidy	
		1978	1984
1	Up to 400	200	180
2	400–580	170	150
3	580–850	150	0

NOTE: 1 UF = U.S. $18.
SOURCE: Ministry of Housing and Urban Affairs.

no case could the subsidy exceed 75 percent of the appraised value (later changed to market value).[14] No subsidy was granted to any person who had to devote more than 20 percent of family income to pay off supplemental borrowings. Cooperatives could apply with savings in the form of sites or other assets. Each member of a cooperative was given the average number of points obtained by all members.

In 1984, following reductions in the costs of construction and interest rates, the subsidy for the first bracket was lowered to 180 UF and for the second bracket to 150 UF; the third was eliminated (Supreme Decree 92). Later, the subsidy for the first bracket was reduced to 165 UF, and in 1988 it was modified again to improve targeting (see the discussion of the Unified Subsidy Program following).

Upon granting the subsidy, MINVU, through SERVIUs, issued the applicant a certificate (voucher) in the amount of the subsidy. The beneficiary then looked for a house in the private sector within the appraised value bracket and paid for it with the certificate, his or her savings, and a bank loan. Although the certificates had a limited duration, in practice their maturities were extended because not all the people used the subsidy within the stipulated period. Delays were particularly evident during the 1982–1983 economic crisis, when the income of beneficiaries decreased considerably as unemployment soared, and beneficiaries were reluctant to ask for indexed loans. In these two years, the subsidies effectively used declined by 29 percent and 24 percent in relation to 1981. They increased considerably beginning in 1984.

Other reasons for the lagging pace in voucher use at the beginning of the program were the slowness of the construction industry to begin building this type of housing and the reluctance of commercial banks to provide the small loans. Gradually, however, the private sector did engage in constructing houses and handled the location of sites, the permits, and all the construction work, including urban services, at their own risk and cost. However, MINVU or the State Bank has had to provide the loans. One problem the construction industry has faced is that the vouchers cannot be used to buy a house that is being built, so that the whole project must be financed through the banking system.

The redistributive impact of this program was poor at the beginning but has improved since 1980. The percentage of the total subsidies paid to the poorest 30 percent of the population, the main target, increased from about 10 percent in 1980 to 24 percent in 1986 and to 32.3 percent in 1987 (Table 4.2). The share of the next 30 percent of the population, also a target of the program, rose from 32 percent in 1980 to 41 percent in 1987, while the share received by the richest 40 percent decreased from a peak of 72 percent in 1981 to 27 percent in 1987. This program was recently modified further to improve targeting for the poorest population.

TABLE 4.2 Housing Subsidies Received by Income Group, 1980–1987 (%)

Year	Poorest 30%	Middle 30%	Richest 40%
1980	9.9	31.6	58.5
1981	8.8	19.5	71.7
1982	20.0	18.8	61.2
1983	20.3	29.9	49.8
1984	18.9	37.4	43.7
1985	18.1	35.5	46.4
1986	24.2	38.9	36.9
1987	32.3	40.7	27.0

SOURCE: Calculations as explained in the Appendix to this chapter.

There were two main reasons for the poor initial success with the targeting. First, the relatively high standard of eligible housing attracted middle- and high-income people, as confirmed by the variable subsidy program introduced in 1981, which, despite its regressive rule (the more total points, the lower the subsidy requested), had a strong redistributive impact because of the low standard of housing (units valued at less than 260 UF). This low standard discouraged people with higher incomes from applying. Second, until 1982, beneficiaries could change the subsidy bracket at the time they obtained it. Relatively high-income people would apply for the lower-priced housing for which the number of subsidies awarded was the highest (5,000 of the 10,000 annual subsidies in 1978); then, once they got the subsidy, they would change brackets, thereby losing some of the subsidy (the lowest-priced houses obtained the larger subsidy) but obtaining better housing.[15]

The redistributive impact of this subsidy probably worsens when indirect subsidies, in the form of payments of the difference between the market and face value of the mortgage bonds, are included. This practice was begun in 1984 and ended in 1986, when the mortgage bonds issued by the State Bank began to be sold at more than 100 percent of their face value, because of the reduced market interest rates and security provided by this instrument guaranteed by the state. The average subsidy peaked at 12 UF in 1985 and then declined to 2 UF in February 1986, when it was ended (ODEPLAN 1987a).

Rural Housing Subsidy Program.   In 1980, the government introduced the Rural Housing Subsidy Program as a pilot plan for rural areas. The rural subsidy was available to people—individuals and cooperatives— with rights to sites in rural areas. The point system granted one point for each UF of value between the subsidy requested and 200 UF. As with other variable subsidy schemes, in no case could the subsidy exceed 75 percent of the value of the house; in addition, the appraised value had to be less than 260 UF. Complementary loans were not part of the scheme.

Most beneficiaries built their own houses or bought a prefabricated unit from the private sector. The maximum subsidy and price varied according to whether the unit was in a rural area without services (110 UF) or in a village, requiring connections to basic services (150 UF and a maximum value of 400 UF). Poor rural families could also apply individually or through cooperatives to the general housing subsidy and contractual savings housing (SAF) programs (a discussion of SAF follows). The redistributive impact of this subsidy has probably been similar to that of the HSP (see the Appendix to this chapter).

Low-cost housing and sites and services units.   In 1982, the municipalities were authorized to build low-cost housing and sites and services units. The low-cost housing units (*vivienda económica*) had to have 18 square meters of floor space and cost less than 220 UF. The sites and services units had to have a minimum floor space of 6 square meters (including bathroom and kitchen) and a maximum cost of 110 UF (including the value of the site). The costs could be 25 to 30 percent higher in the most remote regions where construction costs were greater. The units had to be on sites no smaller than 100 square meters. Both construction types included a design for expansion into a house.[16] The units had to have minimal city improvements with connections to public utilities (electricity, water, and sewerage). Construction of the low-cost houses and the sites and services units could be carried out by direct municipal mandate to the private sector or through the local SERVIU. A credit by the IDB to the Ministry of Interior provided financing for sites and services.

The low-cost houses and sites and services units were to be paid for in monthly installments over a period of twelve years. The monthly installments fluctuated between 0.24 and 0.72 UF for the sites and services units and 0.69 and 2.00 UF for the housing units. If the beneficiaries had some savings, the monthly payment could be smaller, up to an established minimum. The difference between the present value of the payments and the cost of the houses was to be met by a municipal subsidy.

This program has been effective in targeting the poorest 30 percent of the population, which has received all the subsidies. The reasons for this success include the low value of the houses, the fact that beneficiaries were not required to have prior savings, and the ease of targeting the subsidy to entire populations living in extremely marginal areas under poor conditions. As indicated, this program has applied to people who needed no relocation from their present sites but lacked basic urban services.

Emergency programs during the 1982–1983 crisis.   The government instituted two main emergency programs during the 1982–1983 crisis to alleviate the financial condition of the construction industry and debtors: special mortgage instruments provided by the Central Bank, and refinancing of mortgage debts. These programs were important because they represented departures from the policy focus on extreme poverty, as a result of the deep economic crisis and need for economic recovery.

To achieve a large-scale reduction of the stock of unsold houses (about 20,000) accumulated since the second half of 1981, in 1983 the government introduced, as part of the financial restructuring plan, a special program to provide mortgage loans with twenty-year terms and 8 percent annual interest rates (versus market interest rates of about 12 percent). At this time, credit was virtually unavailable. The program, in place from April 1983 to April 1984, proceeded as follows: commercial banks issued mortgage instruments at the specified terms to provide financing for home buyers; the Central Bank bought these bonds at face value (at par) by issuing bonds with twelve-year terms and a 12 percent annual real interest rate; and the Central Bank then assigned administration of its bond portfolio to the issuer bank, paying a commission of 1.2 percent. The commercial banks were not allowed to charge commissions, which had been four percentage points, for originating and servicing the mortgages and for the default risk.

Although high, the four-point spread the Central Bank paid was expected to cover the costs of originating and servicing the mortgages and bearing the default risk. It has been estimated that of the 12.4 million UF issued at 12 percent, home-buyers received a subsidy of about 30 percent (because of the difference between the market and mortgage rates), and the commercial banks and construction firms got a transfer of about 18 percent for issuance costs and in profits (Institute of Economics 1986). Given the characteristics of the houses built by the private sector, the subsidy most likely was highly regressive, going to the highest 40 percent of the income distribution. It did, however, revitalize the construction industry and was instrumental in its quick recovery and expansion in employment after 1984.[17]

The reprogramming of mortgage debts went as follows. In 1983, the government reduced by 40 percent the monthly mortgage payments to be financed by the Central Bank at an 8 percent real annual interest rate, which were paid at the end of the mortgage contract in monthly payments similar to those while serving the mortgage. This 40 percent reduction applied to the first year. Thereafter, the payments were to be increased by ten percentage points each year until the level of the original payments was reached. In 1984, the ten-point annual increase was reduced to 3 percent to alleviate further the situation of debtors, and the interest rate was reduced to 4 percent. Permission was given to those benefiting from the previous rescheduling programs to renegotiate their debts (excluding those incurred under previous programs) according to the more favorable market conditions prevailing at that time.

Most debtors who had contracted mortgages at 12 percent interest rates, including those under the old SINAP system and MINVU, benefited from this rescheduling program. They were able to buy old mortgages with the new mortgages issued at 8 percent. The subsidies involved in these reprogrammings and reschedulings, although they went to middle- and upper-income families, were probably small (because many refinanced their debts with new mortgage bonds at lower interest rates), and corresponded to the difference between the market and the 4 percent interest rate charged on the accumulated monthly payments that were not renegotiated.

Savings and Financing System for Housing (SAF).   In part as a result of the emergency programs introduced during 1982–1983, the government set up the SAF program in 1984 to help finance housing for medium- and higher-income groups formerly served by SINAP. These groups had not been receiving housing benefits because of the policy focus on extreme poverty. Basically, the new system sought to attract people into housing savings plans offered through the banking system. Once in such a plan, a person could apply for a subsidy, ranging from 30 to 130 UF, to complement savings and credit obtained from commercial banks for the purchase of a house, new or used, urban or rural.[18] To become eligible, the interested person had to sign a contract with a bank or other financial institution, in which he or she agreed to save a specified amount in a given period (a minimum of eighteen months) and to maintain in his or her account a specified minimum quarterly balance. Once the subsidy had been awarded, the account was frozen until the actual purchase.

The number of points required for selection for this program was a direct function of the number of family dependents, amount of savings, and number of months the savings account had been open. The subsidy also varied inversely with the quantity of subsidies applied for. Through this system, people can acquire houses valued at up to 2,000 UF (about U.S. $36,000). As with the traditional housing subsidy system, the public sector confined its role to regulating the savings plan and the priority system for assignment of the subsidies. Looking for a house, as well as its actual purchase, was the responsibility of the private parties.

The SAF contained a government guarantee of credit at a fixed interest rate. This credit, which could be obtained from any commercial bank at maturities of twelve, fifteen, or twenty years, had a real annual interest rate of no more than 8 percent. The credits were financed with mortgage bonds issued in UF at 5 percent. MINVU paid upfront the difference between the market (Santiago Stock Exchange) and issued (face) value of the bond through its SERVIUs. There was a limit of 130 UF on the amount paid. The government also guaranteed payment of 75 percent of the loss after foreclosure and recovery of the mortgage guarantees (the latter was given only for unpaid credit below 500 UF).

Despite the guarantees, use of the SAF certificates was initially slow. Of over 15,000 subsidies given in 1984–1985, only just over 100 had been used by the end of 1985. The reasons probably included a fear of credits in UF (given that wages and salaries were increasing much less than CPI) and the reluctance of banks to give credit for this type of operation, because the additional subsidy did not seem sufficient to cover the difference of over 3 percentage points between the government-issued mortgage bonds and the face value of the mortgage bonds issued by the commercial banks. This latter concern appears to have been valid, since the average subsidy was high (about 100 UF in 1985 and 78 UF in 1986) (ODEPLAN 1987a).

Although there was a clear need for a financial mechanism for middle-income housing, there was less justification for a subsidy-type program. This program provided subsidies (although in smaller amounts) even to those who purchased housing units valued at up to 2,000 UF. The figures for 1984 to 1987 show, in fact, that the subsidies have benefited primarily the upper 40 percent of the income distribution: over 95 percent went to that group, as compared with the minimal 3 percent received by the middle 30 percent, a primary target of the program (Table 4.3).

The distributive impact of this subsidy probably worsens when the indirect subsidy (the guarantee of the value of the mortgage bonds) is included, as larger subsidies went to the bigger debtors who could afford higher-priced housing. The per capita indirect subsidy, although it declined from 100 UF to 78 UF from 1985 to 1986, was over six times larger than the indirect subsidies provided under the HSP, which was more redistributive in the period 1984–1986 (ODEPLAN 1987a). In addition, although the amount of resources spent on the SAF was initially small (5 percent of what was spent on the HSP), the trend showed a rapid increase in absolute terms and relative to other

TABLE 4.3 SAF Subsidies Received by Income Group,
1985–1987 (%)

Income group	1985	1986	1987
Poorest 30%	1.2	1.2	1.8
Middle 30%	3.4	2.5	2.5
Richest 40%	95.5	96.3	95.7

NOTE: Excluded are indirect subsidies in the form of payments by MINVU of the difference between the market and face or par values of mortgage bonds. These subsidies were more than half of the direct subsidies in 1985–1986 for which information was available (see Table A4.1).
SOURCE: The subsidy calculations are explained in the Appendix to this chapter.

programs. In 1987, total SAF subsidies were about 16 percent higher than those under the HSP. That total amount is much larger if the indirect subsidies are included. Fortunately, the SAF and the HSP have recently been modified and consolidated to improve their very poor redistributive impact (see the discussion of the Unified Subsidy Program following).

The mortgage market.   As indicated, in 1977, the commercial banks, as well as the State Bank and other financial institutions, were authorized to originate and service mortgage bonds to provide financing for middle- and upper-income families. These institutions issued the mortgage bonds in pesos, constant value units (UF), or foreign currency at fixed nominal interest rates. The bonds could be transacted in the secondary market (Bolsa de Comercio de Santiago). The issuing institution retained the default risk, but the investor acquired the interest risk.

Development of the mortgage market was rapid until 1982–1983, when it slowed, only to pick up rapidly at the end of 1983 and in 1984. At that time, the volume of mortgage bonds outstanding increased fast because of the special programs. Thereafter, the market slowed. One of the main reasons for the low volume of mortgages outstanding was the large difference between the interest rates implicit in the bonds and the interest rates for government-backed assets, such as the mortgage rates of the State Bank. A spread of about 4 percentage points (recently declining to 3 percentage points) existed over most of these years.

Recent studies have attributed this large spread in interest rates to distortionary factors arising from a lack of sufficient competition, because only commercial banks and financial institutions can originate and service mortgages. This rule excludes other potential agents such as insurance companies or mutual fund companies from specializing in originating and servicing these types of instruments. Another distorting factor was the high perceived risk, in that the issuers retain the default risk, while investors cannot assess the risk of mortgage portfolios compared with other portfolios of commercial banks, because the mortgage bonds are not collateralized with a specific portfolio of assets (Institute of Economics 1986).

The expansion potential for the mortgage bond market is great, since the AFPs and insurance companies will be accumulating enormous amounts of funds that they could invest in mortgage bonds. In mid-1988, the AFPs' holdings of mortgage bonds were about 26 percent of their accumulated funds (down from a peak of 48 percent in 1983) (see Chapter 5). As the market for the stock of privatized public companies and debentures of moderate-risk private-sector companies becomes saturated, improved mortgage instruments will be needed for these investments. Further, as the market for the life annuities (*renta vitalicia*) provided by the insurance companies expands, reserves (and the capital of the insurance companies) will need to be expanded considerably (García 1986).

MINVU's mortgage portfolio.   As noted, MINVU has had to provide complementary loans to the beneficiaries of most programs (including a few loans in the SAF program), as the private commercial banks have shown little interest in providing this type of relatively small loan. By 1988, MINVU had accumulated about 300,000 individual accounts in its mortgage portfolio, including a significant number of loans from previous administrations that had been only partially adjusted for inflation.

As with the rest of the financial system holding mortgage portfolios, MINVU had to apply annual reprogrammings during the 1982–1983 crisis to reduce the payment obligations of debtors severely affected by unemployment and loss in real wages. These reprogrammings, along with the complex mortgage structure of MINVU's loans, the nature of the beneficiaries, and a long tradition of poor collection by the agencies consolidated under MINVU, led to severe collection problems. Only recently, in 1988, has MINVU started to address this issue successfully.[19] Measures have included (1) a 25 percent reduction in payments if made on time, (2) computerization of the loan accounts and contracting with a private firm to manage over 80 percent of MINVU's accounts, (3) simplified foreclosure procedures, and (4) facilitation of payments through the branch offices of the State Bank operating in most cities. In addition, MINVU introduced a program of mortgage restructuring to match some of the write-downs or debt reductions obtained through the swap program the government introduced to reduce the external debt. This effort has led to an important reduction in the debt of mortgagees. Through this system, the discount obtained in the transaction (about 30 percent) has been used to reduce the outstanding balances of participating mortgage loans. A maximum of U.S. $6,000 per mortgage borrower is allowed, a restriction that favors smaller loans.

The initial results of these measures have been encouraging. Collections improved in real terms during 1988. By March 1989, MINVU had computerized over 90 percent of the portfolio. With this private-sector arrangement and the incentives given to the SERVIUs, by which they retain a significant part of the increases in collections to finance their own regional investment plans, expectations are that significant further improvements will be achieved in collections in the near future, as promised by MINVU.

Recent housing programs

In the wake of recent studies financed by a World Bank housing loan, the government has redefined and simplified the previously discussed programs to improve the targeting of housing subsidies to the neediest population (Institute of Economics 1986).[20] It has also proposed improved operations of the mortgage market so that interest rates can be reduced and the market expanded to provide housing financing to middle- and upper- income people. These programs were introduced under a housing-sector World Bank loan implemented in 1989. A summary of the programs follows.

Modified Basic Housing Program.   The main modification to the original BHP involves the establishment of three subsidy brackets (previously there was only one) based on the value of the house. The aims are to reduce the amount of subsidy per beneficiary so that more subsidies can be given and to take into account the varying needs and desires of the lowest income groups. As indicated, this program has had an excellent redistributive impact, but the subsidies have been too high given the economic capacity of beneficiaries, the lower construction costs, and the need to service more of the poorest homeless households (Castañeda and Quiroz 1984). Although houses must cost less than 300 UF (U.S. $5,900), the upfront subsidy varies inversely with the value of the house, ranging from 48 to 75 percent. The brackets are shown in Table 4.4.

Unified Subsidy Program.   The Unified Subsidy Program combines the HSP and the SAF. Its purpose is to help finance the housing needs of poor and middle-income families and to increase the redistributive impact of the two previous programs, while providing options for high-cost housing at much lower subsidies. The program contains three price

TABLE 4.4 The Basic and Modified Basic Housing Program
Subsidies (UF)

	House price	Maximum subsidy
Basic program	266	< 200 or 75% of cost
Modified basic		
Level 1	< 215	75% of cost
Level 2	215–259	56% of cost
Level 3	260–300	48% of cost

NOTE: 1 UF = U.S. $18.
SOURCE: Ministry of Housing and Urban Affairs.

brackets for housing with corresponding subsidies, which are lower the
higher the price of the house (Table 4.5). About 90 percent of the
subsidies are to go to the lower bracket, following the existing system of
three calls (*llamados*) per year by region. This approach, if properly
implemented, will most likely reduce the poor redistributive impact of
the programs.[21]

The point system for determining beneficiaries is based on that of
the SAF program, factoring in the amount of savings, which can be in
the form of ownership of a site without a mortgage; length and regu-
larity of the savings effort; family size; and amount of the subsidy
requested. The subsidy consists of a certificate or voucher that MINVU
redeems in cash payable to the builder upon termination and registration of the unit for the beneficiary. The beneficiary can also do the
construction or can use cooperatives or private companies in the open
market. In fact, over 30 percent of the units will be built by cooperatives
and NGOs such as the Hogar de Cristo, a large nonprofit organization
of the Catholic Church.

As it did under the two programs that were combined under the
Unified Subsidy Program, MINVU pays upfront the difference between

TABLE 4.5 Unified Subsidy Program House Prices
and Subsidy Ranges, 1988 (UF)

Bracket	House price	Subsidy
Level 1	< 400	120–150
Level 2	400–900	100–130
Level 3	900–2,000	80–110

NOTE: 1 UF = U.S. $18.
SOURCE: Ministry of Housing and Urban Affairs.

the face or par value and the market value of the mortgage bonds. The difference arises because of the guaranteed interest rates, which can be lower than market interest rates, and the high risk associated with the origination and servicing of mortgage bonds. Given the very low redistributive impact of this indirect subsidy, it should be confined to only the first two brackets.

The Public/Private Association Program.   This special program was initiated in 1987 to provide upfront subsidies to organized homeless groups. The cost of the houses is limited to 210–260 UF (U.S. $3,780–4,680), and the subsidy provided is 60 UF (U.S. $1,080). In some cases, the SERVIUs handled the construction; in other cases, the beneficiaries located their own builders. A credit from the State Bank or other commercial bank at the prevailing market interest rate covers the difference between the subsidy and the cost of the house. MINVU pays the difference between the guaranteed rate and the market rate implicit in the sale of mortgage bonds in the market. Under the World Bank loan, the direct subsidy has been increased to 80 UF, while the indirect subsidies associated with the discount on the mortgage bonds are gradually being reduced.

Rehabilitation program.   This program, to be started on a pilot basis under the World Bank project, provides financing for a tenement (*conventillos*) program, to make deteriorating housing units habitable, and a home-improvement program for poor households. These programs are to be executed primarily by NGOs with related experience. The majority of beneficiary families under the tenement rehabilitation program should fall within the poorest 60 percent of the population. Renovated units are expected to have three rooms, in addition to a kitchen and bathroom, in a site of 100 square meters per family and will be the property of the family. The home-improvement program is expected to benefit families in the poorest 20 percent of the population, with units up to 46 square meters. As in most other programs, financial assistance will include upfront subsidies and credit (in amounts not yet specified).

The Redistributive Impact of Selected Programs in 1980–1986 and Comparisons with 1969

The programs selected for the analysis of the redistributive impact and comparison with 1969 include those described previously except for the cooperatives program and the emergency programs initiated in response to the 1982–1983 crisis. Also excluded are several programs such as neighborhood sanitation, community equipment, colonization housing, and legal assistance to poor families for titling (some of these have been financed by the Ministry of National Assets). In all the calculations it was assumed the beneficiary complies with the payments agreed to and does not receive (or will not receive) additional subsidies for less than full payment of the debts.

Subsidies resulting from the discount value of the mortgage and any subsidies arising from the renegotiation of mortgages during 1983–1987 or the incentives offered by MINVU for prompt payment of debts were also excluded. The benchmark income distribution comes from the Employment and Unemployment Surveys of the University of Chile. The subsidies included account for about 60 percent of MINVU's total expenditures and for about 80 percent of its investment budget. (A summary of the methodology for these calculations is provided in the Appendix to this chapter).

Principal findings

Figure 4.1 shows the significant increase in the proportion of subsidies received by the poorest population since 1982. Before then, the distributive impact remained more or less the same as in 1969, despite major changes in the programs to improve targeting. In 1982, the share of subsidies that went to the poorest 30 percent of the population—50 percent—was more than double the figure of about 20 percent in 1969 and 1980. Their percentage remained at this level until 1986, the last year for which information was available for the calculations. In contrast, the subsidies received by the middle 30 percent income group (the third to

FIGURE 4.1 Housing Subsidies Received by Income Groups, 1969 and 1980–1986

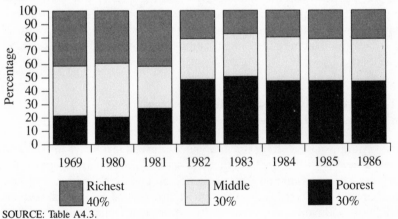

SOURCE: Table A4.3.

the sixth deciles of the income distribution) dropped from about 40 percent to 33 percent, and those received by the richest 40 percent of the population were halved. In absolute real terms, the subsidies received by the poorest 30 percent increased over four times between 1980 and 1986, while those received by the next 30 percent rose by about 50 percent; the level for the richest 40 percent in 1986 was similar to that in 1980, following recent increases (Figure 4.1). Most remarkable is that in comparison with 1969, the subsidies received in 1986 by the poorest 30 percent were 55 percent higher, while those received by the middle 30 percent and the richest 40 percent were 40 and 60 percent lower, respectively.

The main reason for the improved success in targeting subsidies has been the emphasis given to very basic housing programs that do not attract middle-income groups and to improvements in the screening of the poorest groups, along with a tightening of controls to avoid subsidies going to nontarget groups. In fact, as Table A4.1 in the Appendix shows, the social and basic housing and the sites and services programs, which gained in importance, have the highest redistributive impact, as contrasted with the applicants, housing subsidy, and SAF programs, which had little relative redistributive impact.

As mentioned, the differences in the redistributive impact of the programs can be attributed to different identification criteria and selection procedures for beneficiaries and to the type of housing unit offered under each program. In the case of the Social and Basic Housing and the Sites and Services Programs, for instance, eligible beneficiaries lived in camps (easily identifiable by MINVU and by municipalities); most were settled in the same place or relocated elsewhere *as a group*. In the case of the applicants and housing subsidy systems in particular, the requirement for savings and the more costly housing units for which a person could apply (up to 850 UF) determined the relatively low redistributive impact. The least redistributive of all the programs has been the SAF, which provides subsidies for high-priced houses affordable only to high-income groups (the richest 40 percent), who got over 95 percent of all subsidies.

Impact of the Housing Programs

As a result of these systematic programs, the housing situation has improved considerably in recent years. Estimates for the period 1982 to 1987, based on the 1982 Population and Housing Census and recent household surveys (such as the CASEN Survey) measuring living standards, show there has been a considerable reduction in the housing deficit and improvements in housing conditions. According to these estimates, the housing deficit, defined as the difference between the total number of households nationwide and the number of acceptable houses, fell from 480,000 units (19 percent of households) in 1982 to 356,000 (13 percent) in 1987.[22] Although comparisons of housing conditions for the years before 1982 are not possible, the 1982 census information and the 1985 CASEN data indicate that the housing situation of over 85 percent of the Chilean population in 1982 and 1985 was good, surely one of the highest percentages in Latin America. Housing units classified as "fair" or "poor" (needing replacement) amounted to about 14 percent, according to both sources.

The greatest advances, however, have involved the provision of basic services such as water and sewerage, advances that have aided the rapid decline in infant mortality since 1976 (see Chapter 3). The coverage of potable water in urban areas increased from 78 percent in 1976 to 98 percent in 1987, and coverage of sewerage increased from 51 percent in 1976 to 79 percent in 1987 (Table 4.6). This progress has been made in the context of the massive slum rehabilitation, titling, and city improvements programs. For instance, between 1979 and 1987, about 450,000 titles were issued to people in upgraded slum areas. As has occurred in most countries, Chilean cities have been plagued with massive peripheral slum areas with no basic services, resulting from illegal "invasions."

TABLE 4.6 Urban Coverage of Potable Water and Sewerage Services, 1976–1987 (%)

Year	Coverage[a]	
	Potable water	Sewerage
1976	78.2	51.1
1977	80.6	55.9
1978	86.0	56.3
1979	92.1	62.4
1980	91.4	67.4
1981	91.5	68.2
1982	92.1	70.0
1983	92.7	70.6
1984	94.3	72.9
1985	95.2	75.1
1986	97.0	77.0
1987	98.0	79.0

a. Includes both in-house connections and access to water at a nearby source.
SOURCE: Ministry of Public Works, National Service of Sanitary Works.

During the 1960s, the Operation Site Program was created to provide slums with basic urban services, and about 120,000 such sites were created between 1965 and 1970. However, at the beginning of the 1970s, there was a rapid increase in invasions on municipal and private unoccupied lands, along with unfinished construction, as a result of the political radicalization under the government of President Allende. At the end of 1973, it was estimated that over 100,000 families (not counting some from the old Operation Site Program) were living illegally without urban services.

Despite the considerable advances, wide differences in in-house water supply and sewerage coverage persist among different income groups. In 1985, these differences ranged from about 58 to over 97 percent across the income distribution in the case of water, and from about 60 to 97 percent for sewerage (Table 4.7). Pockets of slums still exist in the major cities such as Santiago; they could be upgraded with basic urban services. More difficult is upgrading the old *operación sitio* projects, which are scattered in different parts of the city, each one requiring specialized studies.

Summary and Conclusions

Chile's interventions in the housing sector in the past fifteen years have involved major structural reforms of institutions and legislation and a changed role for the public sector. In 1975, MINVU started to operate

TABLE 4.7 Potable Water (In-House) and Sewerage by Income Decile, 1985 (%)

Income decile (low to high)	Coverage	
	Potable water (in-house)	Sewerage
1	57.9	59.6
2	60.0	62.5
3	69.2	68.7
4	70.4	71.3
5	76.3	77.5
6	82.0	79.9
7	84.2	84.2
8	90.7	90.1
9	95.3	95.5
10	97.4	97.4

SOURCE: University of Chile, ODEPLAN, CASEN Survey, 1985, cited by MINVU.

through decentralized and autonomous regional services (SERVIUs), in close coordination with the municipalities. The housing legislation was simplified and reordered to permit more competition and a bigger role for the private sector in land development and subdivision, construction of housing units for government-subsidized programs, private leasing contracts, and land titling. The role of the public sector changed from active involvement in construction, financing, and development to the provision of direct, upfront subsidies to households that, after their own efforts, still needed state assistance. Although not originally intended, MINVU also became involved in providing mortgage financing to the poorest households.

These reforms are still being fine-tuned, as new programs are introduced to improve targeting. So far, they appear to be highly successful. First, the efficiency of resource use appears to have improved significantly, given that fewer government expenditures have been used to mobilize larger resources for housing. Since 1973, over 420,000 housing units have been built, mainly through the private sector, while government expenditures have declined considerably. In 1983, public spending on housing was only about 30 percent of what it had been in 1970. Second, cost-effectiveness has improved, in the face of the high priority given to basic programs such as land titling, slum upgrading, and urban rehabilitation, including the provision of connections to potable water and sewerage. These efforts have been of enormous benefit to the population. Third, equity improved considerably, with the proportion of subsidies received by the poorest 30 percent of the population increasing from about 20 percent in 1969 and 1980 to about 50 percent in 1982 through 1986.

Designing programs targeted to the poorest groups has proven difficult. It has required establishing a delicate balance among the criteria of the beneficiary's own effort, the ability to pay, and the type of unit offered. The optimal formula has been learned through experimentation with different programs and incentive schemes aimed at reducing the allocation of subsidies to higher income groups. For instance, the Applicants System and the Housing Subsidy Programs initially benefited middle-income groups, because they offered relatively expensive housing (up to 850 UF) and required high savings and a minimum income. In addition, a lack of control early on led to house appraisals below market values. Beneficiaries bought unfinished housing units with appraised values lower than those of the finished products. In this way, higher-income people were able to circumvent the rules on the house values eligible for subsidies, and more costly finished housing units were subsidized.

The greater share of subsidies that has gone to the poorest 30 percent of the population has resulted from the strong impetus provided by the Sites and Services and the Basic Housing Programs as part of the urban rehabilitation and slum-upgrading effort. These programs have had a large impact because of the type of units they offer (rather low standard) and the way in which the beneficiaries are selected (primarily by regional targeting of complete slum and camp neighborhoods that were "legalized" and upgraded, or from which residents were moved to suitable lands). Key to the success of the programs has been the fact that, while sites and services were provided to people in slum areas that could be settled and upgraded, the more adequate solution of a basic house was given to people in slums who had to be relocated. This approach gave families an incentive to move and provided a ready place for them to go to. Also important has been the role played by MINVU in contracting out projects with private enterprises and in providing complementary credit.

Introduction of the upfront voucher-type direct subsidies to beneficiaries in place of the subsidies given through low nominal interest rates, as was done in the past, has gradually become generalized and has proven to be a functional way to distribute housing subsidies. Under this system, beneficiaries pay for the value of a specified house with their own savings, the voucher, and a credit obtained from commercial banks at market interest rates. Initially this mechanism did not work well, because there was no private supply of very low-cost housing and the commercial banks were not interested in financing the poorest households. Later, when there was a substantial supply of private-sector low-cost houses, MINVU and the State Bank provided mortgage financing. Moreover, the private sector, including cooperatives, has become so active and specialized in low-cost housing (from sites and services to house building) that the costs have dropped appreciably.

Because of an initial lack of information and prompt evaluation of the programs, the subsidies appear to have been too large in view of the economic capacity (and willingness to pay) of beneficiaries. Some of the poorest families (who were eligible for the Basic Housing Program), for example, received subsidies of 200 UF, which covered a significant part of the total value of the house. These people might have been able to pay at least 80 UF over twenty years at 8 percent annual interest rate, under pessimistic assumptions of no growth in wages and only moderate reductions in unemployment.[23] In 1988, the government reduced both the subsidies and the appraised value of the houses eligible for financing. This step will lead to further significant reductions in the housing deficit over the next few years. In addition, since 1984 the CAS Index poverty measurement instrument applied by the municipalities to prospective beneficiaries has substantially improved poverty screening and information on economic capacity.

Appendix: Methodology for Computing the Subsidies

The methodology used to compute the distribution of housing subsidies by income group is explained in Castañeda and Quiroz 1984. As will be seen, the lack of evaluations of the programs, coupled with inadequate information on the income distribution of beneficiaries under each program and, in some cases, on the amount of the subsidy granted, made a number of assumptions necessary in calculating the subsidies, especially before 1984. Some of these assumptions have been confirmed. The main features of the methodology for the calculations are as follows.

Housing programs in 1969

Information on the distribution of subsidies by income group for the housing programs, including the Operation Site, in effect in 1969 is provided by Arellano (1976), who used income data from the National Institute of Statistics (INE) for 1969. This information source is old; but for purposes of comparison, Arellano's subsidy data were used with the benchmark income distribution derived from data from the Department of Economics of the University of Chile employment and unemployment surveys. The data on subsidies pertain to actual subsidies granted, including both direct and indirect, the latter involving below-market interest rates on loans.

The assumptions made were that beneficiaries paid the amounts they owed on time and received no additional subsidies because of a failure to pay in full or because of less than full indexation of the debts. The programs considered were CORVI, CORHABIT, CORMU, and SINAP. The cutoff points of the income levels (that is, the maximum incomes for the poorest 30 percent and the intermediate 30 percent) were, according to Arellano, one and two living wages, respectively. According to data from the Department of Economics, the cutoff points were 1.298 and 2.597 living wages for those same income groups.[24] These higher cutoff points significantly raise the redistributive impact of the 1969 programs as compared to Arellano's calculations based on 1969 data.

Housing programs in 1980–1986

The subsidies that went to each program were computed in three steps: first, the percentage of subsidies that would go to each income group was determined based on numerous antecedents about the type of beneficiaries in each program (see Table A4.1); second, the number of housing units provided under each program during the different years was determined with information from MINVU; and then the amount of the subsidy actually received by each beneficiary was obtained with additional (and in some cases partial) information from MINVU. In most programs (with the exception of the Sites and Services, Housing Subsidy, and SAF Programs), it was assumed that until 1983 the subsidy received was 200 UF per beneficiary. From 1984 onward, there is more direct information on the subsidy per beneficiary by program.

Applicants Systems Program.   The income distribution of this program's beneficiaries is not known. What is known, however, is that group A applicants had to give proof of monthly income lower than five times the minimum wage and a minimum of 600 savings quotas, while group B applicants had to show a monthly income in excess of five times the minimum wage and a minimum of 1,000 savings quotas (later increased to 1,600). The minimum income was 182 pesos at the time the regulations were published, an indication that group B applicants were in the highest 40 percent of the population income bracket. The information from the Ministry of Housing also indicates that 70 percent of the housing units finished under this system went to group A applicants, and the balance to group B.

With the above information, it appears safe to assume that half of the group A beneficiaries belonged to the middle 30 percent and the remainder to the highest 40 percent of the income bracket. This information permits calculation of the proportion of benefits that went to each income group. The amount of subsidy per beneficiary was calculated as 200 UF based on MINVU data, which indicated that 95 percent of the beneficiaries had qualified under the terms of Supreme Decree 1,170 of 1977, which enabled them to apply for a 200 UF subsidy for a cash purchase, combined with credit from MINVU.

Social Housing Program.   A study published in 1982 provided information on distribution of subsidies by income group under this program (Arellano 1982). The study used as a benchmark the income distribution information from INE's 1978 consumption survey. To maintain uniformity in the income distribution data used, and because of the inconsistencies detected in INE's survey, the subsidy data are arranged within the income distribution data of the Department of Economics.[25] The assumptions made are that the distribution of beneficiaries by income group did not change from 1980 to 1983, and that the income distribution for the Greater Santiago area is similar to that in the rest of Chile.

Basic Housing Program.   For the most part, MINVU provided basic housing from 1980 to 1986 through the variable subsidy system. Since the income distribution of the beneficiaries is not known, it was approximated by the income distribution of beneficiaries of the variable housing subsidy. This approximation proved to be very good, as indicated by information from a direct sampling provided by a study of the Santiago metropolitan area (Cepa Ltda. 1985b). The reason is that both the assignment method and the value of housing units provided were similar in the two programs. It is assumed that the distribution of beneficiaries by income group did not change in these years. Targeting may have improved in recent years with the introduction of the CAS Poverty Index into the criteria used to determine beneficiaries.

Sites and Services Program.   Because of the type of housing provided and the location of beneficiaries (camps and slums at the periphery of urban areas), all of this subsidy went to the poorest 30 percent of the Chilean population. This assumption was confirmed by direct information from an evaluation study of the slum-upgrading program for the Santiago metropolitan region in 1984 (Cepa Ltda. 1985a). The amount of the subsidy was calculated at 75 percent of the cost of each site and service unit.

Housing Subsidy Program.   This program presented the most difficulties in determining the subsidies by income group. There were twelve calls between 1978 and 1986, but there were delays (especially at the beginning) in claiming and paying the subsidies. The calculations were based on three pieces of information: (1) the amount of the subsidies paid, as published by MINVU by call by year; (2) information on the income distribution of the beneficiaries of the subsidies awarded, also published by MINVU; and (3) the income distribution cutoff points for the third and sixth deciles of the benchmark income distribution used herein. Calculation of the subsidies *paid* by year involved the subsidies that had been *awarded* in different years. The income distribution specific to each call was used in the calculations, so that, in fact, each year's total subsidies by income group were a weighted average of the subsidies paid that year in the different calls (the weights were the income distribution of the subsidies awarded). The assumption was that the distribution of subsidies awarded was the same as that of subsidies paid.

Rural Housing Subsidy Program.   In view of the lack of income distribution data on beneficiaries of this program, the distribution for the HSP was used. There were two considerations regarding the two opposing biases in this assumption. First, the rural subsidy was variable, in that the lower the amount requested, the higher the chance of getting it—a factor that probably made this subsidy more regressive than the HSP. Second, the rural subsidy applied to houses of up to 400 UF, while the HSP applied to houses of up to 580 UF; so that the rural subsidy was more progressive in that the constraint on house values attracted people of lesser incomes.

Savings and Financing System for Housing.   The methodology used to calculate the subsidies by income bracket was similar to that used with the HSP. It involved the income distribution of beneficiaries who had been awarded subsidies in the different SAF calls.

TABLE A4.1 Distribution of Subsidies by Program and Beneficiary Income Group, 1980–1986 (%)

Program and income bracket	1980	1981	1982	1983	1984	1985	1986
Applicants System							
Poorest 30%	0.0	0.0					
Middle 30%	35.0	35.0					
Richest 40%	65.0	65.0					
Social Housing							
Poorest 30%	23.8	23.8	23.8				
Middle 30%	63.9	63.9	63.9				
Richest 40%	12.3	12.3	12.3				
Basic Housing							
Poorest 30%	60.2	60.2	60.2	60.2	60.2	60.2	60.2
Middle 30%	35.6	35.6	35.6	35.6	35.6	35.6	35.6
Richest 40%	4.2	4.2	4.2	4.2	4.2	4.2	4.2
Sites and Services							
Poorest 30%	100.0	100.0	100.0	100.0	100.0	100.0	100.0
Middle 30%	0.0	0.0	0.0	0.0	0.0	0.0	0.0
Richest 40%	0.0	0.0	0.0	0.0	0.0	0.0	0.0
Housing Subsidy and Rural Subsidy							
Poorest 30%	9.9	8.8	20.0	20.3	18.9	18.1	24.2
Middle 30%	31.6	19.5	18.8	29.9	37.4	35.5	38.9
Richest 40%	58.5	71.2	61.2	49.8	43.7	46.4	36.9
SAF							
Poorest 30%						1.2	1.3
Middle 30%						2.5	3.0
Richest 40%						96.5	94.7

Blank cell indicates that program was not available in that year.
SOURCE: Calculations as explained in the Appendix of this chapter.

TABLE A4.2 Subsidies Paid by Program, 1980–1986
(thousands of UF)

Program	1980	1981	1982	1983	1984	1985	1986
Applicants							
System	1,368.0	1,180.4					
Social Housing	886.9	178.0	104.1				
Basic Housing	981.7	1,788.5	2,415.9	2,697.8	2,919.7	3,587.7	3,874.0
Sites and							
Services			84.4	208.0	608.1	627.1	661.0
Housing Subsidy							
Direct	1,352.0	1,480.3	1,065.3	1,194.9	2,405.7	2,428.6	2,750.2
Rural Subsidy						144.4	192.9
SAF							
Direct Subsidy						110.0	469.0
Indirect							
Subsidy[a]						69.7	195.7

Blank cell indicates that program was not available in that year.
a. The indirect subsidy is the amount paid by MINVU to cover the difference between the face or par
value and the market value of mortgages. See the text for explanation.
SOURCE: Calculations as explained in the text and in Castañeda and Quiroz 1984.

TABLE A4.3 Housing Subsidies Received by Income Groups in 1969
and 1980–1986 (millions of 1978 pesos and %)

	Poorest 30%		Middle 30%		Richest 40%	
Year	Amount	%	Amount	%	Amount	%
1969	1,336.0	21.6	2,294.2	37.2	2,542.0	41.2
1980	477.9	20.5	929.9	40.2	933.7	39.3
1981	693.4	27.0	805.1	31.4	1,067.8	41.6
1982	921.7	48.4	584.8	30.7	397.4	20.9
1983	1,108.1	50.6	703.8	32.1	377.9	17.3
1984	1,559.4	47.2	1,086.9	32.9	657.5	19.9
1985	1,845.9	47.2	1,231.9	31.5	833.0	21.3
1986	2,077.6	46.7	1,419.2	31.9	952.1	21.4

SOURCE: Calculations as explained in the Appendix of this chapter.

CHAPTER 5

Reform of
the Social Security System

This chapter reviews why and how the social security (pension) system was reformed in Chile. It begins with an extensive review of the old system, to help explain the rationale for the reforms. The chapter then describes the new system that began in 1981: its main features, the results so far, the fiscal cost, and how the reform has been implemented. A few lessons derived for other countries are presented at the end of the chapter.

The Old and New Systems: An Overview

The old pension system had a number of problems that the new system proposed to correct. First, a high degree of discrimination existed because of the great diversity in the numerous pension institutions, specifically in terms of benefits and retirement requirements that discriminated against weaker groups, particularly blue-collar workers. Second, most institutions suffered a deep financial crisis as a result of decreased revenues caused by excessive contribution rates and a lack of control that induced evasion, excessive expenditures on administration, and other benefits for a few privileged workers (such as housing loans at very low nominal interest rates). As a result of this feature, there was a need for large, untargeted, and increasing subsidies, especially for the pension system of public employees. Finally, services for beneficiaries were poor; many had to wait several months after retirement before receiving any benefit.

Under the new system, there are unified, simple, nondiscriminatory rules regarding benefits to be provided, retirement requirements, and eligibility criteria. Government subsidies are targeted to the poorest workers, whose accumulated funds are not enough to cover the minimum established pension, and to the needy not enrolled in the social security system. An individual capitalization scheme allows workers to save (compulsorily) for their own retirement and to pay for the disability and survivors insurance premium. Retirement funds (10 percent of taxable income) can be deposited in private pension fund administration companies (AFPs) that operate for those purposes. Disability insurance can be bought from private insurance companies at a premium of about 3.4 percent of taxable salary. Competition among the AFPs and insurance companies is expected to lead to higher returns, lower administrative costs, higher pensions for affiliates, and better services for beneficiaries.

The record of the reform

The reforms have had a high short-term fiscal cost (the net long-term cost is much lower), in part as a result of their success, as indicated by the great number of people who transferred from the old to the new system in a very short period. The growth of the new system sharply reduced the revenue of the old institutions and thereby increased their deficits, which were already up as a result of the contraction of the public sector and the increase in pensioners. Implementation has also required several modifications to the original law to correct for problems and gradually to open up capital market investment opportunities to the pension funds. As a result of the massive transfer of participants, the funds grew rapidly from 1.1 percent of GDP in 1981, the first year of the reform, to 17.6 percent of GDP in 1988.

Overall, the social security reform can be described as highly successful in terms of the number of affiliates, the number of pension fund companies in the market, the returns from the pension funds (which on average have been over 3 percentage points higher than the returns from the financial system), and the benefits provided. A major advance of the reform has been that pension funds are being used as instruments for the deconcentration of property in industry and for the privatization of public enterprises. This has been both an inducement and a necessity, as new and expanded investment alternatives are required for proper portfolio diversification of pension funds and to avoid excessive investment in government paper. In fact, a danger is that the government will concentrate the investments of the pension funds or will artificially reduce interest rates to cope with the financial deficit of the old system and to cover payment of the recognition bonds in the new system. Other dangers include overregulation of the AFPs and investment requirements and direct government involvement in the risk classification of the financial instruments permitted for pension fund investments.

Before the Reforms

The Chilean social security system has a long history, beginning in the early 1920s. It was one of the first in the western hemisphere and is the oldest in Latin America. It grew rapidly to achieve one of the highest coverage rates in Latin America (about 60 percent of the work force in 1970). Growth of the system occurred, however, in a fragmented way, a reflection of the influence of social pressures and interest groups.

In 1980, just prior to the reforms, the social security system was composed of thirty-five separate social security institutions (called Cajas), each one covering different groups of workers and subject to different legislation regarding benefits and conditions for their receipt. Moreover, the benefits varied greatly across groups of workers and especially between blue-collar and white-collar workers, the latter generally being the most favored. Payroll contributions by employers and employees became very high (the second highest in Latin America), but increasing subsidies by the state were needed to finance the benefits.

Institutional setting

The legislation resulting from the system of thirty-five different Cajas was very complex. There was a lack of accountability and control and a lack of incentives on the part of these bureaucratic structures to provide adequate and timely services. The three largest Cajas—the Social Security Service (SSS), for blue-collar or manual workers; EMPART, for private-sector white-collar workers; and CANAEMPU, for public-sector employees and newsmen—accounted for over 90 percent of all affiliates.

With the exception of the Cajas for financial-sector employees, the armed forces, and the national railroads, all the others came under the supervision and control of the Superintendency of Social Security, created in 1965. This superintendency did not supervise just these Cajas but also the National Health System, the National Medical Service for Employees (SERMENA), and the welfare services of the public and private sectors. The Superintendency of Banking Institutions oversaw the Caja for financial-sector employees, and the General Office of the Comptroller handled those for the armed forces and railroad workers.

Administration of the Cajas varied markedly, but all followed the tripartite principle that called for representatives from government, employers, and the labor force. The Cajas related to the Ministries of Labor and Defense were each administered by a council and a director or executive vice-president appointed by the president of the Republic. The council was presided over by the respective minister and was composed of representatives from the beneficiaries and employers, the president, and the Superintendency of Social Security, the latter without voting rights. The Cajas tied to the municipalities were administered by councils with representatives from the municipalities. Those tied to the Ministries of Finance and Economy were directed by representatives from those ministries.

In addition to the thirty-five Cajas, numerous other institutions had a role in providing some of the same benefits provided by the Cajas, as well as other benefits. These include the Cajas de Compensación Familiar (employer-promoted welfare organizations) and the Mutuales de Seguridad (employer-funded occupational risk institutions). The Cajas de Compensación were nongovernment institutions charged with paying monetary income subsidies, financed by employers' contributions. These Cajas were created by employers or associations of employers (a minimum of twenty employers and 3,000 employees) and provided other services to beneficiaries such as loans for housing and education. Supervision of these Cajas was handled by a Commission of Family Subsidies, specially created for this purpose.

The Mutuales appeared in the late 1950s, created by the private sector to provide insurance coverage for accidents, rehabilitation services for insured workers, salary benefits during the time out of work (85 percent of salary), indemnizations, and disability and survivor pensions. Financing was provided by an employer contribution of 0.85 percent plus an additional amount between 0 and 3.4 percent, depending on the risk category in which the specific firm was classified based on past accidents. The average contribution for the whole system in 1986 was 1.8 percent of salaries. Administration of the Mutuales was handled by directories, with equal participation by workers and employers. The Superintendency of Social Security performed supervisory and normative functions for all these institutions.

Benefits provided

All insured workers enjoyed the same types of benefits, and Chile had one of the most comprehensive benefit systems in Latin America. There was, however, great disparity in the amount of benefits provided to various types of workers; the system favored the most organized and politically influential groups. For example, public employees, who were not allowed to form unions, formed powerful "associations" of national significance that were key factors in shaping the benefit structure offered by the Caja for public employees, gradually increasing the number and amount of benefits. The first and most favored groups, however, were those in the strategic industries that had the potential to paralyze the country, such as workers in mining and the railroads (Mesa-Lago 1978). Least protected were the blue-collar workers in the Caja de Seguro Obrero (which became the SSS).

An attempt in 1952 to unify the entire system failed because of opposition by the Caja of Employees, the armed forces, and the powerful Medical Association, which had been founded in 1948. Thus, the 1952 reform applied only to the Caja de Seguro Obrero. Two new institutions were created: the National Health System (NHS), which unified and provided health services to blue-collar workers and indigents (such services had previously been provided by public hospitals, clinics, and consultancies of the Caja de Seguro Obrero and state and municipal governments); and the SSS, which provided pensions and other monetary benefits to blue-collar workers.

A description of the benefits provided, with examples of the many discriminatory features, follows.

Old-age pensions.   Old-age pensions varied markedly among occupational groups because of different eligibility criteria, ways of determining the pension, and adjustment criteria. This situation gave rise to thirty-one different pension systems. The eligibility criteria included a specified minimum age and number of payments to a given Caja, payments that could, in some cases, be substituted for by a number of years of service. The minimum age requirements varied from fifty-five years for women, public employees, newsmen, employees of financial institutions, and the armed forces to sixty-five for blue-collar workers in the SSS and private-sector employees in EMPART. These age limits could be reduced up to five years for workers doing what was defined as hard work (*trabajos pesados*), with a one-year reduction for every five years of service.

The criteria for determining the pension amount also varied markedly. For instance, while for blue-collar or manual workers (in SSS) the maximum pension was 75 percent of the base salary, for white-collar workers (in EMPART) it was 100 percent. The base salary for workers in EMPART was calculated on the basis of the previous five years, including inflation adjustments for the first two years, but the base salary for workers in the SSS excluded adjustments for inflation. Once the pension was given, all workers were eligible for adjustments for inflation (in some cases with fiscal funds). However, as in the case of disability and survivors pensions, high-level public-sector employees enjoyed pension increases that were tied to increases in the salaries for the jobs they had prior to retirement (called *pensiones perseguidoras*).

Seniority pensions.   Seniority pensions (*pensiones de antigüedad*) were given to workers completing a certain number of working years or years of contributions to the social security institutions. This pension was not available to blue-collar workers (SSS), however, who accounted for over 60 percent of all beneficiaries in all Cajas combined. Years of service and/or contributions varied markedly among groups, from thirty-five years for private-sector white-collar workers (EMPART) to twenty-three and a half years for employees of financial institutions. A few groups enjoyed special treatment beyond these general rules, such as congressmen and senators, who could obtain this pension with as few as fifteen years of service.

The amount of the pension was 100 percent of the base salary, which differed as discussed among groups of workers. All in all, given the differences in required years of service and contributions and salary base, there were over thirty different pension systems. Differences among groups also existed in that, for some workers, pensions were not periodically adjusted for inflation. Seniority pensions were, in general, greater than the old-age pensions. This disparity encouraged dubious practices by people wishing to obtain early retirement.

Disability and survivors pensions.   The amount obtained in disability and survivors (D&S) pensions varied greatly according to occupational groups because of different eligibility criteria, years of service, base salary for determining pension, nature of the pension (that is, permanent versus temporary or subject to revision), and automatic adjustments for inflation and pay scales. In general, the criteria were relatively unfavorable for lower-paid blue-collar workers as compared with public- and private-sector employees. For instance, while private-sector blue-collar workers had to make a minimum number of payments, no similar requirement existed for the public sector. Further, pensions for workers in the private sector were subject to revision, while those for workers in the public sector were permanent. Another example is that, while all private-sector workers (in EMPART) received periodic pension adjustments, only higher-level public-sector employees had access to readjustments, which were tied to the salary increases in the jobs they had at retirement.

Family assistance. This benefit consisted of income transfers (*asignaciones familiares*) for all insured workers, active and retired, based on the number of dependent family members. It was started in 1942 for private-sector white-collar workers and was extended eleven years later, in 1953, to blue-collar workers. Because these benefits, for which specific payroll contributions were assigned, were distributed by the social security institutions, they became part of the social security benefit system. Nevertheless, institutions such as the Cajas de Compensación Familiar and still others (the welfare offices of enterprises) were also created or used to distribute these benefits.

The amount of the benefits per dependent varied markedly among groups of workers, with the lowest benefits going to blue-collar workers. For instance, by 1960 the income transfers per family member of Central Bank of Chile employees were over six times higher than those given to the dependents of blue-collar workers (in SSS). The ratio for employees of financial institutions and private-sector white-collar workers was over 4 to 1, and that of public-sector employees, including the armed forces, over 2.4 to 1. Moreover, independent workers affiliated with the SSS were not eligible for this benefit.[1]

Unemployment compensation. Unemployment compensation (*subsidio de cesantia*) consisted of money payments of various kinds, including temporary or periodic payments similar to a pension, lump-sum (severance) payments, and loans of various sorts that had to be repaid upon resumption of employment. This benefit was started as early as 1924 for private-sector white-collar workers in the form of a severance payment made by the employer. In 1936 it was further modified by the introduction of payroll contributions (employer and worker) to pay for this subsidy. The amount and type of benefit received varied greatly among and within occupational groups of workers, depending on the reason for unemployment, the number of years of contributions, and a worker's own resources.

A few examples illustrate the differences in unemployment compensation benefits provided. Blue-collar workers in SSS received an advance from the indemnization fund, that is, they received a lump-sum amount in severance pay. White-collar workers in the private sector received a subsidy during ninety days in an amount determined each year by the social security institution. In addition, these workers could ask for the return of their accumulated contributions, which they had to give back upon finding employment. In addition to the subsidy, workers enrolled in Cajas such as that for employees of banking institutions received retirement funds and a special payment, which in some cases could include a life annuity. Public-sector employees in general and the armed forces received no subsidy but were eligible for severance pay financed through the employee's own contribution. In the public sector, some people also received unemployment pensions.

Health and maternity benefits.   Health and maternity benefits were added gradually to the several social security regimes. Blue-collar workers were covered by the Caja de Seguro Obrero until 1952, when it was reformed with the creation of the SSS for social security benefits, and the NHS, which provided preventive and curative health-care services for blue-collar workers and indigents. White-collar workers (private and public) were served by their respective Cajas until 1968, when the SERMENA was created as a preferred provider system (see Chapter 3). All family members were covered in all Cajas and other social security institutions, with no restrictions for previous health conditions or illness. Additional payroll contributions were introduced over time for both workers and employers to finance these new benefits.

Other benefits.   Other benefits included loans for housing at minimal nominal interest rates (in the face of substantial inflation). This benefit was, however, not available to workers in the SSS (over 60 percent of all workers), 93 percent of whom received the established minimum pension.

Financing

Payroll contributions from employers and workers varied widely across the Cajas but were in general among the highest in Latin America. In the early 1970s, contributions varied from 14 to 66 percent of payroll taxes. Of that rate, employers contributed from 2 to 52 percent, workers from 2 to 19 percent, and the state about 5.5 percent. The state contribution involved special taxes collected by the central government and municipalities on tickets to special events, travel, legal documents, imports and exports, bank deposits, and gambling, as well as direct subsidies to cover deficits. Given this great diversity of payments and subsidies, it was almost impossible to determine precisely the amount of total government funding for the Cajas and to identify beneficiary groups of government subsidies within and among Cajas.

The payroll contributions were low at the beginning for most Cajas, but they increased significantly and came to vary widely over time as more benefits (pension, unemployment subsidies, severance pay, money income subsidies, loans, and health services) were added in response to strikes and other social pressure. For instance, payroll contributions in the SSS that totaled 5 percent (2 percent worker and 3 percent employer) from 1925 to 1937 increased to a peak of 51.4 percent (7.3 worker and 44.1 percent employer) in 1975. Contributions to the Caja for banking institutions increased from 28 percent plus 0.25 percent per semester of the average balance of deposits of less than 30 days to a peak of 52.5 percent, plus the above-mentioned 0.25 percent, in 1964. Contribution rates in the Caja for public employees rose from 14 percent in 1925 to a peak of 54 percent in 1974. For the Caja for private-sector employees, the rates went from 10 percent (5 percent employee and 5 percent employer) to a peak of 64.7 percent (12.6 percent employee and 52.1 percent employer) in 1974 (Figure 5.1).

Despite the substantial payroll contribution rates and the favorable age structure of the Chilean population, most Cajas, as of 1979, were in a precarious financial condition, requiring substantial government contributions to finance the deficits and sustain the low level of pensions. About 70 percent of all pensioners (the great majority in the SSS) were receiving the minimum pension. Overall, between 1973 and 1980, payroll contributions represented only about 71 percent of revenues, while government contributions represented over 25 percent, and returns on investment a minimal 2 percent.

FIGURE 5.1 Payroll Contribution Rates by Caja, Old System, 1925–1980

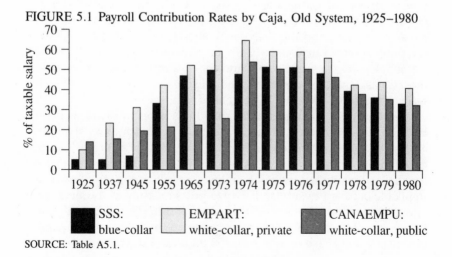

SOURCE: Table A5.1.

Government contributions went to the SSS, to help finance the pensions and especially the family assistance benefits, and to the Cajas for public employees, the armed forces, and national railroad workers. Part of the government's subsidies to the Caja for public-sector employees can be viewed as compensation for its lower contribution rates as employer (compared with the private sector). A large part, however, was a direct subsidy to public-sector employees.[2]

On the revenue side, reasons for the poor financial performance of the Cajas included substantial evasion, in the form of employers' failures to make full payments, claims of lower salary bases, and delays in payments; and very low (and often negative) returns on investments such as housing loans (lent at subsidized interest rates), properties rented to affiliates, and treasury bonds issued at controlled low nominal interest rates. On the expenditure side, the reasons included increased expenditures on early retirement and consequent accelerated aging of the population affiliated with the Cajas; duplicity of pensions; other benefits such as health-related services, which some Cajas continued to provide; and administrative deficiencies (Mesa-Lago 1985).

Evasion lowered revenues considerably, and contribution rates were periodically increased just to compensate for this loss in revenues. However, workers had no incentive to make employers pay on time and declare the full wage amount paid, since pensions and other benefits were unrelated to the amount of pensions received (except in the last five years of employment, which were the wage base, although eroded by inflation). As a result, and because of the laxity of controls, actual contributions were estimated to have been as low as 40 percent of what they should have been in 1960, and about 60 percent in 1980. According to a study by the Catholic University of Chile, this shortfall resulted both from actual contribution rates below what was required and from substantially lower taxable wages in relation to total wages earned, even for public-sector employees (Catholic University of Chile 1981). The Catholic University study also found very low returns on investments in most Cajas, with the exception of those in the financial sector, where the returns represented about 15 percent of total revenues.

Expenditures increased substantially as a result of the generous benefits, especially for early retirement at ages much lower than sixty and sixty-five (for women and men). The ratio of retirees to active contributors almost doubled between 1970 and 1980 (from 0.22 to 0.40) for all Cajas combined, while the ratio of people over sixty years of age to people between twenty and sixty (a gross measure of the labor force aging pattern) remained almost constant at 0.16 (Figure 5.2) (Catholic University of Chile 1981). Particularly noteworthy is the ratio of passive beneficiaries to active ones of over 100 percent observed in the Caja for

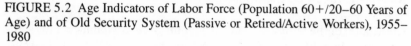

FIGURE 5.2 Age Indicators of Labor Force (Population 60+/20–60 Years of Age) and of Old Security System (Passive or Retired/Active Workers), 1955–1980

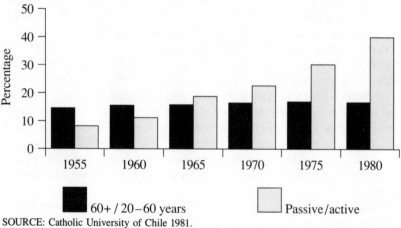

■ 60+ / 20–60 years   ☐ Passive/active

SOURCE: Catholic University of Chile 1981.

railroad workers in 1979. Additionally, although that ratio decreased markedly in the late 1960s and early 1970s in the Caja for public employees (as a result of the rapid expansion of public-sector employment), it has increased rapidly recently as the public sector has been streamlined and retirement has risen as a result of reforms that provided early retirement options to workers being transferred to municipalities (teachers and some health workers). Expectations of the reform may also have induced people to apply for early retirement.

The Reforms

Soon after the military government took power in 1973, it initiated several reforms to simplify and unify the Caja system and to correct some of its most discriminatory and inequitable features. Efforts centered on simplification of the complex legal and institutional structure regulating family assistance and unemployment insurance; on unification of the pension adjustment criteria, ages of retirement, and seniority pensions; and on reduction of the size and disparity of contribution rates in the different Cajas. A major step toward targeting government subsidies to the poorest population was the creation of an assistance pension in 1974. These and other changes took place between 1974 and 1980, before the major reform introduced in 1981.

Reforms between 1974 and 1980

Unification of the family assistance benefits in 1974 established the same amount of benefit for all workers. A fund financed solely by the state, instead of payroll contributions, was created to distribute this benefit. The uniform amount represented an increase for lower-paid blue-collar workers and a reduction for higher-paid white-collar workers and public employees, who, as noted, had been receiving significantly higher amounts. Coverage was also extended in 1980 to all poor children under fifteen years, pregnant women, and the mentally retarded of any age not receiving assistance pensions (a definition of the assistance pension follows). Despite this increase in coverage for the poorest, the bulk of this subsidy remains untargeted. Efforts to eliminate the subsidy for higher-paid workers have met major legal obstacles and opposition from this group, which see this benefit as a hard-won conquest of the past.

Rationalization and unification of unemployment subsidies for all workers were instituted in 1974. The subsidy was proposed to be a temporary monetary benefit amounting to 75 percent of the last salary (an average of the last six months for the private sector), which had to be no less than 80 percent of the two monthly minimum wages in Santiago and not more than 90 percent of four such monthly minimum wages. Payment was to be made by a fund administered by the Superintendency of Social Security, to be financed by a 2 percent payroll contribution (paid by employers in the case of blue-collar workers, and by employers and the respective Caja, each contributing 1 percent, for white-collar private-sector workers). Funds for public-sector employees were to be provided directly by the central government. In 1981, it was also established that the family assistance benefits and unemployment compensation would be financed by direct government contributions instead of payroll contributions, which were eliminated.

An assistance pension system (PASIS) for the uninsured of about U.S. $17.60 was introduced in 1974. It covered all disabled persons older than eighteen years; the mentally retarded of any age, provided they were not receiving family allowance; and all persons older than sixty-five years. All these people were eligible if their own resources were less than 50 percent of the minimum pension. In 1974, the minimum pensions of the different sectors and the Cajas were unified.

In 1979, the government unified the adjustment criteria for pensions and retirement ages, which had been set at sixty years for women and sixty-five for men for all workers irrespective of occupational status and social security institution. These reforms implied elimination of the adjustment of the pensions of high-ranking public-sector employees according to the wage increases for the job held prior to retirement, as well as "seniority" pensions, which could be enjoyed by a few privileged people at an age as young as forty-three.

A reduction in the payroll contribution rates in all major Cajas began in the period 1973–1975 (see Table 5.1). While the contributions were not yet uniform, the dispersion was reduced considerably in 1980. The government further reduced the contribution rates to about 20 percent for all Cajas in early 1981 and assigned the full payroll contribution (worker and employer) to workers just before it announced the major 1981 reform. Since the payroll contributions in the new system were only about 13.4 percent (10 percent for the pension and 3.4 percent for the D&S insurance), workers who changed to the new system would see an increase in their liquid salary, amounting to 10 percent on average for all workers.

The reform of 1981: the new social security system

Notwithstanding these reforms, in 1981 the government started implementing a profound reform of the old system of Cajas (excluding those of the armed forces). The main objectives were to (1) eliminate the differential treatment of different groups; (2) better target government subsidies to the needy through transparent mechanisms; (3) change the incentive structure for workers, whose benefits would now depend on their contributions rather than on political pressure; (4) promote worker responsibility in looking after their social security contributions

TABLE 5.1 Payroll Contribution Rates,
1973 and 1980 (%)

Caja	1973	1980
SSS	49.9	33.2
Workers	9.5	7.3
Employers	40.4	25.9
EMPART	64.7[a]	41.0
Workers	12.6[a]	12.3
Employers	52.1[a]	28.7
CANAEMPU	54.0	32.5
Workers	n.a.	15.5
Employers	n.a.	17.0

n.a. = not available.
a. 1974.
SOURCE: Catholic University of Chile 1981.

through free choice of the pension fund administrator, a measure that could lead to greater savings and a reduction in fraud and evasion; (5) increase the efficiency of administration of social security funds through private-sector management; and (6) promote greater democratization of property through expansion of investment opportunities that could be made with social security funds.

Main features of the new system.   The new system is described in Decree Law 3,500 of March 1981. Several modifications to the law have been made since to improve the modus operandi, increase competitiveness, and expand the range of investments that can be made with pension funds. The main features of the new system as of 1987, with some reference to changes made since 1981, are as follows:

- *Individual capitalization for old-age pensions.* The old pay-as-you-go pension system, by which current pensions were determined and paid by current members of the work force contributing to the different Cajas, was replaced by one of individual capitalization of funds for old-age pensions. Under this system, compulsory monthly contributions of 10 percent by individuals are put in an individual passbooklike savings account that is untransferrable, protected from legal suits, and tax-free, and has a minimum return and security guaranteed by the state. Similar guarantees apply to additional funds that the worker may choose to save in his individual account and that could be used for increasing pensions or attaining early retirement.

- *Private administration of pension funds.* Individual accounts are administered by private for-profit AFPs. The state establishes normative and supervisory roles through the Superintendency of AFPs. The private companies can charge administrative fees. The pension funds cannot constitute the capital of the private company, which is required to observe strict rules on the investment of the funds, as defined by the law and the Superintendency of AFPs.

- *Insurance protection for disability and survivors pensions.* D&S pensions are provided by private insurance companies, which the beneficiaries can choose. The companies provide the necessary funds to complement individual accumulated funds in case of accident or death. The premiums vary across insurance companies but are uniform for all beneficiaries of a given AFP without regard to gender or income level. The pension is equal to 70 percent of the average salary for the last ten years, adjusted by inflation. (Originally, the salary base was that of the last year, a system that created several distortions). Covered are all civilian employed workers and, starting in 1987, unemployed workers for twelve months after dismissal, provided they had paid for at least six months during the year prior to dismissal. To reduce the likely impact this coverage could have on the premiums paid by workers, the pension for the unemployed worker is 50 percent (instead of 70 percent) of the average salary of the last ten years.[3]

- *State guarantees of minimum return and security.* In addition to the inherent checks and balances provided by the AFPs themselves as they compete to attract new members, the state provides a number of safeguards for the pension funds. They are the property of the beneficiaries and are to be managed as separate accounts from those of the AFP. AFPs cannot use the funds for their own expenses. The only source of revenue for the AFPs are commissions and administrative fees. The AFPs must pay a minimum return on the pension funds, established in relation to the average return obtained by all AFPs. If an AFP is unable to pay the minimum return and meet its obligations, it has to dissolve, and its beneficiaries can transfer their funds to other AFPs. As a way of minimizing the risk to the state, AFPs are required to establish reserves, monitored and supervised by the Superintendency of AFPs.

- *Choice of pension fund administrator.* In contrast to previous social security regimes, in which workers belonging to a given Caja could not change except when they changed occupation, the new system gives workers complete freedom to choose among pension fund administrators. Workers have been able to transfer their funds from one AFP to another relatively easily since the modifications of requirements were made in 1988. All civilian workers, including independent workers, can affiliate with any AFP.

- *Choice of pension options.* Upon retirement, disability, or death, the insured or other beneficiaries can choose among three pension options. The first is a life annuity bought from an insurance company, with the accumulated funds to be paid to the insured and survivors. The amount of the life annuity must be equal to at least the minimum pension guaranteed by the state. If the insurance company goes bankrupt, the government is responsible for 100 percent of the minimum pension and 75 percent of the excess amount above the minimum pension; the rest has to be borne by the beneficiary. The second option is a programmed withdrawal of funds based on the life expectancy of the beneficiary and his or her family group, to be paid by the AFP that the beneficiary chooses. If the accumulated funds exceed the minimum limits established, the beneficiary can withdraw additional funds. In case of death and no dependents, the accumulated funds, tax-free up to some limit, will increase the inheritance funds. The final option combines the previous two. It offers a programmed withdrawal for a number of years or months and a life annuity afterward, contracted with an insurance company. Several regulations seek to ensure that the contracted pensions are greater than the minimum pension, thus lessening the risk of state contributions.

Beneficiaries can choose early retirement if they have accumulated enough funds to generate a pension of at least 50 percent (it was 70 percent until 1988) of inflation-adjusted wages for the last ten years, and a pension at least 110 percent of the minimum pension. To achieve this level, beneficiaries can make additional voluntary contributions (with some limits), which enjoy the same exceptions as the required ones.

• *Targeting government subsidies to the needy.* The new system includes a guaranteed minimum pension for all beneficiaries whose accumulated funds are not sufficient for that minimum. The government subsidy equals the difference between the minimum pension and the life annuity for those choosing this option, or the minimum pension for those choosing the programmed withdrawal of funds once these funds have been exhausted. The minimum pension is given to beneficiaries meeting the retirement age who have contributed for at least twenty years (adding the number of years contributed to the old system and the years of unemployment compensation received). To receive benefits in case of disability or death, the worker must have paid two years and contributed to the new system for at least six months.

The minimum pension is 85 percent of the minimum wage (increasing to 90 percent for those over seventy years old). This is more than 40 percent of the average wage in Chile; that is, the average worker has a guaranteed pension of over 40 percent of his income while active in the labor force. This level of benefit is relatively high: in the United States it is given to people retiring at normal ages (Myers 1986). The state provides an assistance pension of about 50 percent of the minimum pension to the needy who are not affiliated with the system or who have contributed less than the required amount for the minimum pension.

• *Uniform and lower payroll contributions to finance benefits.* A uniform payroll rate of 10 percent for the old-age pension and an insurance premium of about 3.4 percent for D&S pensions were established for all civilian workers. This rate marked a significant reduction in the payroll contributions, from over 20 percent (depending on the Caja) to 13.4 percent, for those willing to change to the new system. The most significant change, however, was that the old-age contribution was transformed from a typical payroll tax into a contribution that can appropriately be viewed and treated as compulsory savings for old age. Early actuarial calculations made by ODEPLAN indicated these payroll contributions, net of commissions and administrative fees paid, would be sufficient to generate a pension close to the recent salary of most workers.[4]

Institutional and regulatory framework.   The AFPs are private companies whose only business is the administration of pension funds. The requisites for forming an AFP company include capital requirements that increase with the number of beneficiaries as follows: 5,000 UF (about U.S. $92,896 in 1989), which increases to 10,000 UF if the number of affiliates reaches 5,000, 15,000 UF if the number reaches 7,500, and 20,000 UF if the number reaches 10,000 affiliates. The capital must be paid in full before the AFP can operate. Originally, a single minimum of 20,000 UF was established (in place until 1987), but it was later considered too high to encourage new pension fund companies and more competition. AFPs must send to all beneficiaries an updated statement of the accumulated funds and commissions every four months.

To meet the established return requirements each month, AFPs must set up two reserves: one for "return fluctuation," formed with excesses over the specified limits on monthly returns, which is the property of the fund; and a capital reserve requirement of 1 percent of the accumulated funds minus the value of investments in other funds, and short-term (less than thirty-day) Treasury and Central Bank paper held in custody. This reserve requirement is calculated daily and must be placed in financial instruments as determined by the Central Bank. Each AFP has to pay a minimum return each month that is no less than the lower figure given by the average return on the last twelve months of all pension funds, minus two percentage points; and 50 percent of the average return of all funds in the last twelve months.

AFPs are permitted to charge administrative commissions and fees for

- the monthly deposit, a fixed amount the AFP charges to all affiliates (it has to be the same amount for all beneficiaries but can vary across AFPs; any change in commission has to be announced at least three months before it takes place)

- transfer from one AFP to another

- withdrawals of pension funds under the programmed withdrawal option

- D&S insurance that AFPs must contract for beneficiaries (the commission is estimated as a percentage of the salary)

AFPs cannot charge commissions for maintaining the accumulated funds of dependent workers who are not contributing at that moment (for example, the unemployed) or of independent workers who have contributed no money for twelve consecutive months.[5]

Created in 1981, the Superintendency of AFPs is charged with controlling and supervising the AFPs and with enforcing the regulations and norms. It is an autonomous agency that is linked to the government through the Ministry of Labor and Social Security. Its main functions are to (1) authorize the creation of AFPs and register them; (2) ensure that AFPs deliver the required services; (3) establish regulations and norms for implementation of the law; (4) enforce the establishment and lawful use of required reserves and their investment requirements; (5) serve as Technical and Executive Secretariat of the Risk Classification Commission (RCC); (6) enforce the procedures regarding portfolio composition and risk of pension fund investments in financial instruments as classified by the RCC; and (7) supervise the primary and secondary markets in invested pension fund instruments, notwithstanding the supervision of the Superintendency of the Stock Market and Insurance (SVS).

Created in 1985, the RCC is charged with approving, modifying, or rejecting proposals by companies for the risk classification of instruments in which pension funds can be invested. The RCC consists of three superintendents (that of AFPs, who presides; the banking and financial institutions; and the stock market and insurance companies) and four representatives of AFPs. One representative of the Superintendency of AFPs serves as secretary and legal witness at all meetings.

Instruments can be classified into five categories (A to E), depending on the risk assigned, which is based on the probability of default (capital and interest), liquidity, and other characteristics. Category A, with a value of 1.0, has the lowest risk and D (0.0) the highest. E is for instruments for which there is no information. All government paper and that with state guarantees is in category A. The classifications must be made at least monthly and are published in the *Diario Oficial*, the official daily newspaper.

Risk classification is carried out for all instruments offered to the public. However, instruments of corporation are ranked only on request. Once the instruments have been classified, issuers are obliged to provide all the information necessary for updating the classification whenever pension funds are invested in those instruments. If the issuer gives no information, the instruments will be classified as E or will be disapproved for investment.

The law also permits risk classification by private companies, which can challenge the official classification and request revisions. These private companies can classify all types of instruments, including those suitable for AFP investments. Private risk classification companies are starting to appear in the market.

Laws 3,500 of 1981 and 18,646 of 1987 establish guidelines and regulations regarding the instruments in which pension funds can be invested. As a general rule, pension funds should only be invested in marketable assets and in securities not restricted to particular investors, and they should not be lent directly to customers. The number and variety of instruments have been increased gradually and cautiously over time so as to afford regulators, AFPs, and the public a learning period, as the economy has recovered from the deep financial crisis of 1982–1983.

As of 1988, investment instruments were classified into seven categories: A is government paper (Treasury and Central Bank) and bonds issued by the Regional Housing and Urban Affairs Services (SERVIUs) to finance housing; B, term deposits in banks; C, instruments guaranteed by financial institutions; D, letters of credit from financial institutions; E, bonds issued by public and private enterprises; F, instruments (*cuotas*) of other pension funds; and G, shares of public limited companies (*sociedades anónimas abiertas*) approved by the RCC. All instruments in categories B, C, D, and E must have an RCC risk classification.

The Central Bank is responsible for determining limits of investments within and among categories and the weighted average maturity of investments made in fixed-yield instruments. It can, however, establish only maximum (not minimum) limits within the guidelines of the law. The maximum limits should not be less than

- 30 percent of funds for investments in categories B and C combined if the average maturity is less than a year, and 40 percent if at least one-fourth of this sum has a maturity of more than a year

- 40 percent for investments in category D

- 30 percent for investments in category E

- 20 percent for investments in category F

- 10 percent for investments in category G

Additionally, investments in categories A and G can be no larger than 50 percent and 30 percent, respectively, of the fund's portfolio. (In the original law, there was no limit for investments in category A, and investments in category G were not permitted).

To avoid concentration of the AFP industry and possible conflict of interest, pension fund resources cannot be invested in shares of AFPs, life insurance companies, and mutual fund companies. Additionally, AFPs themselves are not allowed to own shares in companies in which pension funds can be invested.

A few of the other most important regulations that promote deconcentration and public-sector divestment in public enterprises are that pension funds cannot be invested in companies where one person has direct or indirect control of more than 50 percent of the shares; companies where less than 10 percent of the subscribed shares are in the hands of minority owners; and companies where at least 15 percent of the shares are not subscribed by more than 100 unrelated shareholders, each one owning a minimum of 100 UF (about U.S. $1,848 in 1989). Pension funds can be invested in public limited companies in which the state, autonomous decentralized agencies, or municipalities own 50 percent or more of the stock only if the companies sell or promise to sell 30 percent of their stock. A written agreement must be signed, including a specified time frame for selling the first 25 percent.

There are also strict limits for investments in instruments issued by financial institutions that take several factors into account, including assets or the patrimony of the institutions and the riskiness of the portfolio, calculated on the basis of the RCC classification of instruments. Beginning in 1987 with Law 18,646, pension funds can also be invested in shares of financial institutions up to a limit given by the product of a "concentration factor" and the total value of the company.[6]

Arrangements for the transition from the old system. One of the most difficult aspects of the reform was how to deal with the old system—its beneficiaries, pensions, and the past contributions made by those willing to transfer to the new system. The old system will only disappear when there are no more pensioners in it (around the year 2030). The arrangements and commitments made are as follows: (1) The old civilian Cajas (the Cajas of the military are not included in the reform) were combined into three (collapsing in 1988 into one), with only a few small ones remaining independent, under the jurisdiction of the Ministry of Labor, which appoints their directors. The tripartite administration was eliminated. (2) The requisites for obtaining benefits were unified, although the amounts of most benefits follow the different regimes established. (3) Individual accounts were set up for calculating a proxy amount of the accumulated funds to be paid upon retirement, accident, or death of beneficiaries who had contributed to the Cajas and decided to transfer to the AFPs. This amount, called the "recognition bond" (*bono de reconocimiento*), earns a 4 percent inflation-adjusted annual return until it is paid.[7] (4) The deficits of all Cajas were paid, with the funds coming from fiscal contributions, sales of assets, and investments of the Cajas.

These rationalization and financial arrangements are the responsibility of the Institute for Normalization of the Social Security System (Instituto de Normalización Previsional) created in 1980. In 1988, the institute was also given responsibility for unifying under its jurisdiction the regrouped Cajas of the old system into one single entity (Law 18,689 of January 1988).

Implementation of the Reforms

So far, implementation of the reforms can be characterized as highly successful, given not only the difficulty of the task but also the number of objectives achieved. It also has been costly for the government, requiring strict fiscal discipline, and has needed a considerable number of clarifications and modifications of the original law: more than 400 regulatory measures (*directivas*) for the AFPs and fourteen new laws have been issued to correct unforeseen problems, such as the high commissions for D&S insurance, the inappropriate salary base, and the need to expand the investment alternatives for the funds gradually. It is in the latter area where the government has been the most cautious, given the number of guarantees involved and the need to allow for a learning period for all parties.

The following are some of the developments with respect to the number of affiliates and coverage of the system; the number of AFPs and their concentration; the amount of accumulated funds relative to GDP, bank deposits, and national savings; the fees charged and benefits provided; and the fiscal cost of the reform.

Beneficiaries and coverage under the new system

As of May 1981, people began to transfer massively to the new system, which grew rapidly to include 1.4 million beneficiaries at the end of 1981 and 3 million (about 74 percent of the employed civilian labor force) in 1988. As a result, enrollment in the old Cajas declined from 2.2 million in 1980 to 0.5 million (about 12 percent of the employed labor force) in 1988. The reasons for the shift included an increase in take-home pay of about 10 percent under the new system, which resulted from the lower contribution rates and was transferred entirely to the workers; and disillusionment with the old system, which provided low pensions and bad services and was highly segmented, discriminating against lower-paid and weaker groups.

The people who moved first and in large numbers were the relatively young. For older groups, the decision has not been as easy, since they are closer to retirement and some can enjoy some of the generous benefits of the Cajas. New members of the labor force are required to enroll in the new system.[8] Overall, coverage of the social security system remained at about 80–85 percent of the employed labor force between 1980 and 1988 (Figure 5.3), except in the crisis years of 1982–1983, when open unemployment reached more than 20 percent.[9]

One problem of the old system, which the new has not been able to solve, is the low coverage of the self-employed. In theory, self-employed workers were expected to contribute to the system, as they would be the direct beneficiaries of their contributions, which could be increased by the government in case the accumulated payments were insufficient for the minimum pension. Several reasons could explain the lack of interest. (1) The system is new, and workers still may not see or trust the benefits. It is worth mentioning that only a few pensions (mostly D&S) have been given so far. (2) The self-employed may prefer to save in the form of capital accumulation (investing in a home, upgrading a small business or store) that could give them more ex ante return or independence, rather than in savings for retirement under government programs. (3) Independent workers are not allowed to contribute just for pensions and D&S but must also contribute for health insurance. The combined contribution, although low compared with the old system,

FIGURE 5.3 Employed Population Covered by Old and New Systems, 1980–1988

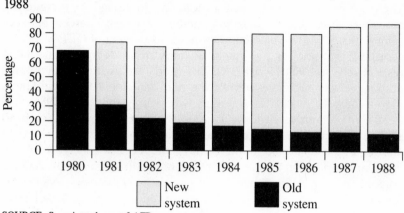

SOURCE: Superintendency of AFPs.

is still about 20.4 percent of their earnings. (4) Many poor families rely on the solidarity of their extended families for protection against disastrous events (sickness, disability, and death) and for old-age protection, the same events that are protected by the formal system.

Under these circumstances, especially considering reasons 2 through 4, compulsory contributions, which are frequently proposed by critics of the system, are not the solution, since they will not be enforceable. Probably a more efficient and cost-effective solution is to continue the voluntary affiliation, granting assistance pensions to the needy uninsured self-employed population, and low-cost fee-for-service medical attention (especially for catastrophic events such as cancer or accidents) in public hospitals (see Chapter 3).

Number of AFPs

There are twelve AFPs, most of them operating since 1981. Since the financial crisis of 1982–1983, most have become profitable. The two largest covered 49 percent of beneficiaries in 1988, a decline from about 53.3 percent in 1981. Concentration of the industry will most likely continue to decline as a result of recent changes reducing the capital requirements. There are essentially two types of AFPs: open, which seek to attract workers from all industries and enterprises; and closed, which seek workers in a given occupation (for example, teachers). However, workers are free to affiliate with any AFP they want.

Accumulated fund size

The size of the accumulated funds has increased by staggering amounts—from about 18 percent of national savings, 3 percent of fixed-term deposits in the financial system, and 1 percent of GDP in 1981 to about 54, 43, and 18 percent of savings, time deposits, and GDP, respectively, in 1988 (Figure 5.4). The funds are expected to continue growing at very high rates beyond the year 2000, when they could be as high as 40 percent of GDP (Iglesias, Echeverría, and López 1986).

There is controversy, however, as to whether the new pension fund system has increased net national savings. This question is hard to answer because, although there may have been an increase in net voluntary savings on top of the compulsory contribution to the savings accounts held in AFPs, a better and more efficient pension system (as the new system is expected to be) may induce people to save less in other forms of asset accumulation. What is clear in the few years that the new system has operated is that the government has had to generate a surplus in other expenditure items to finance the deficit of the old social security system. Although more exploration of this point is needed, it appears this responsible government behavior means that the accumulation of pension funds indicates, in fact, an increase in national savings.

Accumulated funds: investments by type of instrument

Since the beginning, the funds have been invested in great proportion in government paper and fixed-term bank deposits. Gradually, however, investments in other instruments have increased, as permitted by the RCC. Only in 1985 were AFPs permitted to invest in the shares of public and private enterprises.

In 1988, the funds were invested as follows: 35.4 percent in government paper (Treasury and Central Bank), down from the peak of 47 percent in December 1986; 28.5 percent in fixed-term deposits, down from 61.9 percent in 1981; 21.6 percent in mortgage bonds; and 8 percent in shares, debentures, and corporate debt (Figure 5.5).

These trends show a consolidation of the system and growing independence from official instruments as the capital market has developed. They also show that the government has so far been able to resist the temptation to finance increases in the deficit and debt-service obligations through increased emissions of government paper or manipulation of interest rates. Large increases in government paper in the pension funds would affect their credibility and ultimately returns, risk, and interest rates. Another temptation that so far has been resisted

FIGURE 5.4 Pension Fund Size as a Percentage of GDP, Savings, and Bank Deposits, 1981–1988

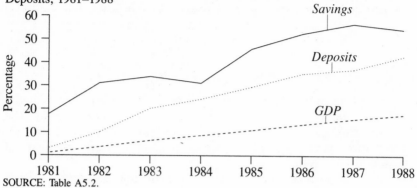

SOURCE: Table A5.2.

FIGURE 5.5 Pension Fund Investments by Instrument, 1981–1988

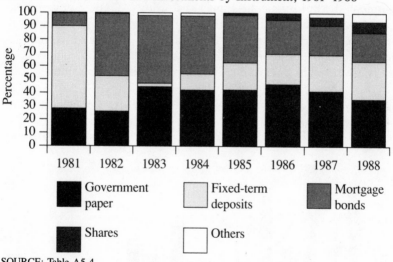

SOURCE: Table A5.4.

is to allow AFPs to provide credit directly to beneficiaries or the public. This was a disastrous policy under the old Cajas, which had provided credit (for housing, for instance) to their beneficiaries that the Cajas would not recover because of the very low nominal interest rates and their lack of administrative capacity to do so.

Average return from the accumulated funds

One of the most impressive records of the AFPs has been the high real returns obtained, even in the worst years of the financial crisis. The returns averaged over 14 percent per annum between 1981 and 1988, about three percentage points higher than those from the financial system (Figure 5.6).

As a result of the commission structure, which includes a fixed commission, the returns have varied by level of taxable income. Higher income levels have received higher returns. This system has attracted criticism and put pressure on regulators to eliminate the fixed commission. However, if the fixed commission corresponds to charges for the fixed cost of administration and account handling and the cost of reserves (as it appears to be), it is a proper pricing instrument that, were it eliminated, could generate higher distortions. Thus, a government subsidy paid at retirement to those whose accumulated funds are insufficient to merit minimum pension (as a result of the fixed commission) may be a better alternative in terms of overall resource allocation than is government intervention to eliminate the commission.

FIGURE 5.6 Real Returns of Pension Funds and Bank Deposits, 1981–1988

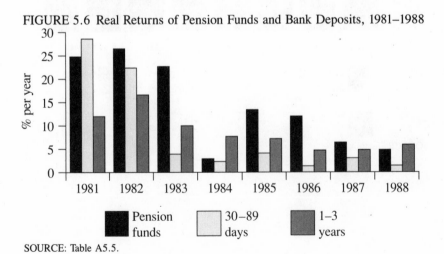

SOURCE: Table A5.5.

Evolution of charges and commissions

The commissions and fees charged by the AFPs have declined markedly since 1981 as a result of stiff competition, which has induced a sharp reduction in their operating costs. The fixed commission fell from an average of 288 constant pesos in 1981 to 146 pesos in 1987, a drop of 50 percent (Figure 5.7). The commission on accumulated funds declined from an average of 0.99 percent in 1981 to 0.52 percent in 1987 (Figure 5.8). The additional contribution for D&S insurance rose from 2.44 percent in 1981 to 3.59 percent in 1983 but declined gradually to 3.4 percent in 1987 (Figure 5.9).

The increased contributions for D&S have been the result, to some extent, of an increase in the number of pensions granted, induced by the fact that the base salary for this pension was that of last year. As a result, people near retirement pressed for attaining a D&S benefit rather than an old-age pension. This practice also put a heavy burden on the medical boards, under the Superintendency of AFPs, which are charged with determining disability.[10] Additionally, a transitory article of law that was eliminated in 1983 prohibited old-age pensions under the new system in the case of affiliates with less than five years of contributions. The salary base for D&S pensions was modified in 1987 to take into account the inflation-adjusted salaries of the last ten years.

Another reason for the increase in D&S contributions has been the attempt by AFPs to compensate, through these contributions, for the decrease in fixed and variable commissions. The latter commissions have been the most visible and advertised feature of AFPs and have been the basis for competition among them. As a result, D&S contributions, of which AFPs have retained a large part as a commission for

FIGURE 5.7 Fixed Commissions Charged by AFPs, 1981–1988

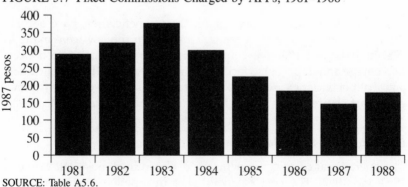

SOURCE: Table A5.6.

FIGURE 5.8 Commission on the Balance Accumulated of Funds Charged by AFPs, 1981–1988

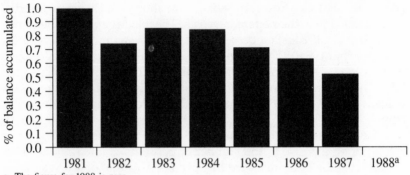

a. The figure for 1988 is zero.
SOURCE: Table A5.6.

FIGURE 5.9 D&S Insurance Contribution Rates, 1981–1988

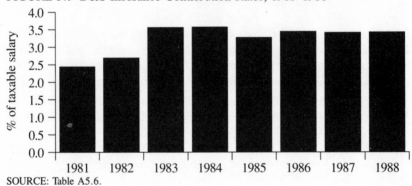

SOURCE: Table A5.6.

arranging the insurance coverage for their beneficiaries, have become the largest source of AFP revenue. Changes in the law were made in 1987 to establish that the commission must be clearly stated (as a percentage and in pesos) to facilitate cost comparisons by beneficiaries, and that beneficiaries are free to choose their insurance company (previously that choice was made by the AFP on behalf of the beneficiaries).

Operational costs of the AFPs

The operational costs per beneficiary declined by almost half between 1982 and 1987. The cost of advertising dropped the most (from 18 percent of operational costs in 1982 to 4 percent in 1987), as the companies have made a name in the market and the system is better known. A rapid decline has also taken place in sales personnel since the new rules regulating the transfer of beneficiaries among AFPs were established.

Several recent measures seeking to induce further reductions in administrative costs are being implemented: (1) the amount of information requested by the Superintendency of AFPs has been reduced and the report period lengthened; (2) AFPs can transfer among themselves contributions that were not properly addressed (previously these contributions had to be returned to the employer for proper remission); and (3) separate payments for contributions and deposits in personal savings accounts are allowed (Superintendency of AFPs 1988).

A major remaining problem that has increased the operational costs of AFPs and thus the commissions charged is the burdensome process of collecting contributions. Current arrangements require an enormous amount of paperwork for employers, who have to deduct the contributions and make payments to over forty separate institutions, including AFPs, the Cajas remaining in the old system, private health insurance companies (ISAPREs), and the National Health Fund (FONASA). Employers also have to pay to mutuality companies contributions for occupational hazards and, until recently, unemployment compensation to the Cajas de Compensación (this requirement was eliminated in 1988). In their competition to attract workers, the AFPs have offered to pay some of the collection expenses incurred by commercial banks (typically U.S. $.50 to $1.00 for each form they process) for contributions paid through the banks, and some have created their own collection agencies.

Benefits provided

In the new system, old-age pensions are determined by funds accumulated during the affiliates' working life. In the first years of the system, however, the larger component of the accumulated funds and of the pension for those retiring will be the recognition bond, which is paid by the government. It has been estimated that for those retiring before the year 2000 (about 100,000 people), the recognition bond will account for over 70 percent of total accumulated funds (García 1986).

Given the newness of the system and a provision that prohibited retirement before five years of contributions had been made to the new system, few pensions have been given so far. The average pension under the new system has been more than 20 percent higher than in the old system. This increase can be largely explained by the differences in the wage bases of retirees under the two systems and the fact that, under the new system, wages are fully indexed. In the long run, it is expected the pensions will be higher under the new system (despite the lower contribution rates) as a result of better administration, higher returns, and the complete indexation of accumulated funds (Cheyre 1988).

D&S pensions have been substantially higher under the new than the old system. Figures for 1987 show disability pensions over 100 percent higher, and survivors pensions about 50 percent higher (Cheyre 1988). The reason is the differences in the salary basis and percentage of salaries covered under the two systems. As indicated, the salary base under the new system was changed in 1987 to include the last ten years of salaries adjusted by inflation, instead of the last year, the basis that prevailed until then. Since wages were increasing in these years and most likely will continue doing so, the new salary base will be lower than the last year's salary.[11] Future pensions are, nonetheless, expected to be higher than under the old system because of greater efficiency and returns on accumulated funds and the full indexation of the pension funds.

Evasion in the payment of contributions

In 1986, about 68 percent of beneficiaries were paying contributions to the AFPs. This percentage is below what was expected, based on the assumption that workers would force employers to pay their contributions promptly. Although part of the low percentage can be attributed to unemployment, migrants, and people who have left the labor force, most of it can be attributed to the relatively low rate (57 percent) of employers who pay on time. This delay is most likely the result of (1) increased paperwork and the absence of a unified collection system (firms have to fill out as many different forms as there are beneficiaries belonging to different AFPs); (2) lack of a strict control system for early detection of delay and enforcement of regulations; and (3) the fact that a guaranteed minimum pension removes the incentives for many low-wage workers to press for accurate and prompt payment of contributions by employers, especially when the labor market is slack. This latter condition, which occurred with the old Cajas, has been observed among independent and low-wage workers such as domestic employees. Besides, because of its novelty, people still have no close attachment to the new pension fund system.

Fiscal Cost

The reform has entailed a large fiscal cost. Additional government transfers have been necessary, first, to meet the increased deficit of the

FIGURE 5.10 Estimates of the Deficit of the Old Cajas and Recognition Bonds, 1985–2015

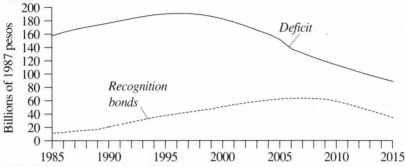

NOTE: This figure excludes the armed forces.
SOURCE: Table A5.3.

old Cajas, which lost most of their revenue as people transferred to the AFPs; second, to pay the recognition bond, which the government promised to pay at the retirement of beneficiaries, accumulated at an annual real rate of return of 4 percent; third, to pay the minimum pension supplement to those workers with accumulated funds insufficient to cover the minimum pension; and fourth, to meet government obligations arising from guarantees in the case of default by the AFPs and insurance companies. Payment of the assistance pensions is not a cost of the reform, since the government was already paying it separately under the old Cajas. The fiscal cost attributed to the first and second elements, that is, the deficit of old Cajas and the recognition bonds, which are relatively easy to project (Figure 5.10 and details following), was as high as 4 percent of GDP in 1986 and could run over 5 percent in 2000 (assuming GDP growth of 3 percent per annum).

The *net* fiscal cost of the reform, however, is much lower, since the government subsidies that would have to have been provided to the old Cajas must be deducted. Estimates by ODEPLAN indicate that the net costs will be high at the beginning but will gradually decline until the year 2000, when the benefits of the reform will start to appear at a rapidly increasing pace.[12] One of these benefits is the savings from the large financial obligations that would have been incurred if the old system had remained unchanged.

Payments for the deficit of the old system

Payments to the old system have been estimated to represent a heavy burden on government finance. According to ODEPLAN, the deficit of the old Cajas, which has to be financed by the national budget, will increase rapidly from about 157.4 billion 1987 pesos (about 3.4 percent of GDP) in 1986 to a peak of about 191.0 billion in 1996 and will gradually decrease thereafter until the year 2015, when it will be about 89.0 billion pesos (ODEPLAN 1986b). This pattern is the result of two opposing trends: first, lower revenues of the old Cajas, as the number of contributors is estimated to decrease from about 1,133,000 in 1985 to 304,000 in 2015, when there will be only passive contributors (that is, the retired); and second, the rapid increase in the number of retired persons over these years as the old system tends to disappear in the next century.

The government's projected payments already reflect a substantial rationalization of the old system, reduction of evasion, sales of property owned by the Cajas, and recovery of past loans. As indicated, some measures are already being implemented. The three Cajas regrouped in 1981 were consolidated into one in 1988 under the Institute for Normalization of the Social Security System. Also, the percentage of affiliates who pay the contributions rose from 68 percent in 1980 to 85 percent in 1986, as a result of increased control and supervision and of the expected increased compliance of people approaching retirement—because pensions are related to income received in the five years prior to retirement. In addition, the recovery of loans and sales of property have increased considerably.

Payments for recognition bonds

Payments for recognition bonds are expected to grow rapidly to a peak early in the next century and then to decrease gradually, when most pensions begin to be financed with workers' accumulated funds under the new system. Calculating the recognition bonds has been very slow and difficult, since the number of years of past contributions has had to be traced on payroll sheets submitted by firms to each Caja, because there were no individual employee accounts. In addition, certain types of workers can return to the old Cajas for retirement benefits.

Payments for the supplement to the minimum pension

Fiscal payments as supplements to achieve the minimum pensions are extremely difficult to estimate because they depend on the real return of funds, trends in commissions and other operating costs, the gains in life expectancy of poorer groups, and the adjustments to the minimum pension. Actuarial estimates indicate a significant number of workers (34 percent for men and 45 percent for women) will need supplements to their accumulated funds at current contribution rates. The estimates are, however, very sensitive to assumptions about returns from the funds, the value of the fixed commission, and unemployment and wage growth. This payment will be a direct targeting of government subsidies to those who are considered the poorest segment of the work force.[13]

Summary and Conclusions

This chapter has reviewed the main features of Chile's old social security system and why and how it was replaced by an entirely new one. Although the reform has entailed a heavy burden on government finances, it has been highly successful in that the new system appears to be meeting the main objectives for which it was created. Implementation has not been easy, however, and further legislation to correct problems in the original law has been necessary.

The main features and advantages of the new system can be summarized as follows:

1. The new system relies on a set of uniform, nondiscriminatory rules regarding contributions, retirement ages, and amounts of benefits provided, in contrast to the old system, which favored stronger and better organized groups of workers. Moreover, given the transparency and uniformity in the rules of the new system, it will be hard for pressure groups in a given occupation, trade, or enterprise to justify claims for special benefits without opposition or similar claims being made by other groups, a process that will exert a counterbalancing force that was absent under the old system.

2. The new system permits a clear targeting of government subsidies to the needy population. It is relatively easy to establish those who are the poorest whose accumulated funds (representing their own effort) are insufficient to cover the minimum pension and thus require a government subsidy. Additionally, it is easy to screen the beneficiaries of the government assistance pension who are not affiliated with the new system. The old system was implicitly based on solidarity, but in practice it may have been regressive, given that the largest benefits and government subsidies went to the strongest groups.

3. The new system relies on private-sector administration and operation of the pension funds and the D&S insurance. The

private sector's response to the opportunity has been very positive, considering that over 74 percent of affiliated workers have transferred to the new system. Management of the funds, with close supervision by the Superintendency of AFPs, has been very efficient, as indicated by returns over three percentage points higher than those of the financial market between 1981 and 1987. Moreover, the AFPs survived the financial crisis of 1982–1983. They also reduced their commissions and fees and have taken measures, as required by the superintendency, to improve information for beneficiaries. Recent reforms reducing the amount of capital required to set up AFPs are expected to increase their number and improve competition and the services provided.

4. The new system gives responsibility to workers to look after their own pension funds and allows for voluntary additional contributions or additional savings for retirement. This system may have a net positive effect on aggregate savings upon consolidation, offering proof that it operates with no major distortions. However, a better and more efficient social security system may induce people to save less than otherwise. The control beneficiaries have over their own funds will be a strong force preventing the government from introducing regulations regarding interest rates and partial adjustment for inflation. This force was lacking before because, while it was easy to identify the beneficiaries, it was difficult to identify the groups who paid.

5. The new system has promoted the development of a stronger capital market in Chile, as the pension funds can be invested in private enterprises, mortgage bonds, and public enterprises being privatized. The share of government paper decreased from 46 percent of the funds' portfolio in 1985 to 40 percent in 1988 as new instruments became eligible for investment and new regulations and limits were set. The government has also used the pension funds to induce the deconcentration of firms. Given the enormous increase in accumulated funds, which could reach about 40 percent of GDP in the year 2000, a large part of private-sector investments will be financed and owned by the pension funds over the next few years.

Several lessons are suggested by this review. First, reforming social security systems is extremely difficult. Not only are political considerations important in terms of the power of interest groups, but, in the absence of a responsible government, the short-term fiscal implications also could threaten the country's fiscal situation and macroeconomic stability. Key to the success in reforming the Chilean social security system are (1) the destabilization of interest groups as a result of the military regime, which introduced new labor legislation and a more competitive environment in the whole economy; (2) a strong will for reform and very capable technical expertise, which has been applied to the preparatory studies since mid-1975 (Chile tried to reform the system several times in the 1960s and 1970s with very little success, however); (3) the rapid deterioration of pensions, in part as a consequence of the fiscal contraction of 1975 and the partial readjustment by inflation, which implied that over 70 percent of workers were receiving the minimum pension; and (4) strong fiscal discipline of the government.

A second lesson is that reforms similar to those of Chile may be easier and cheaper to implement in countries where the current coverage of the social security system is low (about 20 percent). In these countries, it may be a good strategy not to challenge the usually powerful interest groups of the already insured but instead to open new private-sector alternatives for pension funds to the uninsured population, with gradual inclusion, on a voluntary basis, of beneficiaries in the old system. This strategy will have no immediate additional fiscal implications but will face them gradually, as people who transfer need recognition funds from the old system, which may not be able to provide them.

The final lesson suggested here is that privatization of pension funds needs to be accompanied by reforms to create or expand the capital market. Otherwise, the pension funds may end up in government paper or a few privileged stocks (which could artificially increase in value because of the higher demand). In such a case, there is not much advantage to privatization, and no risk diversification is possible. An excellent way to increase pension fund investment opportunities is through privatization of public enterprises. Careful monitoring of the pension funds and investment alternatives is needed to preserve the security and profitability of workers' contributions and capital market stability and credibility, in that the funds may rapidly become a substantial part of national savings. Risk classification is better left in private hands, however, so as to avoid any indication that the government is recommending, or willing to support in default, private-sector investments of pension funds.

Appendix

TABLE A5.1 Payroll Contribution Rates by Caja, Old System, 1925–1980 (% of taxable salary)

| | Blue Collar | White Collar | |
Year	(SSS)	Private sector (EMPART)	Public sector (CANAEMPU)
1925	5.0	10.0	14.0
1937	5.0	23.3	15.5
1945	7.0	31.1	19.5
1955	33.2	42.4	21.5
1965	47.1	52.3	22.5
1973	49.9	59.3	25.8
1974	47.9	64.7	54.0
1975	51.4	59.2	50.5
1976	51.3	59.0	50.5
1977	48.3	56.0	46.5
1978	39.5	42.6	38.0
1979	36.3	44.0	35.5
1980	33.2	41.0	32.5

SOURCE: Catholic University of Chile 1981.

TABLE A5.2 Pension Funds: Size in Relation to GDP, Savings, and Bank Deposits, 1981–1988
(billions of 1986 pesos and %)

Year	Fund size	% of national savings	% of deposits	% of GDP
1981	32.3	17.7	3.1	1.1
1982	100.7	31.0	10.0	3.6
1983	182.3	33.8	20.2	6.4
1984	240.1	31.0	24.2	8.6
1985	330.8	45.8	29.4	10.9
1986	434.4	52.4	35.1	13.4
1987	530.9	56.5	36.9	15.7
1988	607.96	54.1	42.6	17.6

SOURCES: Superintendency of AFPs and Central Bank of Chile.

TABLE A5.3 Estimates of the Deficit of the Old Cajas and
Recognition Bonds, 1985–2015

Year	Affiliates	Deficit (billions of 1987 pesos)	Recognition bonds (billions of 1987 pesos)
1985	1,133,619	157.420	11.238
1986	1,103,688	162.670	12.411
1987	1,073,234	166.907	14.354
1988	1,042,400	170.377	15.589
1989	1,011,297	173.261	16.938
1990	980,009	176.489	20.654
1991	948,488	179.819	24.289
1992	916,722	183.223	27.917
1993	884,703	186.252	31.529
1994	852,484	188.891	35.187
1995	820,122	190.311	37.927
1996	787,787	190.963	40.452
1997	755,588	190.877	42.939
1998	723,626	189.398	45.355
1999	692,094	186.653	47.694
2000	661,167	182.646	51.206
2001	631,016	177.710	54.180
2002	601,765	172.026	56.827
2003	573,514	165.673	59.067
2004	546,348	158.756	60.874
2005	495,572	151.444	62.717
2006	471,951	137.511	63.629
2007	449,431	131.054	63.735
2008	427,971	124.868	63.220
2009	407,526	118.947	62.158
2010	388,052	113.277	58.922
2011	369,506	107.870	54.603
2012	351,845	102.718	49.954
2013	335,028	97.813	45.041
2014	319,014	93.142	39.866
2015	303,765	88.689	34.426

NOTE: Figures are deflated by CPI. The armed forces are excluded. Figures for contributors include
actives and retirees.
SOURCE: ODEPLAN 1987b.

TABLE A5.4 Pension Fund Investments by Instrument,
1981–1988 (%)

Year	Government paper	Fixed-term deposits	Mortgage bonds	Shares	Others
1981	28.1	61.9	9.4	0.0	0.6
1982	26.0	26.6	46.8	0.0	0.6
1983	44.5	2.7	50.7	0.0	2.1
1984	42.1	12.2	43.4	0.0	2.3
1985	42.4	20.4	35.6	1.1	0.5
1986	46.6	22.9	25.5	4.6	0.4
1987	41.4	27.4	22.0	6.2	3.0
1988	35.4	28.5	21.6	8.1	6.4

SOURCE: Superintendency of AFPs.

TABLE A5.5 Real Returns of Pension Funds and Bank Deposits,
1981–1988 (% per year)

Year	Pension funds	30–89 days	1–3 years
1981[a]	24.8	28.6	12.0
1982	26.5	22.4	16.6
1983	22.7	3.9	10.0
1984	2.9	2.3	7.7
1985	13.4	4.1	7.2
1986	12.0	1.3	4.7
1987	6.4	3.0	4.8
1988	4.8	1.4	5.9

a. The value for 1981 corresponds to annualized value.
SOURCE: Superintendency of AFPs, *Monthly Bulletin*.

TABLE A5.6 Fixed Commission, Commission on Balance
Accumulated, and D&S Insurance Contribution, 1981–1988

Year	Fixed commission (constant 1987 pesos)	Commission on accumulated funds (% of balance accumulated)	D&S insurance contribution (% of taxable salary)
1981	288	0.99	2.44
1982	320	0.74	2.69
1983	376	0.85	3.56
1984	299	0.84	3.57
1985	224	0.71	3.27
1986	183	0.63	3.44
1987	146	0.52	3.41
1988	178	0.00	3.42

SOURCE: Superintendency of AFPs, *Annual Bulletin*.

CHAPTER 6

Decentralization and Municipal Reform

This chapter reviews the municipal reforms introduced after 1974. It does so within the context of the broader reforms of the central government that were focused on strengthening the regional, provincial, and municipal governments. Also reviewed are the impact the municipalities had on the provision of social services and the coordination of the safety net. Finally, it outlines several issues for the future.

The municipal reforms included changes in the legal framework begun in 1975 that assigned the municipalities new responsibilities, especially with respect to social services, and specified new and increased sources of funds for carrying out those responsibilities. They also included laws that allowed the municipalities to exercise more flexible and timely management of the budget and of personnel. Subsequently, in 1981, the government instituted a complete change in the structure of municipal staff, which had been regulated by antiquated laws. The new structure included a flexible number of positions (related to the amount of resources and responsibilities), an increased number of positions for professional and technical staff, and a reduction in service personnel.

The municipalities have gradually become important institutionally, operationally, and financially, and are now key players in the government's strategy to combat poverty. Among the services the municipalities provide are primary education and health care (with financing from agencies of the central government), sanitation, low-income housing, child care, recreation, and, until recently, administration and operation of several special employment programs aimed at reducing the social cost during the adjustments of the 1975 and 1982–1983 crises. A key instrument the government has used to target a large number of subsidies to the needy has been the municipal information system, known as the CAS Index, which is derived from socioeconomic information on poor families obtained from a survey in all municipalities nationwide.

Before the Reforms

Until 1974–1975, the municipalities had only limited responsibilities and incomes. They were primarily political institutions rather than providers of municipal services. Although they were to handle solid waste disposal, street lighting, water and sewerage, and several social services such as education, culture, and sanitation (most of which were also responsibilities of the central government), the provision of the services was very limited because of scarce municipal financial resources. One result was that citizens lost interest in municipal affairs. In practice, agencies of the central government provided the bulk of municipal services, having gained much influence and strength through the Constitution of 1925.

As Table 6.1 illustrates, the revenue sources of the municipalities in 1974 included a great variety of taxes and fees, amounting to about 45 percent of revenues. Administration of these revenues was cumbersome, so that, in many cases, the collection costs were extremely high in relation to the income. Other revenue was derived from user charges for waste disposal and rents from the leasing of municipal infrastructure (16 percent) and revenue sharing (transfers) from the central government (29.6 percent). Because municipalities could keep only 25 percent of the property tax they collected, with the rest going to the central government, these monies amounted to only 6.1 percent of municipal revenues.

The municipalities faced several problems in 1974. One was the antiquated legal structure dating back to the beginning of this century, which had been modified only a few times since the 1925 Constitution. That legal structure had been designed to deal with the problems of small and provincial towns rather than those of the large and modern cities that had developed in Chile after rapid migration beginning in the

TABLE 6.1 Structure of Municipal Revenues, 1974

Item	Share (%)
Municipal fees and taxes	44.9
Fees (*patentes*) for vehicles and registration of professional and commerce activities	7.5
Taxes on tourism and public events	11.2
Property tax	6.1
Other	20.1
Sale of services	16.1
Solid waste disposal	3.2
Charges for approval of plans and licenses	9.0
Rents for municipal properties	3.9
Capital revenues	9.4
Central government transfers	29.6

SOURCE: Ministry of Finance 1976.

1950s. A second problem stemmed from the cumbersome and antiquated procedures related to the budget. The budgets of the municipalities were part of the national budget and had to follow its centralized procedures and norms. The general Treasury collected all monies (including those of the municipalities), which were distributed back only after complex and time-consuming accounting and auditing procedures. A third problem was that the responsibilities given to the municipalities were very general and did not specify what corresponded to the different levels of governments. Finally, municipal resources were very limited, and the revenue sharing had minimal redistributive intent.

The Reforms

To address some of these problems, the government introduced major reforms in the municipal regime within the framework of a complete restructuring of the central government. The reforms, which gave more responsibilities to the regions and municipalities, entailed the following:

First, the country was divided into thirteen distinct regions (*regiones* 1–12 and the Santiago Metropolitan Region) in 1974. Each region is overseen by a regional governor (*intendente*) appointed by the president of the Republic. A region comprises provinces, each governed by a provincial governor (*gobernador provincial*), under the *intendente*, and municipalities headed by mayors, who were originally appointed by the president (later changes are discussed following). Before these changes, the administrative divisions were provinces and municipalities, with the provincial governors appointed by the president and mayors elected by popular vote.

Second, within each ministry, a Regional Secretariat (SEREMI) was created for each region (the Secretariats of ODEPLAN are called SERPLACs). The SEREMIs have a dual role, serving as technical advisers to the *intendente* in their sectors and as supervisors to ensure the norms and regulations of the respective ministries are met. SERPLACs help the *intendentes* with project preparation, applying the evaluation criteria and methodologies established by ODEPLAN, and with the coordination of sector investments by the ministries and the National Fund for Regional Development (FNDR) (a description of which follows). SEREMIs and SERPLACs each have a staff of no more than fifteen people located in each region.

Third, the FNDR was created in 1975. This fund is composed at least 5 percent of national revenues from taxes (except property taxes) and foreign trade taxes and tariffs. The property taxes were later allocated to the Municipal Fund (FCM), created in 1979. The FNDR was designed to finance priority investments proposed by the regional governments. In 1983, it was strengthened by an Inter-American Development Bank (IDB) loan for U.S. $250 million. Projects are submitted to the fund by the *intendentes*, with the recommendation of ODEPLAN, which is charged with reviewing all public-sector investment projects to ensure they are properly evaluated and have adequate social rates of return. Project financing is demand driven. ODEPLAN administers a computerized public-sector investment system known as the Bank of Investment Projects (Banco de Proyectos). It classifies all projects according to their stage in the project preparation cycle, from concept to project execution and final evaluation, following uniform methodologies and procedures. Projects costing less than 2.7 million pesos (U.S. $10,000 in 1989) can be approved at the regional level by the *intendente*. The *intendentes* can finance these projects with 4 percent of the FNDR approved for the region, which is given to them for their allocation.

Responsibilities of the different levels of government

The ministries of the central government are responsible for establishing policies, norms, and procedures in their respective sectors. They are also responsible for evaluating and supervising the activities and targets to be undertaken. Investments are circumscribed to large projects of national interest.

The regional governments are responsible for preparing and approving their regions' budgets and for planning and executing the regional investment plans, responsibilities that were previously held by the central government. The regional governments are assisted by Regional Development Councils (CODEREs), presided over by the *intendentes* and composed of the provincial governors and representatives of other government and nongovernment agencies and trade associations. These councils participate in the study and approval of the policies and development plans of the respective regions and in the approval of the regional budgets.

The provincial governments are responsible for supervising the execution of plans, programs, and projects and the delivery of public services by the municipalities in their jurisdictions. They also help with the coordination of municipalities within and beyond the provincial boundaries and with other institutions, including the private sector.

The municipal governments are responsible for providing basic services to their communities, including health and education and typical municipal services such as waste disposal, street lighting, and water and sewerage. Communal Development Councils (CODECOs), which mirror the CODEREs, were created at the municipal level in 1975. Recently, the government authorized the CODECOs to approve the municipal budgets and to select the mayors in certain categories of municipalities. The government also created Planning Secretariats (SECPLACs) at the communal level, mirroring SERPLAC at the regional level, to serve as technical advisers to the mayors.

These institutional arrangements have taken several years to implement fully (especially the CODEREs and CODECOs), and some changes are now being considered by the new democratic government. The system needs, however, to be evaluated to determine how coordination is taking place and the role of community organizations in decision making.

A key to the improvement in regional and municipal management has been the sustained and significant amount of training provided. Two programs have been very important. One is the one-year graduate program offered by the Department of Economics of the Catholic University in Santiago, known as CIAPEP. It has had a major impact in terms of preparing personnel qualified in project-evaluation techniques for ODEPLAN, the SERPLACs, and many of the SEREMIs. This program, probably one of the best of its kind in Latin America, began in 1978, financed initially by IDB and ODEPLAN and later, when the IDB funds were exhausted, completely by ODEPLAN. As part of the training, CIAPEP has conducted evaluations of a great number of national, regional, and municipal projects and has prepared methodologies for project evaluation that have been adapted for the Bank of Investment Projects. Second are the great number of short courses on project evaluation for mayors and other high-ranking municipal officials. These courses were provided under a United Nations Development Program project in conjunction with the government to develop the Bank of Investment Projects at ODEPLAN, with some collaboration from CIAPEP.

The following sections describe in more detail the functions, responsibilities, revenues, and expenditures of the municipalities. An assessment of the municipal role in social services during the last fifteen years and issues for the future is provided in the final section.

The Municipal Reforms

The municipal reforms were enacted through several laws, including the Organic Law 1,289 of 1975 (Nueva Ley Orgánica Municipal), which defined more precisely the organization, responsibilities, and functions of municipalities; the Revenue Law 3,063 of 1979 (Ley de Rentas Municipales), which established the norms and procedures for municipalities' own revenues, set the criteria for distributing the revenue sharing, and created the FCM; and Law 3,551 of 1981, which modified the staff structure of the municipalities, with provisions that included the authorization of more professional and technical staff. Other important and complementary legislation included Law 3,000 of 1979, which established the norms and procedures that gave the municipalities more flexibility in budgetary and financial matters and modified the existing rigid and centralized regime, and Law 1-3063 of 1980, which defined the norms by which responsibility for services such as health and education was transferred by central government agencies to the municipalities.

One of the most important features of the new laws was the progressive flexibility given to municipalities over their budgets. Until 1976, these budgets had been incorporated in the Budget Law of the Public Sector (Ley de Presupuesto del Sector Público). Project execution was therefore subject to the restrictions applicable to the entire public sector. From 1976 to 1986, although the *intendentes* were authorized to approve the municipal budgets, in actuality the municipalities had to await processing of the budgets by the Office of the Comptroller (Contraloria General de la República), a system that delayed the beginning of budget implementation until February or March rather than January. Then, in 1987–1988, new budget laws required that the municipal budgets be studied and approved by the *intendentes* during December of the previous year, with immediate execution. The municipalities only had to give notice (*toma de razón*) to the Comptroller's Office, charged with ex post control and audit functions. Beginning in 1988, the CODECOs were made responsible for approving the municipal budgets, which can be executed starting January 1.

The municipal organic law

The municipal organic law defined responsibilities of the municipalities, mayors, and CODECOs and SECPLACs more precisely. It authorized each municipality to establish its own administrative organization, based on its own characteristics and needs, and to create technical departments for community development, municipal works, transit and transport, evaluation and control, and others, as needed. The law also authorized the municipalities to enter into contracts for the provision of municipal services by private parties and, upon approval by the *intendente*, to hire short-term professional consultants and technicians. In 1981, there was, as noted, a complete restructuring of the municipalities' staffing (*planta de personal*). The measures included more professional and technical staff and a new labor code that was the same as that of the private sector. The municipalities got a new pay scale, with higher salaries for the professional and technical staff; this pay scale differed from that of the public sector (*escala única*) previously applicable to the municipalities.

Municipal revenues law

The municipal revenues law specified the following revenue sources for municipalities:

1. Operation revenues, which the municipalities obtain from charges for services such as solid waste disposal or automobile permits (*patentes*) and from permits for the establishment of lucrative and professional activities. The municipalities can charge any annual fee for waste disposal, with different prices for users according to the frequency of use; users can also contract with other than municipal waste disposal services. The municipalities now get all the proceeds from the vehicle permits, as opposed to only one-third previously. To simplify the issuance of permits for lucrative and professional activities, the law shortened considerably the existing list of up to 400 different trades and their respective charges. It also

eliminated all exceptions to the payment of municipal permits, except for nonprofit or religious organizations.

2. National budget contributions (*aporte fiscal*), which are determined annually in the budget law. The formula for distribution is as follows: 25 percent is distributed in direct proportion to the number of inhabitants in the municipality; another 25 percent is distributed in direct proportion to the number of lots exempt from the property tax; and 50 percent is distributed in inverse proportion to the municipalities' revenues. The richest municipalities—Santiago, Las Condes, Providencia, Viña del Mar, and Machali—do not receive these revenues. In calculating municipal revenues, contributions from the national budget, revenues from the FCM, and transfers are excluded (beginning in 1984, the national budget contributions were channeled through the FCM).

3. The property tax, which goes entirely to the municipalities, 40 percent directly and 60 percent through the FCM based on a redistributive formula (to be described). This tax is collected by the Treasury. Before 1979, the municipalities received only 25 percent of property tax collected in their jurisdictions.

4. The FCM, which was created in 1981 with 55 percent of the proceeds from the property tax. The distribution formula is the same as that used to allocate the budget contributions but includes all municipalities. After 1981, the FCM was given additional funds: first, its share of the property tax was increased to 60 percent; then, starting in 1983, all the budget contributions given to the municipalities were channeled through the FCM; and finally, in 1987, it received 65 percent of the revenues from the permits for vehicles and professional and commercial registration fees (*patentes*) obtained by the two richest municipalities in the country, Providencia and Las Condes. In addition, a given minimum amount now has to be allocated to each municipality, a measure that benefits the smaller municipalities.

5. Other revenues, which consist of small taxes and fees, permits, and concessions that the law simplified and rationalized. Donations made to municipalities are tax-free, in order to encourage this type of contribution by citizens and private organizations.

Municipal Revenues and Expenditures, 1976–1988

Revenues

The overall revenues of the municipalities rose over six times between 1976 and 1988. Operational revenues more than tripled as a result of the increased collection of debts, greater revenues from user fees, and, after 1981, a larger share of the property tax. The redistributive allocation of government funds through national budget contributions and of the FCM rose by almost eleven times between 1976 and 1988. Other income, including transfers for special or emergency programs (for example, the earthquake of 1985), also grew considerably (Figure 6.1).

These revenues *exclude* the substantial amounts of money the municipalities receive for operating and maintaining the schools and primary health-care centers. In 1988, they got about 63 billion pesos for education and 10.08 billion for the primary health-care services they provided. The above revenues also exclude the monies transferred to the municipalities to operate and administer employment programs such as the Minimum Employment Program (PEM); the Employment Program for Household Heads (POJH); the Labor-intensive Employment Program (PIMO); and a few other smaller programs aimed at reducing the social costs of adjustment.

FIGURE 6.1 Municipal Revenues, 1976–1988

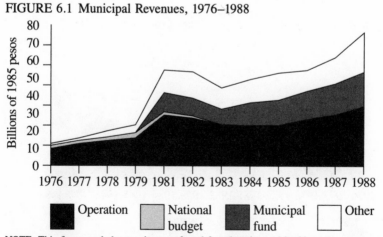

NOTE: This figure excludes monies transferred for education and health care.
SOURCE: Ministry of Interior Affairs, Undersecretary for Regional and Administrative Development.

Expenditures

Overall municipal expenditures also rose considerably between 1976 and 1988 (Figure 6.2). These expenditures *exclude* the bulk of those made for the schools and health posts transferred to the municipalities. The municipalities finance only a small part of education and health-care costs out of their own funds (including revenue sharing). In 1988, the share of the municipalities was 5.5 billion pesos (about 8 percent of the total expenditures on education) and 1.3 billion (about 13 percent of the total expenditures on health care).

The expenditures of municipalities on personnel were very low until 1979 but increased rapidly in the following years. That low level reflected the low qualifications of the staff employed. After 1981, personnel expenditures increased rapidly, reflecting the new responsibilities of the municipalities and new personnel structure. In 1975, the number of technical and professional workers was only 8 percent of the total; the majority were service and auxiliary personnel (*mayordomos y auxiliares*). In 1988, the number of technical and professional workers (excluding teachers and health personnel) increased to 33 percent of total municipal workers (Table 6.2 and Figure 6.3). In 1988, there were 103,033 education personnel and 12,204 health personnel hired by the municipalities and transferred by the respective ministries.

Expenditures on supplies, which were very low until 1979, expanded considerably thereafter, a reflection of the increased number of

FIGURE 6.2 Municipal Expenditures, 1976–1988

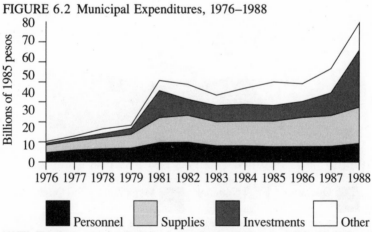

NOTE: This figure excludes the bulk of expenditures on education and health care.
SOURCE: Ministry of Interior Affairs, Undersecretary for Regional and Administrative Development.

TABLE 6.2 Municipal Personnel Hired, 1975 and 1988

Type of personnel	1975	1988
Municipal affairs personnel	20,722	21,564
Professional and technical	1,632	7,107
Administrative	5,296	5,586
Auxiliary personnel	13,794	8,871
Education personnel	0	103,033
Health personnel	0	12,204

SOURCE: Ministry of Interior Affairs, Undersecretary for Regional and Administrative Development.

FIGURE 6.3 Municipal Personnel Hired, 1975 and 1988

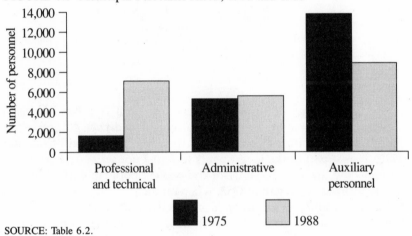

SOURCE: Table 6.2.

services provided by the municipalities. These services included solid-waste disposal and street lighting, among others, which increased considerably after the law mandated full cost recovery for some municipal services. These figures do not reflect, however, the total amount of municipal services provided, because many municipalities contracted out with private companies for the delivery of services such as waste disposal and the cleaning and maintenance of municipal facilities. The central government has encouraged and recommended this practice so that the municipalities can concentrate on providing those services in which no private agent has an interest. This practice is known in Chile as the subsidiary principle (*principio de subsidiaridad del estado*), a key concept underlying government intervention since 1974.

FIGURE 6.4 Municipal Investments (Total and Sites and Services), 1974–1989

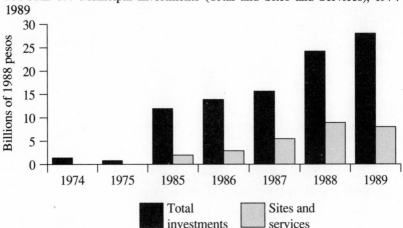

SOURCE: Ministry of Interior Affairs, Undersecretary for Regional and Administrative Development.

Investment expenditures were very low until 1979 but increased substantially thereafter. In 1988, they represented over 40 percent of municipal expenditures, compared with only 12 percent in 1976. After 1982, a great part of the investments has gone for water and sewerage systems and low-cost housing for the poorest population (Figure 6.4). The latter initiative began in 1982, when municipalities were authorized to build sites and services units, using an IDB loan negotiated with the Ministry of Interior Affairs. As seen in Chapter 4, the municipalities' housing programs targeted to the poorest 30 percent of the population have been highly successful: between 1983 and 1989, the municipalities built more than 100,000 housing units, mostly through contracts with the private sector.

Impact of the Municipalities on Social Development

The municipalities have been a key instrument in the government's strategy to reduce poverty, contributing in a number of ways.

1. They deliver specified social services such as primary health care and education based on the infrastructure and monetary resources transferred since 1981 by the respective ministries.

In 1987, the municipalities enrolled nearly 2 million students (64 percent of the total primary and secondary students) in the more than 7,000 schools transferred to them. They are now responsible for the operation of all school and health centers, including the hiring of personnel, purchase of supplies, and maintenance of infrastructure. One interesting feature of the transfer of social services is that the central government provides direct financing through a fee-for-service mechanism (for specified outputs or products) rather than through revenue sharing. (More details on the transfer of the schools and health-care centers are provided in Chapters 2 and 3.)

2. They deliver other social services, such as care for poor children in day-care centers (Centros de Atención Diurna and Centros Abiertos), some school lunch programs, public libraries, and recreation in municipal recreation and youth centers. The municipalities also help in choosing the beneficiaries and in distributing the national government subsidies under the Assistance Pension Program (PASIS) and the family subsidy (SUF) program, among others. They also carry out special social programs such as the minimum employment programs put in place to reduce the impact of the economic crises of 1975 and 1982–1983. Municipalization resulted in substantial savings in the employment programs, amounting to over 500 million pesos in 1985. These savings were transferred to the FNDR for regional and municipal investments.

3. They implement their own social investments, especially in water and sewerage and sites and services programs.

4. They provide a key instrument used to target subsidies to the poorest population, the CAS Index. The CAS Index was initiated in 1980 to identify the beneficiaries of social programs that were to be developed by the CAS, presided over by mayors. The index consists of the results of responses to more than thirty questions on the socioeconomic conditions of poor families in the municipalities. The survey is conducted in all municipalities by social workers or other municipal personnel. An additional benefit of the CAS Index is that it familiarizes municipal workers with community problems and deficiencies in social services.

Issues for the Future

Three main issues that must be addressed in the future emerge from this review. First, the financing arrangements for education and health-care services must be improved to give more incentives to municipalities for increased quality and cost containment. The municipalities receive a payment per student attending school and a fee-for-service payment for primary health-care services provided. Many municipalities are running deficits for both operations, which may affect these services particularly in the poorer municipalities.

Quality in the primary municipal schools is expected to result from competition with the private sector, which receives the same payment from the Ministry of Education as that provided to the municipalities. A key tool in this model is the performance examination to be given regularly to students by the Ministry of Education. If the examination is in fact given, this model should produce the expected results in the long run. To improve quality in the short term, measures directed to the poorest municipalities or where the quality indicators are the worst should be implemented. Among these measures are direct monetary assistance for building laboratories and computer facilities and providing specialized school aids. New facilities should be operated and maintained by the municipalities, not the Ministry of Education. Similar facilities or credit lines can be made available to qualified private schools that are committed to improving the quality of schools in the poorest areas.

Providing incentives for municipalities to improve the quantity and quality of health services is probably more difficult. The fee-for-service scheme used to reimburse the municipalities does not include copayments by users, and it therefore gives an incentive to both municipalities and users to overuse the system. Cost containment requires that some cost be borne by the municipality, the user, or both. Currently, the municipalities bear some of the costs, because the ceiling on total reimbursement has been lower than the total billings for services. A result of this situation, however, may be more inferior services in poorer and rural municipalities, which may find it harder to finance the deficits out of their own resources (including revenue sharing).

There are ways in which the National Health Fund (FONASA) can fully finance basic health services to avoid some of the problems caused by the municipal deficits, while still providing incentives for cost containment by the municipalities. One way is to combine grant financing with the present fee-for-service payment system. Reimbursement could be made by drawing part from the guaranteed grant fund and the rest from FONASA. Funds remaining in the grant fund at the end of the year could be kept by the municipality. Another method is to pay an amount per beneficiary to the municipality for health-care services. The municipalities would then be free to choose what health services to provide and how to provide them, the only condition being that they would have to achieve certain social indicators and quality of services.

The second issue for the future concerns how to preserve needed municipal autonomy to operate the health and education services. One subissue that is being actively discussed is the salaries of teachers and health personnel. In the past, the respective ministries determined the salaries and pay scales; now they are determined by the municipalities. This municipal prerogative should be preserved if the municipalities are to be held accountable for the services they provide. The municipalities can and have made salary adjustments based on performance indicators that were not applied under the previous centralized personnel management system.

The third issue is that improvements must be made to the highly redistributive nature of the current formula for revenue sharing through the FCM, which favors smaller municipalities. The system should include a reward for revenue-raising efforts by the municipalities (under the current formula, the less they collect the more they get). It should also recognize limits on redistribution from the richer to the poorer municipalities, limits that are related to collection costs and efficiency considerations (while the richer municipalities produce more taxes and other revenues, they also demand more services).

CHAPTER 7

Summary and Conclusions

The purpose of this book has been to review the policy changes and structural reforms in the social sectors (education, health and nutrition, housing, and social security) and in municipal administration in Chile in the 1970s and 1980s. I have examined the rationale for the reforms, studied their implementation, and provided rough indications of the results to date.

Chile has experienced remarkable improvements in its social indicators during the past three decades. These have occurred in a period of sharp economic instability and a deteriorating situation in employment and real wages. This fact has given ample room for hypothesis about why the social indicators continue to improve, at rates even faster than in the past. Various researchers have stressed the long history of social programs in the country; the decline in fertility rates; the improvements in programs aimed at mothers and children; and finally, better targeting of social programs to the neediest, most vulnerable groups—made possible, to a large extent, by the policy changes and reforms in the social sectors that are the subject of this book.

This chapter presents a general summary of the reforms carried out in each social sector, the processes by which the reforms were achieved, and the lessons that other countries can draw from the Chilean experience.

The Reforms

Main principles of the reforms

One of the most interesting features of the Chilean reforms is that similar principles, mechanisms, and implementation procedures were applied in all the social sectors. The principles were as follows:

1. Government subsidies should be targeted to the poorest segments of the population—that is, to those who are not able, through their own means, to meet the basic social needs in areas such as health, education, social security, housing, and other basic services. This principle has two components: first, an effort on the part of the beneficiaries is required; and second, the government must seek to equalize basic services, especially in the case of investments in human capital, aimed at providing equal opportunities for all citizens.

2. Social services should be provided by entities that are closer to the beneficiaries than the central government, such as municipalities and the private sector, including nonprofit organizations. The role of the public sector is to provide financing, issue norms and procedures, and supervise and evaluate social programs. Ministries must be reorganized to assume these supervisory and evaluative roles, while the municipalities and private sector must be strengthened to become key players in the delivery of social services.

3. Financing for social services should be based on services provided rather than on historically based budget allocations. The government should define clearly what types of services it wants to finance and should pay any provider for actual services rendered according to specified norms and conditions. The payments should be the same for all providers, whether municipalities or the private sector. Competition will serve to increase the amount and quality of services provided.

4. Subsidies should be given directly to beneficiaries rather than to providers and should be in the form of upfront direct subsidies (vouchers whenever possible) rather than indirect subsidies such as below-market interest rates.

5. The public sector should undertake only those activities that are socially profitable and that no private-sector party is willing to provide. This practice, called the state subsidiary role (*principio de subsidiaridad del estado*), was a key principle for

government intervention in all spheres of economic and social public activity during the military government.

Summaries by sector

Education.   The purpose of the government's education reforms was to increase the efficiency (both internal and external) of public education and expand the opportunities for students by encouraging the private sector to offer more education alternatives and programs. One means by which the government attained this purpose was to decentralize the provision of public education to the municipalities and to change the way the central government transferred resources to the providers of services. The government moved from the old system of giving money to schools and universities based on historical fiscal allocations for teacher salaries and other costs to a new system of channeling resources based on a per-student payment, which was the same for municipal and private schools. At the university level, tuition was raised, but at the same time loans were introduced for needy students.

Implementing the educational reforms has been difficult, the primary reason being the 1982–1983 recession, which occurred just as the reforms were about to be fully implemented. In addition, the system of transferring funds on a per-student basis, although effective at the primary and secondary levels, has not worked well at the university level.

Moreover, although student loans have increased substantially since they were introduced and now constitute more than one-fourth of university financing, several problems remain. These include a high level of subsidization and the fact that loans are not given to students at private universities and professional institutes, who may be as poor as some of those in the public and private subsidized universities.

There has also been a sharp reduction in university financing, a result largely of the government's efforts to maintain and protect the expenditures for the lower levels of education, especially primary, in the presence of acute fiscal constraints. In 1982, the worst year of the crisis, expenditures for primary and secondary education increased greatly because of the decentralization reform and related high levels of expenditures. Although expenditures for nonuniversity education declined in the 1983–1985 period compared with 1982, they still remained at the 1980 level. As a result, the ratio of public expenditures for nonuniversity spending to GDP rose considerably during the crisis. In the case of university spending, it decreased.

The redistribution of expenditures across the levels of education, together with the differential redistributive impact of the different levels of education, has produced a strong relocation, both absolutely and proportionately, in the overall educational subsidies going to the poorest population. The proportion of all education subsidies received by the poorest 30 percent of all families with students rose from about 29 percent in 1974 to 38 percent in 1986, while the proportion going to the richest 40 percent of families decreased from 47 percent to about 35 percent. The proportion received by the middle-income 30 percent increased modestly, from 24 percent to 28 percent. These figures, while showing a strong effort to target the poorest population, nonetheless indicate that much more needs to be done to target subsidies at all levels of education, but particularly at the university and secondary levels.

Health and nutrition. The reforms of the health-care system had two main objectives: to improve the targeting of health services and food supplements to the needy population and to increase the efficiency (in other words, to get more services from a given amount of resources) of the public health-care delivery system. The government expanded and improved primary health care, emphasizing the most vulnerable groups—mothers and young children living in rural areas, where a 1974 map of extreme poverty showed the lowest indicators of health status to be.

To pursue these objectives, the government undertook major institutional and financial reforms of the health-care system. Begun in 1979, they included

- creating a financial institution for the health sector (FONASA), charged with collecting all revenue for health services from the national budget and the payroll deductions for health care, and with distributing money to, or paying, the providers of services

- strengthening the role of the Ministry of Health (MOH) as the policy-making, normative, supervisory, and evaluating agent

- decentralizing the National Health Service (NHS) into twenty-six regional autonomous services capable of providing preventive and curative services in specified geographical areas

- transferring responsibility for primary health-care services and infrastructure to the municipalities, a shift begun in 1981 and completed in 1987

- allowing workers to choose whether to have their payroll deductions for health go to FONASA or to the private health insurance companies (ISAPREs)

The emphasis given to primary health care, health and nutrition-related interventions, and sanitation appears to have been responsible to a large extent for the rapid improvement in health and nutrition indicators since the mid-1970s. The infant mortality rate dropped from 74 per 1,000 live births in 1973 to 20 per 1,000 live births in 1987, a record decline in Latin America. Malnutrition declined from 15.5 percent of children under six years of age in 1975 to 8.6 percent in 1988. Maternal care coverage has increased considerably. Over 98 percent of births are now attended by professionals, as compared with 81 percent in 1970.

The reforms have not been easy and have required considerable negotiation, trial and error, and correction. The targeting of the health and nutrition interventions has also been difficult, requiring the development of good information systems at the central and municipal levels, extensive coordination among programs, and substantial reform of the health-care delivery system to enable it to concentrate on the poorest population. Targeting still needs strengthening, and the fact that the service directors of hospitals have only limited control over the large share of the budget allocated to personnel needs to be addressed. Development of the ISAPRE system has been impressive: in 1988 it enrolled more than 1.4 million people (12 percent of the population).

A major challenge for the future is to consolidate and continue improving the financing mechanisms, incentive structures, and institutional arrangements made during the past fifteen years. Particular attention needs to be paid to revising arrangements to finance primary health care provided by municipalities and to finance hospitals. Some municipalities are financing operation deficits with their own resources, which is affecting poorer municipalities with limited revenue sources. Reimbursement prices need to be adjusted to reflect new and more expensive treatments necessary for older populations. The private sector plays a large role by offering competitive health insurance alternatives for those who can pay, thus allowing the public sector to concentrate its resources on those who need state assistance and who, for the most part, will be served free of charge. This strategy, which appears to be an effective way of targeting health expenditures to the poorest, must be accompanied, however, by a commitment to provide the poor with good-quality services and to protect expenditures for them. The private-sector health insurance companies need to be closely monitored to avoid fraud to users, default, risk preference, and discrimination against older people.

Housing. A major policy change in housing, begun in 1975, involved the targeting of subsidies to some of the poorer population through programs tailored to their needs and economic capacity. The government introduced direct subsidies for down payments to replace the indirect subsidies that had taken the form of lower interest rates or reduced prices for housing units.

The role of the public sector was limited to financing and screening the beneficiaries of subsidies and establishing norms and regulations, functions handled by the Ministry of Housing and Urban Affairs (MINVU) and the municipalities. The private sector was responsible for land development, seeking the connections to urban services (water and sewerage), construction of housing units, and financial intermediation. The private mortgage market was strengthened to provide financing for housing for middle- and upper-income families.

After a long period of trial and error, these reforms were consolidated and appear to have been highly successful. The use of fiscal resources seems to have improved significantly: fewer government expenditures have been needed to mobilize more resources for housing. Since 1973, more than 420,000 units have been built, mainly by the private sector, while public expenditures have declined considerably. In 1983, government spending was only about 30 percent of what it was in 1970. According to the 1982 census and sample surveys made later, the number of homeless households dropped from about 19 percent in 1982 to about 13 percent in 1987.

The cost-effectiveness of government expenditures has also improved, given the high priority assigned to basic programs such as land titling, upgrading of slums and other urban rehabilitation, and the extension of connections to potable water and sewerage, which to a large extent have benefited the poorest population. Equity has improved considerably; the proportion of subsidies going to the poorest 30 percent of the population has more than doubled, from about 21 percent in 1969 and 1980 to about 50 percent in the 1982–1986 period. Furthermore, in 1989 the government modified the less redistributive programs to improve the targeting of lower-income groups.

Targeting the subsidies has not been easy. Initially, programs directed to the poor benefited primarily middle-income people, because of the excessive requirements for prior savings, poor means testing of applicants, and high value of the houses being applied for. These conditions created an incentive for relatively well-off people to apply for the subsidies. Moreover, because of a lack of information on the economic capacity of prospective target groups, the subsidies appear to have been excessive.

Implementation and consolidation of recent programs are strongly needed that seek to reduce the housing deficit, overcrowding, and the problem of "family members living with relatives" (*allegados*) and to improve housing conditions of tenements through rehabilitation programs. Also needed is continued and stronger action by the MINVU to improve collections on its loan portfolio and reduce its default rate, so that it can speed the reduction in the housing deficit.

Social security (pension system).   Chile was one of the first developing countries to establish a social security system, dating back to 1924. Over time, several problems became evident. A high degree of discrimination existed against weaker groups, particularly blue-collar workers, in terms of benefits and retirement requirements. Most institutions experienced a deep financial crisis, the result of decreased revenues caused by the evasion of contributions because of high rates and a lack of control, and by excessive expenditures on administration and benefits for privileged workers (such as housing loans at very low nominal interest rates). As a result of this crisis, there was a need for large, untargeted, and increasing subsidies, especially for the pension system of public employees. A final problem was poor services for beneficiaries, who had to wait several months after retirement before receiving their benefits.

The salient features of the new system are as follows. First, it has unified, simple, nondiscriminatory rules regarding the benefits to be provided, retirement requirements, and eligibility criteria. Second, government subsidies are targeted to the poorest workers (defined as those whose accumulated funds are not sufficient to cover the minimum established pension) and for the needy not enrolled in the social security system. Third, individual capitalization means that workers save (compulsorily) for their own retirement and to pay for the disability and survivors insurance premium. Retirement funds (10 percent of taxable income) can be deposited in private companies (AFPs) whose function is to administer pension funds. Disability insurance can be bought from private insurance companies at a premium of about 3.4 percent of the taxable salary.

The reforms have had a high short-term fiscal cost (the net long-term cost has been much lower), in part as a result of their success, as indicated by some 3 million people (about 74 percent of the civilian labor force in 1988) who have transferred from the old to the new system in a very short period. The growth of the new system sharply reduced the revenue of the old institutions, increasing their deficits and the need for government contributions. Implementation has also required several modifications to the original law to correct problems and gradually to open up investment opportunities in the capital market to the pension funds. As a result of the massive transfer of participants, the new funds grew rapidly from 1.1 percent of GDP in 1981, the first year of the reform, to 17.6 percent of GDP in 1988.

Overall, the social security reform can be described as highly successful in terms of the number of affiliates, the number of pension fund companies in the market, the returns from the pension funds (which on average have been over 3 percentage points higher than the returns from the financial system), and the benefits provided. A major advance has been that the pension funds are being used to reduce concentration of property in industry and to privatize public enterprises.

Decentralization and municipal reforms. The municipal reforms, beginning in 1975, included changes in the legal framework that assigned the municipalities new responsibilities, especially with respect to social services, and specified new and increased sources of funds for carrying out those responsibilities. They also included laws that allowed the municipalities to exercise more flexible and timely management of budget and personnel. Subsequently, in 1981, the government instituted a complete change in the structure of municipal staff, which had been regulated by antiquated laws. The new structure included a flexible number of vacancies (related to the amount of resources and responsibilities) for professional and technical staff and a reduction in service personnel.

The municipalities have gradually become key players institutionally, operationally, and financially in the government's strategy to combat poverty. Among the services the municipalities provide are primary education and health care (with financing from agencies of the central government), sanitation, low-income housing, child care, recreation, and, until recently, administration and operation of several special employment programs aimed at reducing the cost of adjustment for the 1975 and 1982–1983 crises. A key instrument the government has used to target a large number of subsidies to the needy has been the municipal information system, known as the Committee for Social Action (CAS) Index, which is derived from socioeconomic information on poor families gathered from a survey conducted by all municipalities nationwide.

Issues for the future include (1) improving the mechanisms for financing the education and health-care services to improve their quality and promote cost containment by the municipalities; (2) preserving municipal autonomy over personnel administration, including the authority to raise salaries, so as not to jeopardize the municipalization of services; and (3) improving the revenue-sharing formula of the highly redistributive Municipal Fund (FCM) to introduce incentives for municipalities to increase their own efforts to raise revenues (under the current formula, the less a municipality collects in its own revenues, the more revenue sharing it gets).

The Reform Process

The following are some key aspects of the reform process in Chile that are useful in understanding how these reforms were possible and what the prospects for their survival are in the democratic government that took office in March 1990.

The presence of a leading institution for policy change

Soon after the military government took power, the National Planning Office (ODEPLAN) took a leadership role in the design of the economic and social principles and policies that the new government wanted to apply. After 1974, a small group of conservative economists began influencing major policy decisions not only in economic areas but also in social policy design.

ODEPLAN exerted a tremendous influence over the public sector through the law that required its approval for all public-sector investment projects. With the purpose of introducing homogeneous project-evaluation criteria, ODEPLAN developed many methodologies for cost-benefit and cost-effectiveness analysis to be followed by all public agencies (including public enterprises).

ODEPLAN was also the coordinator of the government's social policy and safety net until about 1984, when the new Secretariat for Social Development was created. ODEPLAN has, however, remained the responsible normative, supervisory, and evaluating agency of the information systems designed for targeting subsidies at the municipal level (CAS Index) and for analysis and evaluation of social policy (the living-standard measurement survey, known as the CASEN survey, conducted in 1985 and 1987).

The continuity of policies and reforms

The continuity of the reform efforts was remarkable in Chile, particularly in view of the sharp budget restrictions that obliged the government to suspend temporarily major policy decisions (such as the transfer of schools and health posts to municipalities) and that gave time and ammunition to opposing groups. To a great extent, the continuity of the reforms resulted from the perseverance, stubbornness, and single-mindedness of key personnel in the ministries and the fact that a substantial number of people had been trained and were working in all the public-sector agencies (central, regional, and municipal).

The role of training

The role played by training of high- and middle-level officials was fundamental. In 1975–1976, ODEPLAN started a scholarship program to send students abroad, especially to the United States, to study economics, business administration, education, and other disciplines. In addition, students were sent to a few well-designed programs in Chile, including a project-evaluation program called CIAPEP at the Department of Economics of the Catholic University in Santiago.

Another program that had a great influence and complemented CIAPEP offered training for municipal officials. This program was supported by the United Nations Development Program in Chile. It had a component for mayors, including several weeks of intensive training on economic analysis and basics of project evaluation, and a component for high- and medium-level municipal officials, who were trained to perform project profiles and to understand and fill the formats provided by ODEPLAN. More than 1,300 municipal officials have been trained since the program's creation in 1978–1979.

Preparation of the reforms.   Having a body of newly trained people facilitated the government's preparation and planning of the reforms. The reforms actually began in 1980, six years after the government took power. From 1974 to 1980, the government undertook a series of studies, realized important policy changes in health and education, and unified criteria for benefits in the existing numerous pension fund systems.

The role of incentives.   Part of the preparation for the reforms was the introduction of incentives and "golden parachutes" for those affected by the reforms. For instance, the government gave severance pay to and, in many cases, authorized early retirement for teachers and health workers who were transferred from the public sector to the municipalities, ruled by the new private-sector labor code. The government also gave a 3–5 percent increase in the education budget to those mayors willing to accept the transfer of schools soon after the decentralization law was passed.

Another incentive developed to help the reform process mandated that workers willing to transfer to the new pension fund system received an increase on average of 10 percent in their monthly take-home check. This was made possible by the government lowering the payroll contribution rates for old-age pension and disability and survivors insurance (from about 23 to 13.5 percent) and giving all the reduction to workers. This move produced a massive transfer of affiliates to the new system, but it was costly to the government, which had to increase the fiscal contribution to the old pension fund system so that it could pay its pension obligations.

The role of information systems

The Chilean government has made the development of information systems for targeting social assistance a high priority. The poverty map made in 1974 by ODEPLAN with the Catholic University of Chile was used initially for targeting health and nutrition benefits and school lunch programs by geographical location. Another key instrument for targeting health and nutrition benefits has been the growth-monitoring system for children and pregnant women implemented by the Ministry of Health in 1975 to identify undernutrition and groups at risk.

The CAS system is a living-standard measurement instrument designed by ODEPLAN and used by the municipalities to identify the poorest 40 percent of the population. It started in 1980 and is based on a regular survey of poverty areas by municipalities and contains up-to-date information on characteristics of family members (age, sex, education, employment status, income, and wealth) and housing conditions. It has become an important tool for selecting beneficiaries for money income subsidies, such as the family subsidy (SUF) and the assistance pensions for the poor.

ODEPLAN has gradually improved the CAS system. In the beginning municipalities were not prepared for information-gathering functions or for classifying the poor. Both the municipalities and the beneficiaries tended to overstate poverty conditions, to receive more subsidies. In 1983, ODEPLAN started to redesign the CAS system, improving the formulary and providing supervision and quality control. Since 1987 the system has been computerized in most municipalities, and the Poverty Index is calculated in a way that minimizes the tendency to exaggerate poverty conditions. ODEPLAN now has a strong normative and supervisory role to ensure the quality and uniformity of the information gathered, nationwide.

Another information system that has been designed to improve subsidy targeting is a comprehensive national survey containing information on all subsidies received by all families in Chile, which was conducted in 1985 and 1987. These surveys have provided reliable information on the amount of subsidies received by different income groups and the redistributive impact of social spending, and the data have been used to formulate corrective actions.

Finally, although not for targeting purposes directly, the government has introduced a national test aimed at evaluating students' achievement in the fourth and eighth grades of primary school. The test results provide information to parents on the quality of the schools educating their children. Tests were administered in 1982, 1984, and 1987, but the results have not been disseminated widely.

The information systems developed have been costly and have represented an important administrative burden for the municipalities and other responsible institutions. However, thanks to technical advances and institutional development, the government has been able to improve these systems gradually while decreasing their costs. The cost of targeting benefits, for example, has been reduced greatly as the different government agencies come to use the same information systems to target and coordinate the distribution of subsidies, thus eliminating duplication of effort.

Lessons for Other Countries

Some of the most important general lessons that the Chilean experience holds for other countries are summarized here.

First, efficiency and equity problems, common in the delivery of social services in developing and developed countries, cannot be solved with "quick fixes." Instead, they often require large institutional changes, resulting in new roles for central government bureaucracies and changes in the way social services are financed and operated.

Second, once the previous point is recognized, a strong commitment for reform is needed from the government, leading to continuity of efforts over a number of years and determination to overcome setbacks and pressures of interest groups. Social reforms that target social services to the poor typically require a long time to yield fruit, while powerful interest groups who enjoy benefits are most likely to be adversely affected by reforms in the short term.

Third, in making reforms, there is a strong need for a leading institution, such as ODEPLAN or the Ministry of Finance, with some budget allocation powers, which can give technical support to the usually weak social ministries and can break their natural resistance to change.

Fourth, it must be recognized that the reforms can lead to high short-term fiscal costs to pay for personnel relocation and incentives, which serve to reduce the resistance from institutions and individuals.

Fifth, reforming central government institutions to undertake primarily policy-making, normative, and supervisory roles and allowing municipalities to operate social services can be a slow process, given personnel issues to be solved and the usually weak municipal administrative structures. Complex legal issues need to be addressed to change municipal personnel structures and budget execution laws.

Sixth, the municipalities and the private sector can play a significant role in poverty-alleviation strategies by providing social services previously offered only by the central government. Municipalities can gradually become safety-net coordinating agencies, identifying beneficiaries of subsidies and social programs, helping avoid duplication of programs and benefits, and monitoring progress in poverty alleviation. A strong normative and supervisory role needs to be played by specialized central agencies to ensure that poverty maps are accurate and comparable across municipalities.

Seventh, financing decentralized municipal primary health care and education is a complex issue that requires cost-containing measures, allowances for differences in cost of provision of services, and special care not to aggravate differences in services provided by rich and poor municipalities. Although the Chilean model is still imperfect and needs to be improved, it has several features that can be useful for other countries attempting similar decentralization of services. Among these features is the introduction of payments for services rendered that are equal for all municipalities (with some allowances for rural and dispersed municipalities), financed directly by the central government. This requires close supervision to avoid fraud and ensure a similar amount of spending per beneficiary across the country. Another feature is the introduction of strict project-evaluation criteria applied to the financing of health and education investments through grants from the central and regional governments. This limits municipalities from making investments that are not strictly needed, as is common when municipalities are totally free to make their own investments using funds from the revenue-sharing system.

Eighth, the programs that benefit the poor most are those most carefully tailored to their needs and situations. Programs that are attractive to those with higher incomes, such as costly housing solutions, are difficult to target to the poorest population, because middle-income people, who have more influence and better social connections, will tend to crowd out the poor. Examples of programs that best target the poorest are land titling (where a severe problem of this nature exists), provision of sites and services, and connections to basic services of potable water, sewerage, and electricity.

Finally, but not least important, is that for targeting the poor and improving social-project coordination, there is a need for two types of information systems: one for identification of beneficiaries and other for regularly measuring the impact of social programs. The latter is key for policy design and for establishing priority groups and programs.

Notes

Chapter 1, "Introduction"

1. In the French SEMPE scale, mild undernutrition corresponds to −1 standard deviation (SD) from reference mean, moderate malnutrition is −2 SD, and severe malnutrition is −3 SD.

2. Ffrench-Davis and Raczynski (1985) indicate that during the period 1974–1985 there was a marked increase in infectious diseases such as typhoid fever and hepatitis compared with 1970–1973. This, however, appears to be the result of increased water contamination, especially of the Mapocho River and beaches of the central region, accompanied by a lack of strict food quality control measures by the Ministry of Health, rather than a result of the economic crisis and adjustment programs.

3. Wisecarver (1986) provides a very interesting review of the political economy of deregulation in Chile from 1973 to 1983. A review of the economic and trade liberalization reforms, some of the controversies surrounding them, and their effects appears in Lüders 1988.

4. Estimates in the United States, for instance, range from 10.5 percent of the population (when all in-kind transfers are counted) to 24.1 percent (considering only money income and changed patterns of consumer spending). See Spencer Rich, "Drawing the Line on Poverty: Census Bureau Sparks Criticism from Many Quarters," *Washington Post*, February 20, 1990.

5. Underestimation of income may be as high as 20 percent for these workers, as seen by the discrepancy between aggregate income calculated by the national accounts and extrapolation of survey information.

6. Another indication is that the purchase of durable goods increased considerably in all income brackets between 1970 and 1982. Possession of black-and-white TV sets increased from 20 percent to 68 percent; radios and radio cassettes from 74 percent to 84 percent; and refrigerators from 29 percent to 49 percent. Ffrench-Davis and Raczynski (1985:35) indicate that this has resulted from declines in prices and the economic "model's emphasis on 'competition' and the market that increased the advertising for all kinds of goods, particularly the modern durable ones, expanded installment plans (credit) and opened easier access to them. These factors encouraged the population of all social strata to acquire these goods, thereby diverting funds that otherwise could be destined for food and other basic needs."

7. Estimates for Central American countries following ECLA (Economic Commission for Latin America) methodology, followed by Rodríguez-Grossi (1985a) and Torche (1987), for people whose income is not enough to meet basic food needs around 1980 are as follows: Costa Rica (24.3 percent); El Salvador (68.3 percent); Guatemala (69.4 percent); Honduras (65.7 percent); Panama (54.9 percent). This methodology leads to overestimates of poverty when there are abundant direct social programs (Costa Rica and Chile) and significant remittances (El Salvador, Guatemala, Honduras), which are usually not captured in employment surveys.

Chapter 2, "Reforms in Education"

1. This provision was specified in the Ley de Subvenciones [Subvention Law], Decree Law 3,476 of 1980.

2. Monthly Taxing Unit is a unit of account that increases monthly with inflation.

3. The exchange rate of thirty-nine Chilean pesos per dollar prevailing in 1980 was generally thought to be overvalued. Starting in 1982, the peso was devalued and the payment in dollar terms was substantially reduced, as indicated later in the text.

4. Although the transfer of vocational schools started in 1978, it was done informally until the legislation regulating all transfers was enacted in 1980.

5. Ley de Subvenciones, Article 3, h.

6. A new CASEN survey was undertaken in 1987, but the information had not been published at the time of this writing. The situation probably improved somewhat between 1985 and 1987, as implementation of the programs was generally better in light of new information for improving targeting.

7. These two trends are related. An econometric study for the Greater Santiago area found a strong inverse relationship between the number of live births to a woman and the average effective age at which her children entered school (i.e., taking into account repetitions and dropouts). Moreover, the more

education a woman has, the lower the number of live births and the lower the age at which her children enter school. See Castañeda 1986a.

8. On Chile, see Castañeda 1984b.

9. A recent study found that repetition rates in Chile were the lowest among a group of countries including Argentina, Bolivia, Brazil, Colombia, Ecuador, Paraguay, Peru, Uruguay, and Venezuela. Furthermore, the Chilean repetition rates declined considerably after 1980. See Schiefelbein 1989.

10. There are two main differences between the public and private subsidized universities. First, the former are controlled financially by the Office of the Comptroller (*Contraloria General de la República*), while the private universities are not. Second, the personnel at the public universities are public employees paid and promoted based on the public employee pay scale (*escala única*). Consequently, the private universities have more freedom in allocating their resources and contracting with employees.

11. In fact, the universities could offer a wide range of undergraduate degrees. The twelve degrees were, however, those believed to have university status. It was expected that the universities would stop providing the non-university degrees that, according to the government, had proliferated.

12. The Academic Aptitude Test (Prueba de Aptitud Académica, or PAA) is a prerequisite to seeking university admission. It has been administered to high school graduates since 1967. In 1984, 122,201 students took the test to obtain one of the 34,447 university places offered.

13. These changes are reviewed by Sanfuentes (1985).

14. In fact, there was an explosion in engineering because of that field's student payment. Enrollment in civil engineering at the universities increased overall from 8,413 students in 1981 to 17,148 in 1985.

15. University authorities made this claim several times to the press in 1985.

16. The Risk Classification Commission is described in Chapter 5.

17. Other reasons for the high dropout rates in Chile include (1) the selection process, whereby, in many cases, students are not enrolled in the discipline of their first choice for lack of space; and (2) the highly specialized curricula of all disciplines, which penalize students who change disciplines after studying a few semesters in a given discipline.

18. Student loan management has proved very difficult in most countries. In the United States, for instance, where the student loan programs total about U.S. $10 billion a year, half of all college financial aid programs are in deep financial trouble because of high default rates. Of the 8,284 schools that have been in the program, nearly 1,100 had cumulative default rates of over 40 percent and another 1,100 over 20 percent (*Wall Street Journal*, March 15, 1988). The reasons include the low income of poor minority students, who tend to have high dropout rates; poor screening (and subsequent high dropout rates) and fraud by colleges, especially at the for-profit trade schools that teach a range of subjects from hairdressing to computer programming and seek to attract students and student loans to get financing; fraud on the part of some financial institutions that provide the credits guaranteed by the federal government; and

poor collection efforts by financial institutions before default is accepted and guarantees claimed. Proposals to cut federal aid to schools with default rates above 20 percent and to enforce tougher new collection standards before defaults are reimbursed are being hotly debated.

19. These data are for the fall semester of 1984, according to a report by the dean of the school.

20. There has been some debate over the effect of the reforms on the proportion of students attending universities in Chile. See Briones et al. 1984.

21. "Reportajes," *El Mercurio*, August 23, 1987.

22. See "Decrece Interes de Alumnos por Entrar a Universidades" (Interest in University Education Decreases), *El Mercurio*, July 16, 1989.

23. The 1983 study was carried out by J. Rodríguez-Grossi, based on sample information for eight regions in Chile. The results were also published in a comparative study by Petrei (1987).

24. Rodríguez-Grossi (1985b) indicates higher percentages of about 50 percent of expenditures on preprimary and primary education received by the poorest 30 percent in 1982. This does not necessarily indicate that targeting worsened from 1982 to 1985 (to which the data in the table refer), but is most likely the result of the higher sampling error in the 1982 survey. While the 1985 survey covered more than 20,000 households nationwide, the 1982 survey covered fewer than 4,000 in eight (out of thirteen) regions of the country.

25. Under the FONASA system, affiliates get a flat amount in the form of a voucher that they can use to pay providers of health care, paying out of their own pockets any difference between the voucher amount and the price charged by the provider they choose.

Chapter 3, "Reforms of Health and Nutrition Programs and Delivery Systems"

1. The map of extreme poverty was prepared in 1974 using 1970 census data.

2. Breast-feeding was widely encouraged through education campaigns in the media and at health centers and posts. Fragmentary information indicated that about 25 percent of all infants were breast-feeding in 1967, as compared with 85 percent in 1940, the result, in part, of the rapid urbanization of the country and the change to an "urban culture." In 1986, the percentage of mothers breast-feeding their children for up to three months had increased to over 50 percent.

3. Previously, children served through the offices had to have their health-care attendance certified and had to get regular checkups, but any licensed physician could provide the certification without adequate follow-up of the children's health.

4. JUNAEB, an autonomous agency within the Ministry of Education, administered a variety of other programs (see Chapter 2).

5. The CAS Index system is based on a socioeconomic survey the municipalities have administered since 1980. The survey, which is carried out by social and other municipal workers, involves over thirty questions used to determine the living standard of poor people in the municipality. This index is widely used to determine the beneficiary populations of the welfare programs administered by the municipalities or the central government.

6. In 1988, the daily cost of a complete ration (breakfast and lunch) was U.S. $0.40, or $69.80 annually.

7. In 1979–1980, the MOH alleged that doctors were misusing the PPS or SERMENA system. It even tried to prosecute some cases.

8. Designing relative-value scales is not easy. A recent study by Harvard University for the U.S. Congress measured physicians' work on the basis of an equation containing four variables: time, mental effort, technical skill, and stress. Researchers then surveyed about 3,000 physicians to judge the relative amount of each of the variables involved in hundreds of services and procedures. The major conclusions of the study indicate that physicians can rate the relative value of their work and that those ratings are reproducible and consistent. However, when researchers looked at the ratings and compared them with customary charges for a given task, they found considerable discrepancies. This information comes from "Medicare Plan Would Shift Doctors' Pay," *Wall Street Journal*, September 29, 1988.

9. A proposal in the U.S. Congress, based on the study cited in footnote 8, seeks to introduce a "relative-value" schedule for reimbursing physicians under Medicare (so-called part B) that would favor general practitioners at the expense of surgeons. The fees would vary by region to account for the differences in doctors' expenses (labor, rent, utilities) and would rise annually with inflation. To contain costs, a cap has been proposed for total payments to physicians. It has been strongly opposed by the American Medical Association. See *Washington Post*, June 19, 1989.

10. The payroll contributions increased from 4 percent in 1982, 5 percent in 1985, and 6 percent in 1986 to 7 percent thereafter.

11. The biomedical indicators, which are given a weight of 50 percent, are a series of ratios, including undernourished children less than one year old to total number of children under one year; the number of normal live births to total births; the number of consultations to the number of hospital discharges; the number of consultations for morbidity to total emergencies; and the number of dental treatments to dental extractions. The financial indicators, which are weighted the other 50 percent, include income-to-expenditures and debt-to-income ratios.

12. FONASA has fine-tuned the FAP payments very skillfully so that the total payments to the SNSS (for personnel, goods and services, and net FAP) are about equal to the payments that would have been made if the FONASA had reimbursed 100 percent of the services billed by the SNSS using level 1 prices.

13. Fragmentary evidence indicates that some workers on the border of the income brackets where copayments increase ask their employers to declare lower wages. As such, their contributions to the social security system are

lower. Although the accumulated social security funds belong to the workers under the new social security system (see Chapter 5), the government guarantees a minimum pension if those funds are insufficient to pay for it.

14. Many municipalities buy medicines from local pharmacies rather than from the Central Warehouse of the MOH, a system that provides them with ready access but has been criticized for higher costs.

15. Usually, there is a limit to progressivity in the revenue-sharing formula in most countries, because the municipalities that produce more taxes also demand the return of more revenues to meet the increased demand for infrastructure and other expenditures.

16. What happens in many countries is that, because the public health insurance system is deficient, firms offer workers a variety of double health-coverage benefits, especially for outpatient services, including medical services at the welfare offices or insurance protection in private companies. This system raises the cost of labor to firms and consequently lowers employment more than a formal and well-functioning health insurance system does.

17. Real wages were calculated as the nominal ISS (with 1983 = 100) divided by the CPI (with 1983 = 100), which was also used to deflate the supply price index.

18. There is a limit of 10 percent on wages that can be used to pay off these loans, which earn no real interest rate.

19. Unfortunately, there is no easy solution to this problem. In the United States, similar selection problems occur with the federal employee insurance system, because the health maintenance organizations (HMOs) have attracted the less risky affiliates, leaving the others to the traditional insurance companies. Companies such as Aetna Life and Casualty Co., which held long-term contracts with the federal government, are ending them because of the adverse selection problem. See "Aetna Pullout from US Plan Heralds Reform," *Wall Street Journal*, June 2, 1989.

20. In Costa Rica, for instance, payroll contribution rates to finance health care are about 15 percent (compared with 7 percent in Chile) because payroll contributions finance all curative care in the country, including that for indigents.

21. There is some controversy about the main factors responsible for the mortality decline. Monckeberg, Valiente, and Mardones (1987) stress the long tradition Chile has had in social programs and targeted interventions for malnourished children. Taucher (1982) attributes the decline in mortality to a decline in fertility rates. Raczynski and Oyarzo (1983) attribute the decline in mortality rates to a decline in fertility of high mortality groups.

Chapter 4, "Reforms in the Housing Sector"

1. This well-established quarterly survey began in 1957 for the Greater Santiago area. It contains income data for the second quarter of each year and is the most consistent source of income information. It has been used in several econometric studies on earning functions, income distribution analysis, and the

impact of minimum wages. Castañeda and Quiroz (1984) present an assessment of its quality, coverage, and bias.

2. SINAP had two fundamental problems: loans were adjusted by the CPI or ISS, whichever was lower, while deposits followed market interest rates; and there was a considerable mismatch between liquid capital and obligations.

3. The UF is a unit of account that is adjusted daily with inflation. In June 1980, the value of the UF was approximately U.S. $24.40.

4. Iglesias, Echeverría, and López 1986. Major assumptions underlying the projections include GDP growth of 3 percent, real return on pension funds of 5 percent, and contributions of 75 percent of the beneficiary population (the current figure is about 60 percent).

5. When the CHCs ceased to operate in 1979, this function was extended to the basic program system as well.

6. The CAS Index is based on a formulary applied by municipal social workers nationwide to people applying for a great number of subsidies. The CAS Index was first implemented in the late 1970s and was applied to housing subsidies in 1984. The formulary includes more than thirty questions on family composition, socioeconomic status, and housing conditions. The index is heavily weighted by lack of or poor housing.

7. The savings quotas were units of account indexed to the ISS, plus an interest rate of 3 percent per year.

8. These units were called *unidades previsionales reajustables* (UPR).

9. It should be pointed out, however, that the information underlying these results was deficient and requires numerous assumptions. See the Appendix to this chapter for summary of the methodology for the calculations.

10. The figures are from Castañeda and Quiroz (1984). The Appendix to this chapter also updates the main tables to 1986.

11. However, the 5 percent house tax (*impuesto habitacional*) received by the CHCs was transferred to general fiscal revenues. Private enterprises permitted to administer this tax to build social housing for their workers continued doing so until 1983, when the tax was abolished to conform with the general policy of eliminating earmarked taxes.

12. Funds under the Variable Housing Subsidy Program, created in 1981 and designed to operate entirely through the private sector, were disbursed very slowly because only a few beneficiaries were able to find a house and use the vouchers.

13. The relocation programs of the BHP have raised several complex issues. First is the availability of social services in areas that have been net receivers of people, and the burden the newcomers have imposed on local government finances. The second is the effect that relocating large numbers of poor people has had on property values in the origin and destination municipalities. Some of these issues are discussed in Catholic University of Chile 1985.

14. This modification was made in 1982 to correct some deficiencies in targeting that resulted from people getting houses whose appraised value was much lower than the market value, a practice that attracted middle- and higher-income people to apply and show savings for this subsidy.

15. This behavior may explain why the average subsidy granted was higher than the subsidy *paid*, as seen in MINVU statistics, and why a more redistributive allocation of benefits was observed in the sixth round of the housing subsidy, when changing brackets was not permitted and housing units were appraised at their market value.

16. Several municipalities have taken an active role in giving technical advice and support to help people upgrade the initial unit quickly. NGOs have also been involved in this process by trying to organize people and looking for donations of materials from the private sector.

17. Another factor was the reestablishment in 1982 and increase in 1983 of the subsidy for incremental labor employment (*subsidio a la contratación adicional de mano de obra*), a program widely used by the construction industry.

18. A used house could be bought with this subsidy during the last quarter in which the certificate was valid. The subsidy certificates were valid for one year.

19. In 1987, for instance, about 75 percent of the mortgagees were more than three months behind in their payments.

20. A study done in 1985 recommended significant reductions in subsidies and reorientation and redesign of the less redistributive programs. See Castañeda and Quiroz 1984.

21. As indicated in Castañeda and Quiroz 1984, a key to reducing the allocations to higher-income groups is strict control of the appraised and market values and of the characteristics of the finished product. In the past, one way to reduce the appraised value was for the beneficiaries to receive a house that lacked some expensive finishings.

22. These figures take into account the number of households living with parents, relatives, or friends in overcrowded conditions who cannot afford to rent or buy a separate house. In 1982, these *allegados* were estimated at 148,000 households. See MINVU 1987.

23. The calculations are in Castañeda and Quiroz 1984.

24. The data from the Department of Economics for the decile income boundaries were taken from Heskia 1980. According to these data, the poorest 30 percent earned less than $960, and the next highest 30 percent, less than $1,921, in 1976 pesos. Converting these figures to 1969 pesos and taking a living wage of 0.4775 pesos for that year (based on socioeconomic indicators published by the Central Bank), the boundaries for the third and sixth deciles were 1.298 and 2.597 living wages, respectively. The 1969 figures were updated to 1978–1986 by using the ISS.

25. The inconsistencies in INE's survey are discussed in Castañeda and Quiroz 1984.

Chapter 5, "Reform of the Social Security System"

1. Figures calculated based on Comisión Prat 1964–1965.

2. It could be argued that this subsidy, represented in a higher lifelong

expected salary, was necessary (equilibrating differential) to attract public-sector employees. This explanation is unlikely. A discussion of the issue of the low government contribution as employer can be found in von Gersdorff 1985 and Arellano 1986.

3. Although some groups experience a higher probability of unemployment than others, this additional payment represents no cross-subsidization among workers since, to receive benefits during unemployment, the event needs to occur. While probabilities for disability could be assumed similar for members of the affiliate population, death probabilities are higher for the older population.

4. Later estimates using actual fees and charges indicate that a high proportion of workers, especially women, will not be able to reach the minimum pension and will require a supplement from the state.

5. These new regulations on commissions were introduced by Law 18,646 of August 1987. The original regulations also included a commission expressed as a percentage of the accumulated funds and a fixed percentage established for disability and survivor insurance, a system that made it difficult to figure out the amount of commissions effectively paid by beneficiaries.

6. The "concentration factor" (ranging from 1.0 to 0.2) is given by the concentration of property regulations for each institution. The factor values are as follows: (1) 1.0 is given to all institutions where no one directly or indirectly is allowed to control more than 20 percent of the shares; (2) 0.8 to all institutions where the maximum control permitted is between 20 and 30 percent; (3) 0.6 to all institutions where the maximum control is between 30 and 40 percent; (4) 0.4 to all institutions where the maximum control is between 40 and 45 percent; and (5) 0.2 to all institutions were the permitted concentration in a single share-holder is between 45 and 50 percent.

7. The recognition bond is paid to all beneficiaries who had contributed to the old Cajas for at least twelve months during the last sixty months before the new system started. Its size is 80 percent of the average salary of the last twelve months before June 1979, adjusted for inflation, multiplied by the ratio between the number of years of contribution (up to a maximum of thirty-five), and thirty-five. The result is then multiplied by a factor reflecting the cost of an annuity (10.35 for men and 11.36 for women). The value of the bond is adjusted by the CPI from June 1978 until the date on which the affiliate changed to the new system. From then on, the bond is expressed in UF and earns a 4-percent annual interest rate. It is paid at legal age of retirement.

8. The original law (3,500) gave a deadline of August 1986 for members of the old Cajas to transfer to the new system. This deadline was later eliminated, and members can now transfer at any time.

9. The figures on enrollment in the new system were very deficient during the early years of operation because of duplicity and inclusion of people who had left the labor force. This occurred because of the massive transfer, the numerous changes in AFPs affiliates made, and the initial lack of an adequate information system.

10. These boards (seventeen plus a Central Board) consist of three physicians

appointed and paid by the Superintendent of AFPs. Resolutions of the boards can be contested before the Central Board by the beneficiary, the AFP in which he is enrolled, and the insurance company.

11. An effect of this change in the salary base may be a reduction in premiums paid, since there will be fewer beneficiaries and a lower pension.

12. The deficits of the Cajas of the armed forces are excluded because they were excluded from the reform. See ODEPLAN 1986b.

13. The estimates are cited in Lacey 1987.

References

Anderson, Maria E. 1984. "Agricultural Sector Study." Draft working paper, September. Washington, D.C.: World Bank.

Arellano, J. P. 1976. *Distribución de los Beneficios Proporcionados por el Sector Público en Vivienda y Urbanismo en Chile, 1969* (Distribution of Housing and Urbanization Benefits by the Public Sector in Chile). Santiago: CIEPLAN. Mimeo.

————. 1982. "Políticas de Vivienda Popular: Lecciones de la Experiencia Chilena" (Policies of Low-income Housing: Lessons from the Chilean Experience). *Colección de Estudios, CIEPLAN*, no. 9.

————. 1986. "Una Mirada Crítica a la Reforma Previsional de 1981." (A Critical Review of the 1981 Social Security Reform). In *Análisis de la Previsión en Chile* (Analysis of Social Security in Chile), ed. S. Baeza. Santiago: Centro de Estudios Públicos.

Briones, G., et al. 1984. *Las Transformaciones de la Educación bajo el Regimen Militar* (Education Transformation under the Military Regime). Vols. 1 and 2. Santiago: PIIE (Education Research Institute).

Castañeda T. 1984a. "Evolución del Gasto Social en Chile y Su Impacto Redistributivo" (Evolution of Social Spending in Chile and Its Redistributive Impact). Department of Economics, University of Chile, Santiago, Mimeo.

————. 1984b. "Fertility, Child Schooling, and Mothers' Participation in the Labor Market in Greater Santiago." *Revista de Economía*. Department of Economics, University of Chile, Santiago.

————. 1984c. "El Impacto de las Inversiones en Educación en Chile, 1960–83" (Impact of Education Investments in Chile, 1960–83). *Revista de Economía*. Department of Economics, University of Chile, Santiago.

————. 1985a. "Los Determinantes del Descenso de la Mortalidad Infantil en Chile, 1975–82" (Determinants of Infant Mortality Decline in Chile, 1975–82). *Cuadernos de Economía* (Santiago), no. 22 (August): 195–214.

————. 1985b. "El Impacto Redistributivo del Gasto Social en Chile" (The Redistributive Impact of Social Spending in Chile). Department of Economics, University of Chile, Santiago. Mimeo.

————. 1986a. *Fertility, Child Schooling and the Labor Force Participation of Mothers in Santiago, Chile.* Discussion Paper, Education and Training Series, no. EDT34. Washington, D.C.: World Bank.

————. 1986b. *Innovations in the Financing of Education: The Case of Chile.* Discussion Paper, Education and Training Series, no. EDT35. Washington, D.C.: World Bank.

————. 1990. "Financing Health Systems: Alternatives and Dilemmas." *Cuadernos de Economía* (Santiago), no. 81 (August): 183–99.

Castañeda, T., and J. Quiroz. 1984. *Políticas de Vivienda en Chile y Su Impacto Redistributivo, 1969 y 1980–1983,* (Housing Policies in Chile and Their Redistributive Impact, 1969 and 1980–1983). Santiago: Centro de Estudios Publicos.

Catholic University of Chile. 1981. *Estudio de la Reforma Previsional: Previsión Social Chilena, Antiguo Sistema 1925–80* (Study of Social Security Reform: Chilean Social Security, the Old System, 1925–80). Santiago.

————. 1985. *Costo Nacional Diferencial de Localizar Viviendas Básicas* (Differential National Cost for Location of Basic Houses). Santiago: CIAPEP/ODEPLAN.

Central Bank of Chile. 1983. *Indicadores Económicos y Sociales, 1960–1982* (Social and Economic Indicators, 1960–1982). Santiago.

————. 1987. *Indicadores Económicos y Sociales* (Economic and Social Indicators). Santiago.

————. 1988. *Boletín Estadístico Mensual* (Monthly Bulletin). December. Santiago.

————. 1989. *Boletín Mensual* (Monthly Bulletin). December. Santiago.

Cepa Ltda. 1985a. "Estudio de Evaluación del Programa de Saneamiento de Campamentos" (Evaluation Study of the Slum-Upgrading Program). Unpublished draft. Santiago: Metropolitan Region Government (*Intendencia*).

————. 1985b. "Estudio de Evaluación del Programa de Vivienda Básica" (Evaluation Study of the Basic Housing Program). Unpublished draft. Santiago: Metropolitan Region Government (*Intendencia*).

Cheyre, Hernán. 1988. *La Previsión en Chile: Ayer y Hoy, Impacto de una Reforma* (Social Security in Chile: Yesterday and Today, Impact of the Reform). Santiago: Centro de Estudios Públicos.

Comisión Prat. 1964–1965. *Informe sobre la Reforma de la Seguridad Social Chilena* (Report of the Reform of the Chilean Social Security System). Santiago: Editorial Jurídica.

FONASA. 1985 and 1988. *Memoria Anual* [Annual Report], *1984* and *1987*. Santiago.

————. 1989. *Boletín Estadístico Anual del Sistema ISAPRE* (Annual Statistical Bulletin, ISAPRE System). Santiago.

Ffrench-Davis, R., and D. Raczynski. 1985. "The Impact of Global Recession on Living Standards: Chile." Revised draft (October). Santiago: CIEPLAN.

García, J. 1986. "Renta Vitalicia y Bono de Reconocimiento" (Annuities and

Recognition Bonds in the Social Security System). In *Análisis de la Previsión en Chile* (Analysis of the Social Security in Chile), ed. Sergio Baeza. Santiago: Centro de Estudios Públicos.

Haindl, E., and C. Weber. 1986. *Impacto Redistributivo del Gasto Social* (Redistributive Impact of Social Spending). Santiago: University of Chile.

Harbert, L., and P. Scandizo. 1985. "Distribución de Alimentos e Intervención en Nutrición: El Caso de Chile" (Food Distribution and Nutrition Interventions: The Chilean Case). *Cuadernos de Economía* (Santiago), no. 66 (August): 215–46.

Heskia, I. 1980. *Distribución del Ingreso en el Gran Santiago, 1957–1979* (Income Distribution for Greater Santiago). Document Series Investigation no. 53, Department of Economics, University of Chile.

Himmel, E., S. Maltes, and P. Gazmuri. 1985. *Efectos de la Política Educacional en el Rendimiento en Chile* (Effects of Educational Policy on School Achievement in Chile). Santiago: Catholic University of Chile.

Hojman, David E. 1989. "Neoliberal Economic Policies and Infant and Child Mortality: Simulation Analysis of Chilean Paradox." *World Development* 17, no. 1: 93–108.

Hurtado, H., E. Muchnik, and A. Valdes. 1987. "A Comparative Study of the Political Economy of Agricultural Pricing Policies: The Case of Chile. Final Report." Washington, D.C.: World Bank. Mimeo.

Iglesias, A., A. Echeverría, and P. López. 1986. "Proyección de los Fondos de Pensiones" (Projections of the Pension Funds). In *Análisis de la Previsión en Chile* (Analysis of the Social Security in Chile), ed. Sergio Baeza. Santiago: Centro de Estudios Públicos.

Institute of Economics, Catholic University of Chile. 1986. *Estudios de Alternativas de Sistemas Habitacionales*. Capítulo 4, "Politicas de Vivienda, 1973–1985" (Study on Alternative Housing Policies, Chapter 4, Housing Policies 1973–1985). Santiago: Catholic University of Chile.

Jiménez de la Jara, J., and M. Gili. 1988. *Municipalización de la Atención Primaria en Salud* (Municipalization of Primary Health Care). October. Santiago: Corporación de Promoción Universitaria (CPU).

Lacey, Robert. 1987. "The Privatization of the Social Security System in Chile." Unpublished. Washington, D.C.: World Bank.

Larraín, H. 1985. "Nivel Académico en Chile: Bases para una Evalución" (Academic Level in Chile: Basis for Evaluation). In *La Educación Superior en Chile, Riesgos y Oportunidades* (Higher Education in Chile: Risks and Opportunities), ed. M. Lemaitre and I. Lavados. Santiago: Corporación de Promoción Universitaria (CPU).

Lemaitre, M. J., and I. Lavados. 1985. "Antecedentes, Restricciones y Oportunidades de la Educación Superior en Chile" (Antecedents, Restrictions, and Opportunities of Higher Education in Chile). In *La Educación Superior en Chile: Riesgos y Oportunidades* (Higher Education in Chile: Risks and Opportunities), ed. M. J. Lamaitre and I. Lavados. Santiago: Corporación de Promoción Universitaria.

Lüders, R. 1988. "Veinticinco Años de Ingenieria Social en Chile, 1963–1988" (Twenty-Five Years of Social Engineering in Chile, 1963–1988). *Cuadernos de Economía* (Santiago), no. 76 (December): 331–80.

Mesa-Lago, Carmelo. 1978. *Social Security in Latin America: Pressure Groups, Stratification and Inequality.* Pittsburgh: University of Pittsburgh Press.

———. 1985. *La Seguridad Social en América Latina* (Social Security in Latin America). Santiago: CEPAL.

Ministry of Finance. 1976. *Estructura de Ingresos y Gastos Municipales 1974–76* (Structure of Municipal Revenues and Expenditures, 1974–76). Santiago.

MINVU. 1987. "Vivienda Como Entorno Micro-Ambiental en Chile: Diagnóstico y Politicas" (Housing and Its Environment in Chile: Diagnosis and Policies). Santiago. Mimeo.

Miranda, E. 1990. "Descentralización y Privatización del Sistema de Salud" (Decentralization and Privatization of the Health System). *Estudios Públicos,* no. 39 (Winter): 5–66.

Monckeberg, F., S. Valiente, and F. Mardones. 1987. "Infant and Pre-School Nutrition, Economic Development, versus Intervention Strategies: The Case of Chile." *Nutrition Research* 7: 327–42.

Muchnik, E., and I. Vial. 1988. *Evaluación del Programa de Alimentación Complementaria en Santiago: Participación, Cobertura y Aceptabilidad de la Leche Ceral* (Evaluation of the Complementary Feeding Program: Participation, Coverage and Acceptance of the Milk Cereal). Santiago. Mimeo.

Myers, Robert J. 1986. "Privatización en Chile del Sistema de Seguridad Social" (Privitization of the Social Security System in Chile). In *Análisis de la Previsión en Chile* (Analysis of Social Security in Chile), ed. S. Baeza. Santiago: Centro de Estudios Públicos.

National Institute of Statistics (INE). 1982. *Proyección de Población* (Population Projections). Santiago: INE-CELADE.

ODEPLAN. 1981. *Informe Social 1980* (Social Report 1980). Santiago.

———. 1985a. *El Financiamiento de la Educación Subvencionada* (Financing of Subsidized Education). Santiago.

———. 1985b. *Informe Social 1984* (Social Report 1984). Santiago.

———. 1986a. *Informe Social 1985* (Social Report 1985). Santiago.

———. 1986b. *Proyecciones del Déficit Previsional, 1985–2015, Parte III: Evaluando Algunos Aspectos de la Reforma de 1980* (Projections of the Social Security Deficit, 1985–2015, Part III: Evaluating Some Aspects of the 1980s Reform). Santiago.

———. 1987a. *Informe Social 1986* (Social Report 1986). Santiago.

———. 1987b. *Proyecciones del Déficit Previsional* (Projections of the Social Security Deficit). Parts 1, 2, and 3. Santiago.

Petrei, H. 1987. *El Gasto Público Social y Su Impacto Redistributivo: Un Examen Comparativo de Cinco Paises Latinoamericanos* (The Redistributive Impact of Public Social Spending: A Comparative Study of Five Latin American Countries). Document Series no. 6. Rio de Janeiro: ECIEL.

Raczynski, D., and C. Oyarzo. 1983. "Porque Cae la Tasa de Mortalidad Infantil en Chile?" (Why Is There a Drop in Infant Mortality in Chile?). In *Colección de Estudios, CIEPLAN,* no. 6 (December), 45–84.

Riveros, L. 1989. "The Economic Return of Schooling in Chile: An Analysis of Its Long-Term Fluctuations." Washington, D.C.: World Bank.

Rodríguez-Grossi, J. 1985a. "La Distribución del Ingreso y del Gasto Social en Chile, 1983" (The Distribution of Income and Social Spending in Chile, 1983). Santiago: ILADES.

————. 1985b. "Effects of the Decentralization Reforms in Chile." Santiago: ILADES. Mimeo.

Sanfuentes, A. 1985. "Financiamiento y Universidad: Antecedentes y Alternativas" (University Financing: Antecedents and Alternatives). In *La Educación Superior en Chile, Riesgos y Oportunidades* (Higher Education in Chile: Risks and Opportunities), ed. M. Lamaitre and I. Lavodos. Santiago: Corporación de Promoción Universitaria (CPU).

Schiefelbein, E. 1989. "Repetition: The Real Issue in Latin America." Draft document. Washington, D.C.: World Bank.

Secretaría de Desarrollo y Asistencia Social. 1989. "Reformas en el Campo de la Nutrición" (Reforms in Nutrition Programs). Unpublished paper. Santiago.

————. 1988. *Traspaso de Establecimientos Primarios de Salud a las Municipalidades* (Transfer of Primary Health Care Centers to Municipalities). January. Santiago.

Superintendency of AFPs. 1988. *Reducción de Costos de las AFP* (Reduction of the Costs of AFPs). October. Santiago.

Taucher, E. 1982. "Effects of Declining Fertility on Infant Mortality Levels: A Study Based on Data from Five Latin American Countries." Report to the Ford and Rockefeller Foundation. Santiago: CELADE (Latin American Demographic Center).

Torche, A. 1985. "Una Evaluación Económica del Programa de Alimentación Complementaria" (Economic Evaluation of the Supplementary Feeding Program). *Cuadernos de Economía* (Santiago), no. 66 (August): 174–94.

————. 1987. "Distribuir el Ingreso para Satisfacer las Necesidades Básicas" (Distributing Income to Meet Basic Needs). In *Desarrollo Económico en Democracia* (Economic Development in Democracy), ed. Felipe Larraín. Santiago: Catholic University of Chile.

UNESCO. 1985. *Anuario Estadístico de América Latina y el Caribe* (Statistical Yearbook for Latin America and the Caribbean). Paris.

UNICEF. 1989. *The State of the World's Children, 1989*. Oxford: Oxford University Press.

Vial, I., E. Muchnik, and J. Kain. 1988a. *Evolution of Chile's Main Nutrition Intervention Programs*. Santiago: INTA (University of Chile Nutrition Institute). Mimeo.

————. 1988b. *Evolution of Chile's Main Nutrition Intervention Programs: A Synthesis*. Santiago: INTA (University of Chile Nutrition Institute).

von Gersdorff, H. 1984. "La Reforma de la Seguridad Social en Chile" (Social Security Reform in Chile). *Revista de Economía*. Department of Economics, University of Chile, Santiago.

Wisecarver, D. 1986. "Regulación y Desregulación en Chile: September 1973–September 1983" (Regulation and Deregulation in Chile: September 1973–September 1983). *Estudios Públicos*, no. 22 (Fall): 116–67.

World Bank. 1988. *Social Indicators of Development*. Washington, D.C.

————. 1989. *Social Indicators of Development*. Washington, D.C.

————. 1990. *World Development Report, Poverty*. Washington, D.C.

List of Abbreviations and Terms

AFP: Pension Fund Administration Company (Administradora de Fondos de Pensiones)

ASP: Applicants System Program (Sistema de Aplicantes)

BHP: Basic Housing Program (Programa de Vivienda Básica)

CADEL: Program for Nutritional Intervention and Language Development (Centros de Intervención Nutricional y Desarrollo del Lenguaje)

Cajas: state pension fund companies

CANAEMPU: Caja for public-sector employees and newsmen (Caja de Empleados Publicos y Periodistas)

CAS: Committee for Social Action (Comité de Acción Social)

CASEN: Living Standards Measurement Survey (Encuesta de Caracterización Socioeconómica)

CHC: Community Housing Committee (Comité Habitacional Comunal)

CIAPEP: one-year graduate program on project evaluation offered by the Catholic University of Chile (Curso Interamericano de Preparación y Evaluación de Proyectos)

CODECOs: Communal Development Councils (Consejos Comunales de Desarrollo)

CODEREs: Regional Development Councils (Consejos Regionales de Desarrollo)

CODESER: Corporation for Rural Social Development (Corporación de Desarrollo Social Rural)

CONIN: Corporation of Infantile Nutrition (Corporación de Nutrición Infantil)

CORFO: Industrial Development Corporation (Corporación de Fomento de la Producción)

CORHABIT: Housing Services Corporation (Corporación de Servicios Habitacionales)

CORMU: Urban Improvements Corporation (Corporación de Mejoramiento Urbano)

CORVI: Housing Corporation (Corporación de la Vivienda)

COU: Urban Works Corporation (Corporación de Obras Urbanas)

CPI: consumer price index

D&S pensions: disability and survivor pensions

EEP: emergency employment programs

EMPART: Caja for private-sector white-collar workers (Caja de Empleados Particolares)

FAP: billing for services rendered (Facturación por Atención Prestada)

FAPEM: billing for services rendered by municipalities (Facturación por Atención Prestada por Municipalidades)

FCM: Municipal Fund (Fondo Comun Municipal)

FNAC: Foundation for Community Help (Fundación Nacional de Ayuda a la Comunidad)

FNDR: National Fund for Regional Development (Fondo Nacional de Desarrollo Regional)

FONASA: National Health Fund (Fondo Nacional de Salud)

GDP: gross domestic product

HSP: Housing Subsidy Program (Subsidio Habitacional)

IDB: Inter-American Development Bank

ILADES: Latin American Institute on Social Teaching of the Church and Social Studies (Instituto Latinoamericano de Enseñanza Social de la Iglesia y Estudios Sociales)

INACAP: National Institute of Training and Employment (Instituto Nacional de Capacitación Profesional)

INE: National Institute of Statistics (Instituto Nacional de Estadísticas)

INTA: Nutrition and Food Technology Institute, University of Chile (Instituto de Nutrición y Tecnología en Alimentos)

ISAPRE: private health insurance company (Institución de Salud Previsional)

ISS: wage and salary index (Indice de Sueldos y Salarios)

JUNAEB: National Board of School Assistance and Scholarships (Junta Nacional de Auxilio Escolar y Becas)

JUNJI: National Board of Kindergartens (Junta Nacional de Jardines Infantiles)

MOH: Ministry of Health (Ministerio de Salud)

MINVU: Ministry of Housing and Urban Affairs (Ministerio de Vivienda y Urbanismo)

NGO: nongovernment organization

NHS: National Health System (Sistema Nacional de Salud)

ODEPLAN: National Planning Office (Oficina de Planificación Nacional)

OFASA: a Baptist international assistance program

PAA: Academic Aptitude Test (Preuba de Aptitud Académica)

PASIS: Assistance Pensions (Pensión de Asistencia)

PEM: Minimum Employment Program (Programa Empleo Mínimo)

PER: School Achievement Test (Programa de Evaluación de Rendimiento)

PIMO: Labor-Intensive Employment Program (Progama Intensivo de Mano de Obra)

PNAC: National Program of Food Supplementation (Programa Nacional de Alimentación Complementaria)

POJH: Employment Program for Household Heads (Programa de Empleo para Jefes de Hogar)

PPS: Preferred Provider System (Sistema de Libre Elección)

SAF: Savings and Financing System for Housing (Sistema de Ahorro y Financiamento para la Vivienda)

SECPLAC: Planning Secretariat (Secretaría de Planificación y Coordinación)

SENCE: Employment and Vocational Training Service (Servicio Nacional de Capacitación y Empleo)

SEREMI: Regional Ministerial Secretariat (Secretaría Regional Ministerial)

SERMENA: National Medical Service for Employees (Servicio Médico Nacional)

SERPLAC: Regional Planning Office (Secretaría Regional de Planificación y Coordinación)

SERVIU: Regional Housing and Urban Affairs Service (Servicio Regional de Vivienda y Urbanismo)

SFP: School Feeding Program (Programa de Alimentación Escolar)

SHP: Social Housing Program (Programa de Subsidio Habitacional)

SIGMO: Hospital Information System (Sistema de Información Gerencial Hospitalario)

SINAP: National Savings and Loan System (Sistema Nacional de Ahorro y Préstamos)

SNS: National Health Service (Servicio Nacional de Salud)

SNSS: National Health Service System (Sistema Nacional de Servicios de Salud)

SSS: Social Security Service (Servicio de Seguro Social)

SUF: Family Subsidy (Subsidio Familiar)

SVS: Superintendency of the Stock Market and Insurance (Superintendencia de Valores y Seguros)

UF: unit of account adjusted daily with inflation (Unidad de Fomento)

USAID: U.S. Agency for International Development

USE: Unit for Subvention in Education (Unidad para Subvenciones en Educación)

UTM: Taxing Monthly Unit (Unidad Tibutaria Mensual)

VHSP: Variable Housing Subsidy Program (Programa de Subsidio Habitacional Variable)

WHO/FAO: World Health Organization/Food and Agriculture Organization of the United Nations

About the Author

Tarsicio Castañeda has been a senior economist for the World Bank since 1985. He is now working on the Regional Unit for Technical Assistance (RUTA) project in Central America. From 1981 to 1985, he served the Organization of American States in Santiago, Chile, where he advised the Chilean government on methods of evaluating social projects. He was also a professor and researcher in the Department of Economics at the University of Chile. In 1979–1980 he was a professor and researcher in the Department of Economics at the University of the Andes in Bogotá, Colombia. A native of Colombia, Castañeda has published many studies on employment, education, health, nutrition, and decentralization. Castañeda received his Ph.D. in economics from the University of Chicago in 1979.

Index

ICEG Academic Advisory Board